Futurity in Phenomenology

John D. Caputo, *series editor*

PERSPECTIVES IN
CONTINENTAL
PHILOSOPHY

NEAL DeROO

Futurity in Phenomenology
Promise and Method in Husserl, Levinas, and Derrida

FORDHAM UNIVERSITY PRESS
New York ∎ 2013

Publication of this book was supported in part by a grant from the Andreas Center for Reformed Scholarship and Service at Dordt College in Sioux Center, Iowa.

Library of Congress Cataloging-in-Publication Data

DeRoo, Neal, 1951–
    Futurity in phenomenology : promise and method in Husserl, Lévinas, and Derrida / Neal DeRoo. — 1st ed.
        p. cm. — (Perspectives in Continental philosophy)
    Includes bibliographical references (p.   ) and index.
    ISBN 978-0-8232-4464-5 (cloth : alk. paper)
    1. Phenomenology.   2. Forecasting.   3. Husserl, Edmund, 1859–1938.
4. Lévinas, Emmanuel.   5. Derrida, Jacques.   I. Title.
    B829.5.D434 2013
    142'.7—dc23

                                                              2012035753

Printed in the United States of America

15 14 13   5 4 3 2 1

First edition

Contents

Abbreviations

Of Husserl's Works

Hua I   *Cartesianische Meditationen und Pariser Vorträge.* Ed. S.
Strasser. The Hague: Martinus Nijhoff, 1950. Translated
by Dorion Cairns as *Cartesian Meditations: An
Introduction to Phenomenology.* Dordrecht: Kluwer
Academic, 1999.

Hua II   *Die Idee der Phänomenologie: Fünf Vorlesungen.* Ed. W.
Biemel. The Hague: Martinus Nijhoff, 1950. Translated
by Lee Hardy as *The Idea of Phenomenology.* Boston:
Kluwer Academic, 1998.

Hua III   *Ideen zu einer Phänomenologie und phänomenologischen
Philosophie. Erstes Buch: Allgemeine Einführung in die
reine Phänomenologie.* Ed. W. Biemel. The Hague:
Martinus Nijhoff, 1950. Translated by F. Kersten as
*Ideas Pertaining to a Pure Phenomenology and to a
Phenomenological Philosophy.* Book 1: *General
Introduction to a Pure Phenomenology.* The Hague:
Martinus Nijhoff, 1983.

Hua IV   *Ideen zu einer Phänomenologie und phänomenologischen
Philosophie. Dreites Buch: Phänomenologische*

	Untersuchungen zur Konstitution. Ed. W. Biemel. The Hague: Martinus Nijhoff, 1952. Translated by Richard Rojcewicz and André Schuwer as *Ideas Pertaining to a Pure Phenomenology and to a Phenomenological Philosophy.* Book 2: *Studies in the Phenomenology of Constitution.* Dordrecht: Kluwer Academic, 1989.
Hua VI	*Der Krisis der europäischen Wissenschaften und die transzendentale Phänomenologie: Eine Einleitung in die Phänomenologische Philosophie.* Ed. W. Biemel. The Hague: Martinus Nijhoff, 1954. Translated by David Carr as *The Crisis of European Sciences and Transcendental Phenomenology.* Evanston, Ill.: Northwestern University Press, 1970.
Hua X	*Zur Phänomenologie des inneren Zeitbewusstseins (1893–1917).* Ed. R. Boehm. The Hague: Martinus Nijhoff, 1966. Translated by John Barnett Brough as *On the Phenomenology of the Consciousness of Internal Time.* Dordrecht: Kluwer Academic, 1991.
Hua XI	*Analysen zur passiven Synthesis: Aus Vorlesungs- und Forschungsmanuskripten 1918–1926.* Ed. M. Fleischer. The Hague: Martinus Nijhoff, 1966. Translated by Anthony J. Steinbock as *Analyses concerning Active and Passive Synthesis: Lectures on Transcendental Logic.* Dordrecht: Kluwer Academic, 2001.
Hua XII	*Philosophie der Arithmetik: Mit ergänzenden Texten (1890–1901).* Ed. L. Ely. The Hague: Martinus Nijhoff, 1970.
Hua XVII	*Formale und Transzendentale Logik: Versuch einer Kritik der logischen Vernunft.* Mit ergänzenden Texten. Ed. P. Janssen. The Hague: Martinus Nijhoff, 1974. Translated by Dorion Cairns as *Formal and Transcendental Logic.* The Hague: Martinus Nijhoff, 1969.
Hua XXIV	*Einleitung in die Logik und Erkenntnistheories.Vorlesungen 1906/1907.* Ed. U. Melle. Dordrecht: Martinus Nijhoff, 1984.
Hua XXVII	*Aufsätze und Vorträge (1922–1937).* Ed. T. Nenon and H.R. Sepp. Dordrecht: Kluwer Academic, 1989.

Hua XXXI   *Aktive Synthesen: Aus der Vorlesung "Transcendentale Logik" 1920/21.* Ed. R. Breuer. Dordrecht: Kluwer Academic, 2000. Pp. 3–83 are translated by Anthony J. Steinbock in *Analyses concerning Active and Passive Synthesis: Lectures on Transcendental Logic.* Dordrecht: Kluwer Academic, 2001. 275–355.

Hua XXXIII *Die Bernauer Manuskripte über das Zeitbewusstsein (1917/1918).* Ed. R. Bernet and D. Lohmar. Dordrecht: Kluwer Academic, 2001.

EU   *Erfahrung und Urteil. Untersuchungen zur Genealogie der Logik.* Ed. L. Landgrebe. Hamburg: Meiner, 1948. Translated by James Churchill and Karl Ameriks as *Experience and Judgement: Investigations in a Genealogy of Logic.* Evanston, Ill.: Northwestern University Press, 1973.

LI   *Logical Investigations.* Translated by J.N. Findlay. New York: Routledge, 2001.

Of Levinas's Works

DEH   *Discovering Existence with Husserl.* Trans. Richard A. Cohen and Michael B. Smith. Evanston, Ill.: Northwestern University Press, 1998.

DR   "Diachrony and Representation." In *Time and the Other.* Trans. Richard A. Cohen. Pittsburgh: Duquesne University Press, 1987. 97–120.

EE   *Existence and Existents.* Trans. Alphonso Lingis. Pittsburgh: Duquesne University Press, 2001.

EI   *Ethics and Infinity.* Trans. Richard A. Cohen. Pittsburgh: Duquesne University Press, 1988.

GDT   *God, Death, and Time.* Trans. Bettina Bergo. Ed. and annotated by Jacques Rolland. Stanford: Stanford University Press, 2000.

IM   "Intentionality and Metaphysics" (1959). In *Discovering Existence with Husserl.* Trans. Richard A. Cohen and Michael B. Smith. Evanston, Ill.: Northwestern University Press, 1998. 122–29.

IS   "Intentionality and Sensation" (1965). In *Discovering Existence with Husserl*. Trans. Richard A. Cohen and Michael B. Smith. Evanston, Ill.: Northwestern University Press, 1998. 135–50.

OB   *Otherwise than Being or Beyond Essence*. Trans. Alphonso Lingis. Pittsburgh: Duquesne University Press, 1998.

RR   "The Ruin of Representation" (1959). In *Discovering Existence with Husserl*. Trans. Richard A. Cohen and Michael B. Smith. Evanston, Ill.: Northwestern University Press, 1998. 111–21.

TA   "The Trace of the Other." Trans. Alphonso Lingis. In *Deconstruction in Context: Literature and Philosophy*. Ed. Mark C. Taylor. Chicago: University of Chicago Press, 1986. 345–59.

TI   *Totality and Infinity: An Essay on Exteriority*. Trans. Alphonso Lingis. Pittsburgh: Duquesne University Press, 1969.

TIHP   *The Theory of Intuition in Husserl's Phenomenology*. Trans. André Orianne. Evanston, Ill.: Northwestern University Press, 1995.

TO   *Time and the Other*. Trans. Richard A. Cohen. Pittsburgh: Duquesne University Press, 1987.

WEH   "The Work of Edmund Husserl" (1940). In *Discovering Existence with Husserl*. Trans. Richard A. Cohen and Michael B. Smith. Evanston, Ill.: Northwestern University Press, 1998. 47–87.

Of Derrida's Works

FK   "Faith and Knowledge: The Two Sources of 'Religion' at the Limits of Reason Alone." In *Acts of Religion*. Ed. Gil Anidjar. New York: Routledge, 2002. 40–101.

NM   Jacques Derrida with Richard Beardsworth. "Nietzsche and the Machine." *Journal of Nietzsche Studies* 7 (1994): 7–66.

OG   *Of Grammatology*. Trans. G. Spivak. Baltimore: Johns Hopkins University Press, 1976.

OoG   *Edmund Husserl's* Origin of Geometry: *An Introduction.* Trans. John P. Leavey. Lincoln: University of Nebraska Press, 1989.

PG   *The Problem of Genesis in Husserl's Philosophy.* Trans. Marian Hobson. Chicago: University of Chicago Press, 2003.

SP   *Speech and Phenomena.* Trans. David B. Alison. Evanston, Ill.: Northwestern University Press, 1973.

SM   *Specters of Marx: The State of the Debt, the Work of Mourning, and the New International.* Trans. Peggy Kamuf. New York: Routledge, 1994.

VM   "Violence and Metaphysics: An Essay on the Thought of Emmanuel Levinas." In *Writing and Difference.* Trans. Alan Bass. Chicago: University of Chicago Press, 1978. 79–153.

WD   *Writing and Difference.* Trans. Alan Bass. Chicago: University of Chicago Press, 1978.

Of Works by Other Figures

PA   Jean-Yves Lacoste. "The Phenomenality of Anticipation." Trans. Ronald Mendoza-deJesús and Neal DeRoo. In *Phenomenology and Eschatology: Not Yet in the Now,* ed. Neal DeRoo and John Panteleimon Manoussakins. Aldershot, England: Ashgate, 2009. 15–33.

PCC   Eugen Fink. "The Phenomenological Philosophy of Edmund Husserl and Contemporary Criticism." In *The Phenomenology of Husserl,* ed. R.O. Elveton. Chicago: Quadrangle Books, 1970. 73–147.

DH   James K. A. Smith, "Determined Hope: A Phenomenology of Christian Expectation." In *The Future of Hope: Christian Tradition amid Modernity and Postmodernity,* ed. Miroslav Volf and William Katerberg. Grand Rapids, Mich.: Eerdmans, 2004. 200–227.

Preface

This book is indebted to a great number of people and to conversations that I have had over the years. I can mention only a few of them here, but know that the contributions from all those who have helped are greatly appreciated. I would like to thank the participants of the thirty-eighth and thirty-ninth annual Husserl Circles for their comments on earlier versions of chapter 1 and what would become chapter 2. There are many other colleagues whose comments and discussions were invaluable to the completion of this book, especially Michael Kelly, Kascha Snavely, Noah Moss-Brender, Jerome Veith, and Philip Braunstein. Jack Caputo, Jeffrey Bloechl, Leonard Lawlor, John Panteleimon Manoussakis, and Richard Cobb-Stevens were very patient in answering questions and offering opinions on earlier drafts, and the book is better because of it. Richard Kearney offered his encouragement and support numerous times at various stages of the process, and this book would not be here without his sage advice. For all of those mentioned, I thank you for your insights, your wisdom, and your friendship. I would also like to thank Helen Tartar, Thomas Lay, Stephen Barichko, and everyone at Fordham University Press for their work in getting this manuscript ready to be published. They have done much to improve the book, and any faults that remain are my fault, not theirs.

Finally, I would like to thank Tanya, who not only made it possible for me to finish this project but also made it, and my life in general, enjoyable and worthwhile.

Acknowledgements

Some of the material that appears in this book has appeared in previous forms elsewhere. An earlier version of chapter 1 was published as "A Positive Account of Protention and its Implications for Internal Time-Consciousness," in *Epistemology, Archaeology, Ethics: Current Investigations of Husserl's Corpus*, eds. Pol Vandevelde and Sebastian Luft (London: Continuum, 2010), and is reprinted here by permission of Sarah Campbell and Continuum.

Some parts of chapter 2 found an early airing in "Revisiting the Zahavi - Brough/Sokolowski Debate," in *Husserl Studies* 27: 1 [2011], and appear here by permission of the editors.

Some sections of part 3 can be found in "Derrida and the Future(s) of Phenomenology," *Derrida Today* 4:1 [2011], and are included here with permission.

Chapter 5 grew out of an earlier project, "Re-Constituting Phenomenology: Continuity in Levinas's account of Time and Ethics," that was published in *Dialogue: Canadian Philosophical Review* 49:2 (2010). Those elements that are similar are reprinted here with permission of Cambridge University Press.

Much of the research for this book was done with support from the Social Sciences and Humanities Research Council of Canada (SSHRC), which I hereby gratefully acknowledge.

Futurity in Phenomenology

Introduction

Futurity and Phenomenology

The thesis of this book is that the very understanding of phenomenology itself is at stake in the question of futurity in phenomenology. If this claim seems overstated, this is because the true centrality of the future to the project of phenomenology has not yet been elaborated. Once a positive account of the future in phenomenology is clearly demonstrated, a positive account of phenomenology also develops. A thorough understanding of the methodological significance of the future in phenomenology reveals that phenomenology is, at its core, an essentially promissory discipline.

But before we can make sense of this claim, we must clarify several key terms and moments of the argument of this book. Phenomenology understands the future as a relation of and to the subject. I will describe this relation as futurity, that is, the subject's relation to (or mode of comportment toward) the future. Futurity is constitutive of our experience in the present: I am right now affected in myriad ways by the future and my orientation toward it. This, in summary, is the bold claim of the phenomenological account of the future. The purpose of this book is not to evaluate this claim as an accurate or inaccurate portrayal of the future but rather to lay out clearly and succinctly the fundamental aspects of this claim and to determine what implications, if any, it has for phenomenology, broadly speaking. This is to say that it is phenomenology, more than time, that is the object of study here.[1] The theme of the future will be used to illuminate phenomenology, not vice versa.

Given this focus, a second caveat must be offered: the phenomenological method is the object rather than the means of this inquiry.[2] As such, its concern for the phenomenological method is theoretical, based on its relationship to a particular discipline (i.e., as its ground), and is not concerned primarily with employing that method; this book provides an analysis of the definition and role of the future within phenomenology and decidedly *not* a phenomenology of the future. Although certain futural acts have been investigated phenomenologically,[3] and although nearly all major phenomenological explorations of time privilege—in some significant way—the future (from Husserlian protention to Heidegger's anticipatory resoluteness,[4] Merleau-Ponty's ec-static temporality,[5] Sartre's discovery that the future creates meaning for the past,[6] Levinas's eschatology, and Derrida's messianic), a methodological examination of the significance of the future for phenomenology itself has been lacking.

From this lacuna has developed a schismatic account of the history of phenomenology, in which the boundaries of the discipline are variously drawn. A recent example of this phenomenon is the debate concerning the 'theological turn' in French phenomenology, in which several phenomenologists (especially Janicaud) question the phenomenological orthodoxy of others (especially Levinas, Henry, Marion, Lacoste, and Chrétien).[7] Focusing on the issue of futurity will help us see in what ways the 'theological turn' engages in issues that are necessitated by Husserlian phenomenology.[8] By clearly establishing the phenomenological import of the 'theological' phenomenologists, one is in a position to build a bridge over the chasm that has developed between Husserlian phenomenology, on the one hand, and 'theological' phenomenology on the other.[9] This bridge can help us reevaluate not just our position on phenomenology more generally but also our position on the work of the 'theological' phenomenologists, as I hope the chapters on Levinas will illustrate. The theme of futurity helps us see that Levinas and Derrida work within the bounds of the discipline of phenomenology to "liberate" it from certain nonphenomenological presuppositions that have somehow found their way into this most rigorous of sciences. Once this is asserted, the boundaries of phenomenological discourse seem to change, and a new set of philosophical problems are (re)introduced into the folds of phenomenology. Given, for example, the "interruption" of the present by the future (within the very constitution of the present, in part by that future), an explanation of mediation (i.e., a 'bridging' of that 'interruption') becomes necessary to phenomenology; similarly, if the interruptive force of the future is in part carried out by other people, the importance of a distinctly phenomenological account of intersubjectivity moves again to the forefront of phenomenology.[10] At the same time, insisting on the phenomenological character of several key issues at work in Levinas and Derrida helps us clarify what precisely is meant by phrases such as "ethics as first philosophy," "eschatology," and "messianicity." Our investigation of futurity in phenomenology will help us not only clarify certain key terms of ('theological') phenomenology, but it will also help us realize more fully the scope of phenomenological inquiry.

If I hope to show that a focus on futurity can help us find (not just historically but also philosophically) significant common ground between the various strands of phenomenology, common ground that can help us reevaluate phenomenology as a whole and each strand individually, my focus must be first and foremost on the methodological significance of futurity for phenomenology. In terms of that methodology, I will argue that futurity—concerned as it is with the subject's relation of constitution, or sense-giving, to the world—is able to reveal something unique about this relation that might otherwise be missed: Because the object of any futural act is, by definition, not present, futurity indicates a fundamental openness of the subject that is not a nostalgic lack or regrettable absence but is instead an integral aspect of the subject's constitutive capabilities.[11] The phenomenological claim of intentionality—that the constituting subject must be necessarily "open" beyond itself and its own horizons—emerges only when futurity is considered essential to phenomenology.

This openness of the constituting subject is not only central to the phenomenological method; it also suggests that phenomenology has an essentially nonepistemological (or nonconstituting) focus that is called "ethics." In tracing this thesis, the move from Husserl to Heidegger is not nearly as significant as the move from Husserl to Levinas. It is Levinas who first recognizes the true radicality of Husserl's account of the openness of the subject and brings this radicality to bear on the rest of the phenomenological enterprise. Where Heidegger implicitly acknowledges this openness in his accounts of being-in-the-world, involvement (*Bewandtnis*), facticity, and so on, he still thinks of these things primarily (at least in *Being and Time*) in relation to the primacy of *Jemeinigkeit* (mine-ness),[12] *Eigentlichkeit* (ownness), the self.[13] Hence the "openness" of Dasein onto a world—which is to say intentionality, for Heidegger—ultimately remains the act of Dasein (if not anymore of the subject),[14] since it is Dasein that is ultimately responsible, through its ecstatic temporality, for this openness. When Heidegger moves beyond the focus on *Jemeinigkeit* to more fully account for the openness of the self, he moves away from a self-identification with phenomenology toward the thinking of Being.[15] Heidegger, it seems, cannot account for the openness of the phenomenological subject within the confines of phenomenology. If he is right, then phenomenology is a self-defeating enterprise, as the very openness that it entails requires the move beyond phenomenology to something else (Thought) that phenomenology cannot itself accommodate.

Levinas, on the other hand, reveals *within phenomenology* the radical openness that is inherent in phenomenological constitution. By shifting the ground of phenomenology from the constituting subject to that onto which and by which the subject is open (the Other in the ethical relation), Levinas strives to make phenomenology more rigorously phenomenological. At times, however, in his focus on the alterity of the Other, he seems to risk losing phenomenology precisely in his attempt to revitalize it. Following Levinas, Derrida will see in Husserl a tension between the constituting powers of the transcendental subject and the openness onto the world that constitutes that subject. This tension will ultimately be nothing other than intentionality itself, as both Derrida and Fink can show us. Futurity—properly understood—reveals to us the intentionality that characterizes the phenomenological situation and that grants methodological significance to the reduction, itself the starting point of the phenomenological method. Hence in appreciating the true significance of futurity for the discipline of phenomenology, it is the triumvirate of Husserl-Levinas-Derrida that helps us clarify more sharply what is at stake in the question of futurity than would the triumvirate of Husserl-Heidegger-Derrida[16] or Husserl-Heidegger-Levinas. That this also helps us show the methodological continuities between Husserl, Levinas, and Derrida and therefore helps us in our minor concern of bridging the chasm between Husserlian and 'theological' phenomenologies is a side benefit.

Part of the reason the significance of futurity for phenomenology has not been previously noted is that it has not been sufficiently studied and clarified. Clarifying it, however, will not be without its own level of argumentation; in explaining Husserl's account of protention, for example, it will be necessary to simultaneously disprove the traditional assumption that protention is nothing more than an inverse retention.[17] Similarly my exposition of Levinas's and Derrida's accounts of the future will be both an exposition of those accounts and an argument that those accounts concern issues raised by a broadly Husserlian account of futurity. The establishment of a common ground for future discourse will be in certain instances as central to my aim as is drawing out the implications and significance of the common ground that is established.

The Argument

Having dealt with these methodological concerns, let us now turn to the substance of the book at hand. Let me re-state the conclusion briefly here:

Futurity will show us that phenomenology is an essentially promissory discipline. If this sounds altogether too mystical, not scientific or rigorous enough, let me assure you that the main thrust of this work is methodological in nature. Ethicality and the promise appear only insofar as they help us make sense of temporality, constitution, and intentionality. If, on the other hand, the methodological nature of this text strikes you as too arcane, narrow, or insular to be of value to philosophy as a whole, let me assure you that the results of this work open onto questions that are essential to a wide range of fields and disciplines, including epistemology and ontology, yes, but also religion, politics, ethics, ecology, and animal welfare.

The work is split into three parts. The first part will show that futurity is not only essential to the constitution of transcendental subjectivity,[18] but it also introduces a certain openness or interruption into the very heart of this (self-)constituting subject. The next part will examine this issue of openness in order to determine its significance for the constituting powers of the subject. The third part will bring to light the implications of the essential connection between constitution and openness for the phenomenological method and, through it, for discussions of ethics and philosophy more generally. As each part shifts in its object of inquiry, we will shift in ours: from a preoccupation with Husserl in the first part to Levinas in the second and Derrida in the third. In so doing, we will see that changes in the understanding of futurity go along with the respective differences in the conception of phenomenology (i.e., as transcendental, as intentional, as quasi-transcendentally intentional),[19] thereby further confirming the central place and significance of futurity for phenomenology and phenomenological method.

We begin with the first phenomenological discussion of the future. This takes place in Husserl's well-known account of inner time-consciousness, specifically the account of protention that he develops there. Within his account of time-consciousness, he discusses three distinct levels of constituting consciousness that collectively make up constituting subjectivity: empirical experience, immanent unities, and the absolute time-constituting flow of consciousness (see Hua X, 73). If there is an essential connection between futurity and constituting consciousness, then we should expect to find futurity playing an integral role not just in "time-constitution" but in every level of constituting consciousness.

In the absolute flow of time-constituting consciousness, futurity is described under the familiar rubric of protention. However, it is not enough to understand protention as an inverse retention, as Husserl seems to suggest we do in the lecture notes from 1905 (Hua X, 55) and in *Ideas I*

(Hua III, §§77, 81). Rather by turning to some of his writings on time, and specifically on protention, from 1917 (e.g., Hua XXXIII), we can begin to distill a more positive account of protention within Husserl (chapter 1). This account of protention will help us see the integral role that futurity—via the "striving" character of protention and its relative emptiness that enables the distinction between clarifying and confirming modes of intuition—plays in the level of absolute consciousness. The most fundamental of Husserl's levels of constituting consciousness would not function without the relation to the future known there as protention.

But it is not enough to show that futurity operates on the level of absolute consciousness. Following Husserl, we must also try to establish how the functioning of absolute consciousness affects the functioning of egoic consciousness. To do this we must account for the relationship between the levels of consciousness, most specifically for the level of constituting consciousness known as immanent unities or passive syntheses, which acts as the turning point between time-constituting consciousness and egoic intentionality. In clarifying how this second level of constitution works, we will see that it is predicated in large part on horizons of expectation that embody a distinct mode of futurity and that are essential to the constitution of a world, the most basic aspect of phenomenological 'ontology' (chapter 2).

This leaves us with only one level of constituting consciousness to discuss in order to have clarified the integral role of futurity in the constitution of transcendental subjectivity. This third level is characterized by an active directing of the egoic regard; when directed to the future, we call this act "anticipation." Going beyond the letter of Husserl's texts, we can distill some essential aspects of this act of anticipation (chapter 3): it has a subject, it has an at least partially clarified object that cannot be present, and it is grounded in the present via our horizons of expectation. In examining this last aspect, we see that anticipation shows us something significant about all of our experiences and not just those that are specifically anticipatory: All experience, like anticipation, is experienced in the present but with the promise of something more to come in the future. As such, anticipation plays an integral role in all empirical experience, thereby showing, at last, that all three levels of constituting consciousness are premised in some significant way on their respective accounts of futurity.

Each of these three modes of futurity functions not only on a distinct level of constituting consciousness but they also function, individually and collectively, to show us something important about phenomenology and its operation: Not only does phenomenology provide an account of futurity, but it is also in some important way premised on that account. There is something essentially futural in phenomenology, especially in phenomenology understood as the act of constitution. This essential futurity in turn begins to suggest a nonepistemological manner by which the future affects our understanding of the present. Taking as a point of departure the necessary nonpresence of the anticipated object discussed under the rubric of the "promise," we will see that this nonepistemological function entails openness within the constituting subject, an openness that suggests the possibility of an essentially "ethical" phenomenology.

If we must go beyond a transcendental constituting phenomenology in order to make sense of possibilities and promises that it has itself opened up, then we must first look for the resources for such a going-beyond[20] within that phenomenology itself. We have already found one such resource in the account of anticipation and the openness within constituting subjectivity that it illuminates. Levinas finds additional resources in his interpretation of the relation between intentionality and the notions of materiality, sensibility, and impression. In shifting our focus away from (transcendental) constitution to openness (onto the world), we will see that Husserl's understanding of the latter will repeatedly problematize his certainty in the primacy of the former. This will lead Levinas to posit ethics, not ontology or epistemology, as first philosophy, a move that does not go beyond phenomenology so much as it moves within a broadly Husserlian phenomenology against a conception of phenomenology that would unduly narrow its scope (chapter 4).

Having clarified this move from transcendental constitution to openness onto the world, we are then able to evaluate the significance of futurity for this openness (chapter 5). Levinas finds in his early investigations into the constitution of the solitude of the subject a significant part to be played by futurity, conceived there as relation to the Other. He develops this notion of the relation to the Other into a conception of the subject in which the subject is no longer constituting but is constituted by its relation to alterity. In this movement, *Totality and Infinity* will play a key role in the transition from a subject-Other correlative model to the later model in which the relation between subject and Other happens "before" the subject and makes possible that subject. Rather than reducing the importance of futurity, however, this move to the an-archic or diachronic time of the "pre-history of the I" (GDT, 175) is premised on an account of futurity, now understood as absolute surprise (TO, 77–79), passive awaiting (GDT, 115), eschatology (TI, 22; TA 349), and a "being-for-beyond-my-death" (TA, 349).

This account of the future put forward by Levinas offers something radically new to Husserl's conception of futurity: the notion of the subject as essentially constituted in addition to the subject as constituting (chapter 6). Though this idea is present in Husserl as well, it is in Levinas that its effects are felt most strongly for phenomenology: The constituted subject is open (onto the world and onto Others) in a way that does not merely add to the levels of constituting consciousness proposed by Husserl but also reveals moments of passivity within each of those levels (the "primal impression" of the absolute flow, the openness onto the world of expectation, and the promise and possibility of ethics that characterizes not only anticipation but all of empirical experience in general), passivity that seems to undermine the constituting power of the transcendental subject.

Because the Levinasian account of the future as passive surprise constitutes a radical critique of the power of the constituting subject, but a critique that takes its impetus from within Husserlian phenomenology, the tension between the power of the constituting subject and the vulnerability of the passive subject cannot be done away with—it is a part of phenomenology itself, and phenomenology itself is therefore based on this tension. Derrida highlights the tense aspect of phenomenology in *The Problem of Genesis in Husserl's Philosophy*, where he shows a fundamental tension in Husserl's work between the empirical/psychological and the transcendental/logical going all the way back to the early forays into a philosophy of mathematics.[21] In the introduction to his translation of the "Origin of Geometry," Derrida shows that this tension finds a common root in Husserl's notion of ideality and therefore that this tension remains throughout Husserlian phenomenology. Building on this, he suggests in *Speech and Phenomena* that this tension, as if between two Husserls, manifests itself in *différance*, a differential and deferring space/time that makes presence (and therefore experience, constitution, etc.) possible only by interrupting that presence continually and from within (by an alterity that is "in" me).[22] This idea of *différance*, of a strange unity-in-difference, enables him to suggest that the phenomenology of Husserl and the ethics of Levinas must themselves be held together in a similar type of unity-in-difference (chapter 7). This is not to suggest a synthesis of the two conceptions of phenomenology nor the reduction of the one to the other but a "unity" that preserves the difference of each pole in tension with each other.

The unity-in-difference of *différance* is itself a product of futurity. Beginning with the deferral that is partially constitutive of *différance*, Derrida develops an account of futurity that seeks to hold several distinct aspects together, not as one but as many in relation. In doing so, he develops a way to hold together the horizontal futurity of Husserlian constitution and the "surprising" futurity of Levinasian passivity (chapter 8). Derrida calls this development of a new account of futurity (which is actually an account of how to relate two other accounts of futurity) the messianic, which holds together messianicity (Levinasian surprise) and messianisms (Husserlian constitution). The central aspect of the messianic, and hence of Derrida's account of futurity more generally, is the promise. In the promise, Derrida strives to show the essential relationship between the giver, the receiver, and the content of the promise: All of these are united in the figure of the other in me, a figure that captures the openness onto the world and the constitution (as constituted/constituting) of the subject that together make up the figure of intentionality.

We are returned, then, to the issue of the promise, an issue that first arose in our analysis of the third Husserlian mode of futurity (anticipation). There we saw that the power of constituting subjectivity was interrupted by the promise of something yet to come. This opened us onto the question of passivity, waiting, and the relation to alterity that characterizes our relations with the world as intentional. But, of course, intentionality is not solely passive. It is precisely the unity of passivity and activity that we are seeking; one can find it at times in Husserl, but it is often undercut there by his analyses.[23] This is what motivates Levinas's "internal critique" of phenomenology and Derrida's rhetoric of the "two Husserls." At stake, then, I would argue, is not a revision of phenomenology but a way of understanding phenomenology properly, that is, as an essentially promissory discipline. Futurity provides us a way of doing so (chapter 9).

The centrality of futurity to phenomenology helps us uncover the necessary relationship between transcendental subjectivity and the world that is constitutive of intentionality and hence is necessary for any rigorous understanding of phenomenology. In so doing, it has also helped us see how Levinas's "ethical" project and Derrida's "deconstructive" project draw their impetus from problems within phenomenology. Our analysis of futurity in phenomenology therefore not only provides us insights into the phenomenological method (via the clarification of intentionality), but it also provides us clues to the scope of phenomenology (including "ethical" phenomenology) and to potential objects of future phenomenological inquiry. A promissory understanding of phenomenology helps us think anew about the "scientific" value of phenomenology and its relation to the reduction. With a reexamination of phenomenology's "principle of principles," we see that phenomenology has a central role to play in the self-understanding of communities and institutions. By helping us see the essential connection between transcendental inquiry and empirical conditions, the task of phenomenology emerges more clearly under the rubric of the promise as the clarification and evaluation of the implicit assumptions that go into our passive constitution of the world (conclusion). In so doing, phenomenology is revealed not only to have epistemological, ethical, and political concerns in its very core but also to have an essential role in relating scientific inquiry and cultural institutions to life and to one's tradition. In this way, we can come to see phenomenology as an essentially communal and intersubjective endeavor and therefore as having direct and important contributions to make to the understanding of politics, religion, ethics, and more.

PART I

Futurity in the Constitution of Transcendental Subjectivity

Protention as More than Inverse Retention

To many philosophers, phenomenology cannot be understood apart from the activity of a transcendental, constituting subject. This notion of phenomenology as transcendental subjective constitution is elaborated most significantly in the work of Husserl, who makes the constitution of the internal time of the subject one of the most basic (and therefore simultaneously the most important and most difficult) of phenomenological problems. In his lectures on time-consciousness, Husserl elaborates his infamous tripartite account of both internal time (as retention-impression-protention) and constituting consciousness (as made up of three distinct levels of constitution: absolute consciousness, the constitution of immanent unities, and the constitution of external objects in "objective" time). In this picture, futurity appears in unique and decisive ways in each level of constituting consciousness: as protention on the level of absolute consciousness, expectation on the level of the constitution of immanent unities, and anticipation on the level of the constitution of external objects. In order to properly understand this complex account of futurity and so get a full account of the various constituting powers of the transcendental subject, it is necessary to deal with each aspect in turn.

We will begin at the most basic level of constitution, that of internal time-consciousness. In his lectures on that topic, and the commentaries on those lectures by later thinkers, lipservice is paid to the future in the triadic conception of time that they offer, but by far the majority of the analysis is spent discussing the relationship between the present and the past. It is assumed (and sometimes stated quite explicitly) that the relationship between the present and the future will be the same as the relationship between the present and the past, just working in different directions. In the time-consciousness lectures, this shows itself in the claim that protention (our relation to the future in internal time-consciousness) is nothing more than retention (our relation to the past in internal time-consciousness) working in the other direction. On such an account, there is nothing phenomenologically distinct or important about protention except its direction of focus (i.e., toward the future rather than the past). This entire account of protention, then, can be summed up in five words: Protention is an inverse retention. To make sense of this, we would need to make sense of retention, thereby explaining the significance attributed to retention in Husserl's analysis and the later commentators.

However, the claim that protention is an inverse retention is not only incorrect, but it also risks losing the decisive significance that protention, and futurity more generally, play in phenomenology. Though the account of protention as inverse retention seems to be grounded in Husserl's lectures, this is not the end of the story, as Husserl later remedies the lack of analysis specifically devoted to protention found in those lectures. In doing so, he does not need to provide an entirely new account of internal time-consciousness; rather by paying close attention to the distinctiveness of protention within that account, he is able to escape certain problems that plague his retention-based account while clearly rooting key notions of phenomenological constitution (such as fulfillment and intuition) in protention. It is, we will see, by turning to protention—with its 'striving' character and the two distinct modes of bringing to intuition that it makes possible—that Husserl is ultimately able to place the phenomenological doctrine of constitution on a solid basis. Revealing the significance of protention opens up the entire problematic of the centrality of futurity to phenomenological constitution.

I. Husserl on Time and Constituting Subjectivity

In *On the Phenomenology of the Consciousness of Internal Time*, Husserl is interested in understanding how we can perceive duration and/or succession, when all we sense is a series of temporal moments stuck perpetually in the present. In speaking of our ability to perceive duration (or succession), Husserl, as both Meinong and Stern before him, must confront the problem that duration of perception is not perception of duration.[1] To circumvent this issue, Husserl claims that our perception of an object's duration itself has some level of temporality that remains distinct from the temporality of the object. He outlines three different levels of constitution in regard to time: (1) "the thing of empirical experience in objective time"; (2) "the constituting multiplicities of appearance belonging to different levels, the immanent unities in pre-empirical time"; and (3) the "absolute time-constituting flow of consciousness" (Hua X, 73). While the exact nature of the relation between the second and third levels remains a matter of debate,[2] at the very least the distinction between the first and the third level remains clear: On the one hand, you have the "clock" time by which we temporally measure objects in the world, and on the other hand, you have the flow of consciousness, which cannot be arrested, timed, or temporally measured. This "temporality" of absolute consciousness is metaphorically called "flow" (Hua X, 75).[3] Though we cannot talk about the temporality of this flow without doing so in conformity with the time of objects (75), that is, by using language of succession, of nows, pasts, and futures, Husserl is adamant that the flow is a distinct level of constituting consciousness, with a temporality that is distinct from that of constituted objects.[4]

To explain the temporality of this flow—and therefore to help clarify the levels of the constituting subject—Husserl expounds a threefold notion of internal time-consciousness as primary impression, retention, and protention.[5] On this model, immanent time begins with primary sensation. These primary sensations "remain" briefly in consciousness, in the mode of a "running-off" (Hua X, 27 ff.), and are constantly modified in this running-off: As I am confronted with new sensations in every instant,[6] the immediately previous sensations are not removed from consciousness but remain, albeit in modified form—no longer conceived as present but as just-past. This aspect of consciousness's ability to retain the immediately previous sensations is deemed "retention."

Protention emerges here as the correlate of retention, that which works like retention but in the other, future direction (Hua X, 55).[7] In protention, rather than retaining a past instant, I protend, or "anticipate,"[8] what will be sensed in immediately future instants. If at time D I have a sensation of D and a retention of C, Dc, then I will also have a protention of E, ‘E, that anticipates the next instant E as not-yet-in-the-now (Hua X, 77, 373), such that at the next instant, E, I will sense E, have a retention of D, Ed, and a secondary retention of C, Ec,[9] along with a protention of F, ‘F, and so on.[10]

We can see that retention and protention seem to make possible a temporality of perception, but what is not immediately clear is how they make possible the perception of temporality that Husserl claims for them (Hua X, 42). The first step in moving from temporality of perception to perception of temporality, at least according to the view current in Husserl's time, was to have all past moments be present in the present moment of consciousness.[11] We have already seen that retention was the act that was supposed to achieve this making-present—but how it is able to do this is far from clear, even to Husserl. Early in his lectures on time-consciousness, Husserl believed that retention functioned on the model of content and apprehension: The running-off functions as the content that is apprehended by the present consciousness as just past. However, Husserl would soon realize that this model of retention is unsatisfactory, as apprehension-content can be the content for only one apprehension, and therefore the content that is present to consciousness at A can be used to apprehend only the now-phase of A. In order for my retention of A to be understood as a retention of a past moment, it must already be apprehended as a modification of present content (i.e., I must apprehend it, not just as content, but as content that has been retained from a previous instant, as just-passed content), and hence "A′ is a modification analogous to phantasm (A), and it is itself consciousness of the past of A" (Hua XXIV, 260n.1).[12]

Retention, then, is a modifying and not merely an apprehending consciousness. As a modifying consciousness, however, retention remains nothing other than primal or absolute consciousness. This shift in the understanding of retention signals a larger shift in Husserlian phenomenology away from the content-apprehension schema toward an account in which even "mere experience" is already a constituted consciousness. But this raises the danger of an infinite regress problem: If the first level of consciousness is already constituted, then there must be some other level of consciousness that constitutes that level, and another one again to constitute that level, ad infinitum. To avoid this infinite regress, consciousness must be self-constituting (Hua X, 378–79).

It is precisely to meet this need for a self-constituting consciousness that Husserl employs his notion of absolute consciousness (Hua XXIV, 245). Absolute consciousness can be self-constituting and therefore can avoid the infinite regress problem of constitution because of what Husserl calls the double intentionality of retention: Retentional intentionality is both a transverse (*Querintentionalität*) and a horizontal intentionality (*Längsintentionalität*; Hua X, 380). The first intentionality makes possible the presentation of objects to consciousness; the second makes possible the (self-) presentation of the stream of absolute consciousness in which the perception of temporality is possible, and makes it possible because, by way of this horizontal intentionality, absolute consciousness "constitutes itself as a phenomenon in itself" (Hua X, 381). What this double intentionality makes possible, then, is that one act (retention) constitutes both the immanent objects of consciousness and the consciousness of the different temporal modes of givenness of that object over time.[13]

If protention is really just retention in the other direction, then it should function equivalently to retention. Unlike retention, however, protention does not obviously work as a presentifying act, in the same way as did retention. To more clearly understand this point let us use Husserl's example of hearing a symphony. In hearing a symphony, one can easily conceive of how the preceding note is retained in consciousness, such that I hear the next note differently[14] because it followed the first note than I would hear it if it was played alone. In listening to a piece of music, I have no difficulty in perceiving the many notes that make up that piece of music as successive (one note follows a previous note). Nor do I have any difficulty in perceiving the many notes as part of one piece of music, a piece of music that stretches through time. I do not, in this sense, hear a bunch of disjointed notes but one cohesive symphony, which takes the course of an hour to play itself out. This is because each note hangs around in my consciousness—not as if it were still present but as having just-been-played—into the playing of the next note, which then hangs around into the playing of the following note, and so on, so that the string of notes is tied together into one symphony by this train of "hangings around," this train of notes retained into the next moment. Thus the concept of retention and its impact on my perception of temporality can be easily understood.

Less immediately evident, however, is how my hearing of the present note is affected by protention. The traditional claim of protention would be that, like retention but operating in the other direction, in hearing the current note something of the just-future note prefigures itself, such that I hear the current note differently because of the note that is to follow it: In protention I must hear the first note precisely as a *first* note. In retention I clearly hear the note differently if it follows another note than if it does not; specifically, in the former case, I hear the note *as following* another note—I hear it as the second note (in a string of notes in a scale or symphony, etc.). But can I really hear the difference between two identical notes played at the same time by different musicians, given that one note will be followed by a second note while the other note will be followed by silence, as protention understood as an inverse retention would claim? It does not strike me that the playing of the next note would affect my hearing of the current note, either in its tone or in its mode of temporal givenness (i.e., as preceding a future note). I am suggesting that we do not hear a note specifically as a *preceding* note, that is, as a first note in a string of notes, until we have heard the second note. By this point, of course, the first note is no longer present for us to hear. Properly speaking, then, we do not hear the note as the *first* note at all; rather we hear it as a note and remember later (i.e., after the playing of the second, third, and fourth notes) that it was the first note. Unlike retention, where I hear the note as the second note, in this case I do not hear the note as the first note. Yet I must be able to hear the note as first, that is, as preceding a later note, if protention is to function as an inverse retention.

One could suggest that, in hearing a familiar melody, I hear the current note in part in anticipation of the next note that I know (from past experience) is to follow it. When I hear the first few bars of Beethoven's Ninth (or the first few chords of Nirvana's "Smells Like Teen Spirit," for that matter), I hear them precisely as the first few bars (or chords) of a familiar piece of music. It seems, then, that we have found a situation that supports the notion that protention is an inverse retention. But even if this scenario occurs (and it seems to me obvious that it does), it does not strike me as relevant: What is being described here, while phenomenologically identifiable, is not protention but expectation or the act of anticipation.[15] Protention, if it is to make any sense at all, must operate in every situation of perception of temporality and not just those situations in which past experience yields a certain familiarity that causes me to expect or anticipate what is to come next. Just as retention must be kept separate from recollection (Hua X, §19), so too must protention be understood as distinct from expectation and anticipation. But understood merely as retention in the other direction, it is not immediately clear how protention can be understood as distinct from those other futural acts.[16]

Developing Husserl's symphony example has yielded two essential insights into protention: Protention is something other than an inverse retention. Protention is something other than expectation and anticipation. The first of these insights will guide the remainder of this chapter. The second announces the need for the following two chapters. Together they cry for the development of a positive account of protention.

II. Fulfillment and Protention as (More than) Inverse Retention

In trying to understand protention, then, we are forced to look beyond the notion of an inverse retention.[17] Earlier I said that Husserl understands retention to function, by way of a double intentionality, as one act that simultaneously constitutes objects and the absolute consciousness that makes possible the perception of temporality. In attempting to explain how retention is able to do this, he turns to the fact that every retention "contains expectation-intentions whose fulfillment leads to the present" (Hua X, 52). It is the concept of fulfillment that is able to tie retentions to the present of the stream of consciousness. But this is the case only because of the presence of protention: "Every process that constitutes its object originally is animated by protentions that emptily constitute what is coming as coming, that catch it and bring it toward fulfillment" (52). Though Husserl does not develop this intriguing notion in any more detail in Hua X, he does develop it in more detail in other texts of this time (ca. 1917),[18] and in so doing he begins to realize that in its capacity for fulfillment protention promises to be a more fertile ground for a phenomenological analysis of absolute consciousness than was retention (Hua XXXIII, 225–26).[19]

The notion of fulfillment gives Husserl a strong account of how absolute consciousness is self-constituting. In order to fulfill a protention, an act must be aware of both the preceding act anticipating fulfillment and the constitution of the present object. Hence there is a twofold coincidence between protended and present moments: There is a coincidence between the previous protentional intention and the primal presentation (Hua XXXIII, 25), and there is a coincidence between that toward which both the protention and the primal presentation are directed. The first of these Husserl describes under the rubric of "general fulfillment" and the second under "particular fulfillment" (29–30). General fulfillment plays a role in the self-constitution of the primal stream, thought along the lines of the stream's "self-relatedness" (*Selbstbezogenheit*; 207). Particular fulfillment plays a role in the constitution of the immanent temporal objects. Hence the notion of fulfillment is able to explain why the double intentionality needed to make absolute consciousness self-constituting is united in protention in a way that could not be so easily explained in retention.

Let us examine this idea of fulfillment in more detail.

A. General Fulfillment

General fulfillment provides Husserl with a way of conceiving the constitution of the primal stream of absolute consciousness: Because every moment is the fulfillment of a previous intention, every moment can be connected to the previous moment via this general fulfillment. In describing this general fulfillment by claiming that "fulfillment contains in itself retention of the previous intention" (Hua XXXIII, 25), he indicates that every protention has a retentional aspect, and every retention a protentional aspect (21–22). Every protention grows out of a retentional horizon.[20] Conversely, every point of any momentary phase of consciousness has an essentially protentional aspect, in that every point is directed toward its fulfillment in the corresponding point of the following momentary phase of consciousness.[21] As such, all points along the vertical line of each instant can be viewed as protentions and not just those that I originally called protentions (indicated in my example by the `). Further, it is only because of these implicit protentions that we can speak of retentions as retaining anything at all: It is the character of fulfillment that entails that the previous instant has been retained (see Hua X, 52), and this is true for every point of a momentary phase of consciousness, not just that point which is a primal impression (F) of what had immediately prior been the primal protention (`F).

It is because of the coincidence entailed in this notion of fulfillment that Husserl is able to posit the self-relatedness that characterizes the stream of absolute consciousness and enables it to avoid the problem of infinite regress: Because this coincidence happens *in the very fulfillment* there is no need of another act beyond the coincidence to unite the past to the future (Hua XXXIII, 27). While the sixth of the *Logical Investigations* seems to indicate that consciousness of fulfillment requires three elements (a consciousness that must be fulfilled, a consciousness that fulfills, and a synthesizing consciousness that ties the first two together such that one can be conscious of the fulfillment), the position that Husserl describes in the Bernau manuscripts is that, because of the essential role of protention, this third element (which quickly would lead to a problem of infinite regress) is no longer necessary. Husserl is thereby able to avoid the problem of infinite regress, as there is no longer recourse to an "external" synthesizing consciousness beyond the fulfillment.[22] This self-related fulfillment is continuously occurring in general fulfillment, in which protention protends the mode of givenness of what is to come: E protends its being given in the next instant as a retention, Fe, Ed protends its being given in the next instant as a secondary retention, Fd, and `F protends its being given in the next instant as F. But again the mutual implication of protention and retention is at work, as, conversely, Fe retains the protentional directedness of E as well as its fulfillment, F retains the protentional directedness of `F and its fulfillment, and Fd retains the protentional directedness of Ed and its fulfillment (as well as the protentional directedness of D and its fulfillment in Ed, etc.). This complex relationship between protention and retention is able to do away with talk of primal impression;[23] rather than protending or retaining a particular sensation-content, protentions protend retentions, and retentions retain protentions (as well as the retention of previous protentions).[24] As Husserl puts it:

> That which came before as such is retained in a new retentional consciousness and this consciousness is, on the one hand, characterized in itself as fulfillment of what was earlier, and on the other, as retention

of what was earlier. . . . The earlier consciousness is protention (i.e., an intention "directed" at what comes later) and the following retention would then be retention of the earlier retention that is characterized at the same time as [its] protention. This newly arriving retention thus reproduces the earlier retention with its protentional tendency and at the same time fulfills it, but it fulfills it in such a way that going through this fulfillment is a protention of the next phase.[25]

All this makes Husserl able to say that the "now is constituted through the form of protentional fulfillment, and the past through a retentional modification of this fulfillment."[26]

B. Particular Fulfillment

The emphasis on the "form" or structure of the flow as made up of the movements of protention and retention marks the fundamental difference between general and particular fulfillment. This structural openness is infinite, as every moment would contain a protention, ʽF, of the next instant, F, which itself would protend its givenness in the following moment as Gf, and so on, as well as the protention, ʽʽG, of that next instant's protention, ʽG, of the instant, G, that comes immediately after that, and so on, ad infinitum.[27] To avoid a new problem of infinite regress, Husserl employs the idea of particular fulfillment. If protention via general fulfillment constitutes the self-relatedness of absolute consciousness, thereby avoiding the old problem of infinite regress, protention also, via particular fulfillment, helps constitute the immanent object, thereby avoiding the new problem of infinite regress.[28]

In particular fulfillment, fulfillment occurs gradually, as reflected in the modes of givenness of the temporal object as they differ according to degrees of fullness. The nearer the object gets to me (physically and temporally), the fuller is the intuition I am able to have of it. The givenness of the object, then, tends toward a culmination (Hua XXXIII, 30) or saturation point (39) of greatest fullness, which is also the point of minimal evacuation (30). This point is the primal impression, which functions as the *terminus ad quem* of protentions and the *terminus ad quo* of retentions (38).

The culmination point applies only to what Husserl calls the "domain of intuition." This domain is distinct from the domain of nonintuitive differentiation, which is characterized by an empty, nonintuitive potential for differentiating the points of an immanent temporal object.[29] The limit of the intuitive domain is what Husserl calls the zero of intuition (Hua XXXIII, 227). This limit prevents the problem of infinite regress because of the finite nature of intuition: We cannot intuit an infinite number of things. In the domain of nonintuitive differentiation, however, we can theoretically distinguish an infinite number of potential protentions and retentions attaching to every momentary phase of consciousness. This domain is limited again by the point at which consciousness falls away, a second zero. Here, however, the limit is an open point without differences (227–28), that is, the point in which there exists theoretically an infinite number of points that consciousness cannot practically differentiate (e.g., all the future protentions mentioned above). There is, then, a certain potential infinity in both the protentional and retentional directions. However, this potential infinity does not succumb to the problem of infinite regress because no one, and certainly not Husserl, has claimed that consciousness can retain or protend over an infinite span of time. Indeed quite the opposite: The period of retention and protention is severely limited, tied, as it is, to the "primal impression." This, I would argue, avoids the problem of infinite regress in its most damaging guise, while still leaving consciousness necessarily open in the direction of protention and retention.[30]

III. Differentiating Protention and Retention

The difference in direction highlights what up to now has been the main (perhaps the only) difference between protention and retention: One deals with the future, the other with the past. Even the act of fulfillment in itself does not favor protention over retention, as both are necessary for fulfillment to occur (Hua XXXIII, 46).

But it is not accidental that the discussion of fulfillment occurs at the same time as Husserl increases his focus on protention. There is something essentially different about protention that gives it a unique function in fulfillment and hence a unique function in absolute consciousness, subjective constitution, and phenomenology itself. What makes protention intrinsically different from retention is the "striving" character of protention (Hua XI, 73). Husserl makes clear that the striving characteristic of protention is a passive directedness, a "passive intentionality" (76), with which the ego has no active involvement (86). This "directedness" seems to define the very essence of protention, as when I quoted Husserl equating protention with "an intention 'directed' at what comes later."[31] This intentional character, he claims, belongs intrinsically to protention, and protention alone; while retention may acquire intentionality, it does not intrinsically possess it (77). In other words, though we *can* "cast a backward turning glance" toward the past, this is a subsequent act that is distinct from retention, and we must "clearly differentiate between the direction of the egoic regard, and the direction in perception itself that already takes place prior to the apprehending regard" (74). Indeed Husserl seems to say that an intentionally directed retention ceases to be retention; once "awakened" by a directed consciousness, it "should already be characterized as a remembering" (80) rather than as a retaining.[32] To be directed toward the past, then, is to be remembering, not retaining. Retention retains the past in a temporality that is in the present, always moving toward the future. Hence retention is not directed toward the past.

The other side of this directedness is fulfillment. Fulfillment is "a unity of consciousness . . . that carries out a new constitutive accomplishment" (Hua XI, 75) and as such can be characterized as an associative synthesis (76). Specifically fulfillment is the unity between the full presentation of confirmation and the empty protentional presentation that makes possible the self-relatedness of the primal stream of absolute consciousness. This unity is possible because of a distinction in modes of bringing to intuition that marks the second essential difference between protention and retention. In protention there are two distinct modes of bringing to intuition: the clarifying (picturing) mode and the confirming (fulfilling) mode (79–80). The first of these modes seeks to clarify, picture, or prefigure the intended objective sense; because the "generality of expectation is always relatively determinate or indeterminate" (79), it is necessary to determine more closely (80) the field of possibility for the intended and expected object. Here protention enables expectation[33] to fill some of the emptiness of the intended object so that the intended object can coincide with a confirming or fulfilling intuition in a synthesis. The second mode of bringing to intuition, then, is "the specific fulfillment of intuition" that is the "synthesis with an appropriate perception" (80). Here "the merely expected object is identified with the actually arriving object, as fulfilling the expectation" (80).[34]

Husserl is again adamant, though, that these two modes of bringing to intuition occur only in protention. In retention the synthesis that clarifies the sense of the intended object is simultaneously the synthesis that confirms the object as the fulfillment of the clarified intention (Hua XI, 80). Though remembering *can* be a "picturing" or clarifying, "it cannot merely be a picturing; rather it is simultaneously and necessarily self-giving and thus fulfilling-confirming" (81). This perhaps is another way of marking the "essential difference" that Husserl finds between protention and retention already in marginal additions to *On the Phenomenology of the Consciousness of Internal Time*: Protention "leaves open the way in which what is coming may exist and whether or not the duration of the object may cease and when it may cease," while retention "is bound" (Hua X, 297; cf. Brough's English translation, 309n.42). In short, unlike retention, protention can remain essentially open. If the directed character of protention is especially necessary for general fulfillment, then this openness to the future—characterized by the distinction between clarifying and confirming intuitions—is especially necessary for particular fulfillment.

We can see that protention is and must be distinct from retention. It is *not* merely an inverse retention but is characterized by essential differences that help explain the possibility of the self-constitution of the stream of absolute consciousness. Protention, and protention alone, is necessarily directed (and thereby intentional) and able to bring to intuition both a clarifying and a confirming synthesis (and thereby make possible the particular fulfillment of objects). Hence not only is protention essentially different from retention, but protention as one mode of futurity has a key role to play in absolute consciousness.

Conclusion: Rethinking Internal Time-Consciousness

Developing the implications of this positive account of protention for an account of futurity in phenomenology is one of the projects of this book. For now I would merely like to draw out the implications of a positive account of protention for Husserl's account of time-consciousness, especially for the concept of retention internal to that account. Doing so will help us begin to see the importance that this new account of protention will have in time-consciousness and hence the importance of futurity to a phenomenological account of constitution.

As discussed in section I above, Husserl's account of internal time-consciousness is necessary to establish what he will call "absolute consciousness" and hence avoid problems of infinite regress that plagued the earlier accounts of time-consciousness put forward by Meinong and others. Retention was the key to establishing absolute consciousness, as its double intentionality enabled one act to be simultaneously self-constituting and constitutive of objects. However, our new account of protention gives us reason to question this move. Specifically it causes us to question to what extent retention can be described as "intentional" at all, let alone doubly intentional.

The problem arises from the lack of directedness or striving that marks one of the essential differences between retention and protention. If retention is not directed, if it does not strive in the way that protention does, it is difficult to conceive of how it can be intentional, as an essential aspect of intentionality is its being necessarily directed.[35] Indeed Husserl himself states that "retentions, as they arise in their originality, have no intentional character" (Hua XI, 77).[36] But if retentions are not intentional, as Husserl himself says, then surely they cannot be doubly intentional, as Husserl also states.[37] Yet the double intentionality of retention was key to establishing the need for and viability of his account of absolute consciousness. Hence if one denies that (double) intentionality, one seems to lose the justification for Husserl's discussion of absolute consciousness, and the possibility of transcendental phenomenology itself is called into question.

But this extreme conclusion need not be reached. Rather a clarification of our terms at this point helps us to avoid this damning consequence while at the same time deepening our understanding of internal time-consciousness in general and retention more specifically. This can be done by paying close attention to the "fundamental stratification" of cognitive life (Hua XI, 64). The key distinction at work in this stratification is that between "modal modifications of passive *doxa*, of passive intentions of expectation, their inhibitions passively accruing to them, and the like" (52), on the one hand, and, on the other, the "spontaneous activity of the ego (the activity of *intellectus agens*) that puts into play the peculiar accomplishments of the ego," for example, in judicative decisions (64). This stratification enables us to distinguish between conscious acts constituting the active level of the ego and that which passively constitutes those conscious acts.[38] Retention and protention belong properly in the passive sphere and as such cannot be considered acts, properly speaking. Therefore retention cannot possibly be the act that is doubly intentional. Rather retention and protention (i.e., internal time-consciousness) make it possible that acts can be doubly intentional; retention and protention are necessary constitutive factors of the acts of consciousness, which themselves constitute the objects of our experience.

This clarification helps us adequately understand the place of internal time-consciousness in Husserl's thought. It also helps us understand that retention—which is not yet an act—cannot possibly be intentional in the standard sense, namely as consciousness of. It is more accurate to say that conscious acts are able to be intentional because of retention and protention, that is, because of internal time-consciousness. Within internal time-consciousness, it is protention that strives for fulfillment,[39] and hence protention is more easily connected with intentionality, including the double intentionality that makes possible absolute consciousness.

The implications of the above are twofold. First, *retention and protention are not something we do*. Because they are not acts but are constitutive of acts, retention and protention are not something that we consciously "do." It is therefore difficult at best and inaccurate at worst to talk of retaining, for example, a note. Rather we *perceive* the note as temporal, as part of the symphony, and are able to do so because of protention and retention. What exactly is retained, then, becomes difficult to discuss, as it is all too easy to conflate the retained and the perceived, though, properly speaking, what we can talk of as perceived cannot be that which is retained, as that which is retained is necessary for perception to occur (Hua XI, 53). With this caveat in place, it would seem that *both* the hyletic datum of some particular tone (say, C sharp) and the protentional directedness of that tone as temporal, directed again both to the object (particular fulfillment) and to the different modes of that object's being given to consciousness (general fulfillment), are retained. They are retained not in the act of retention but in the act of perception (here, specifically, the perception of the note). This distinction between acts of consciousness and that which constitutes those acts (including internal time-consciousness) must be rigorously maintained.

Second, *it is especially, though not exclusively, because of protention that our acts can be doubly intentional.* As this conclusion runs contrary to Husserl's claims that retention is doubly intentional (cf. Hua X, 380–81), we should not affirm it too quickly. I have already shown that protention and retention, taken together as internal time-consciousness, enable us to both perceive objects and conceive of ourselves as conscious of objects.[40] Hence internal time-consciousness makes us able to be doubly intentional in the way necessary for absolute consciousness. However, within internal time-consciousness, we can see that it is protention that strives for fulfillment, both because it is inherently directed and because it differentiates between clarifying and confirming modes of bringing to intuition. Hence it is protention that is tied more closely to intentionality in general and, by extension, to double intentionality as well. Of course, this is not to say that retention has no role to play in intentionality, as retention and protention necessarily refer to and employ each other, as discussed above. It is merely to say that protention bears some necessary relationship to intentionality that requires further analysis before any investigation into intentionality—single or double—can be said to be complete.[41]

Given these two implications, it is misleading to speak of retention as doubly intentional. If one means by this that retention is the doubly intentional act called for by Husserl to avoid infinite regress and thereby ground absolute consciousness, this immediately runs contrary to the first implication of our analysis of protention, which shows that retention and protention are not acts but are constitutive of acts. On the other hand, if one wants to use the term "act" loosely here and thereby mean only that retention is that which enables our consciousness to be doubly intentional (even if it is, properly speaking, other acts that have this doubly intentional character), we see that this too is not quite correct, as it runs contrary to the second implication of our analysis of protention. In fact if one wanted to speak loosely and thereby attribute double intentionality to either retention or protention, it seems more accurate, if one is forced to choose between the two, to ascribe this doubly intentional characteristic to protention rather than retention.

We can see that the positive account of protention discussed in this chapter helps us to clarify internal time-consciousness in general and retention in particular. But it is specifically an account of futurity that I am interested in pursuing here. We have seen that an analysis of futurity will be necessary to any attempt to understand intentionality within phenomenological discourse. To do this, we must first complete our analysis of the essential relationship between futurity and constituting consciousness. In order to see how the positive account of protention fits into this analysis, we must turn now to an account of the relationship between the different strata of constitution discussed above, to see how protention in the most passive sphere of constitution impacts other aspects within the passive sphere and ultimately impacts the active sphere as well. On all three of these levels of constituting consciousness, we will find a different account of the subject's relation to the future. Taken together, these will give us a more robust account of the role of futurity in phenomenology.

2

Expecting the World

In developing his positive account of protention, Husserl is forced to alter his understanding not just of time-consciousness but also of transcendental subjective constitution itself. We encounter the world as always already constituted rather than as some raw content or hyletic data in need of subsequent apprehension. The potentially infinite chain of subsequent constituting acts of consciousness can be arrested only by the self-constituting nature of absolute consciousness. But as self-constituting, absolute consciousness seems to fail to open us onto the world, leaving us instead protending retentions and retaining previous protentions. Husserl's account of transverse intentionality is supposed to get us beyond this problem, but we cannot understand how until we more clearly understand the relation between the different levels of constituting consciousness he suggests.

But it is not enough to understand each level on its own, as Husserl himself came to see. In his genetic phenomenology, Husserl emphasizes the importance of genesis and history to the functioning of the subject.[1] In this approach, it is no longer enough to distinguish between levels of consciousness; now one must be able to tell the tale of how X leads to Y, how earlier levels of constitution enable or lead us to our present lived experiences. Such a project seems to cry out for an account of how we can move from the absolute flow of consciousness to the constituted acts of the ego.[2] We cannot make this move without passing through the second level of constituting consciousness, called that of 'immanent unities'[3] in Hua X. In making clear the nature and role of the constitution of 'immanent unities,' we will see that this level of constituting consciousness requires a certain relation to the future that I will call 'expectation.' In trying to clarify the function of constitution in phenomenology, we will see that expectation plays a key role as the mediating step between absolute consciousness and the thematic acts of the active ego.

I. The Levels of Constitution and the Bifurcation of Consciousness

A problem arises early on in any attempt to clarify the role and function of the different levels of constituting consciousness. In *Analyses concerning Passive and Active Synthesis*, Husserl claims that the "fundamental stratification" of consciousness is its split into passive and active levels (Hua XI, 64); however, in *On the Phenomenology of the Consciousness of Internal Time*, discussed in chapter 1, he clearly gives us a threefold stratification of consciousness:

> Now that we have studied time-consciousness . . . it would be good to establish and run through systematically for once the different levels of constitution in their essential structure. We found:
>
> 1. the things of empirical experience in objective time (in connection with which we would have to distinguish still different levels of empirical being, which up to this point have not been taken into consideration: the experienced physical thing belonging to the individual subject, the intersubjectively identical thing, the thing of physics);
> 2. the constituting multiplicities of appearance belonging to different levels, the immanent unities in pre-empirical time;
> 3. the absolute time-constituting flow of consciousness.
>
> (Hua X, 73)

We are left to consider how to proceed: Do we assume that Husserl gives us two different accounts of the stratification of consciousness? If so, then we must answer the question of which of the two is better suited to Husserlian phenomenology. This would require a close examination of each of the different accounts, as well as an analysis of the relative merits of each account for the later accomplishments of Husserl and the phenomenological tradition that follows him.

Such attempts have been made, but I think they ultimately prove to be misguided.[4] A closer examination of Husserl's analyses in Hua XI shows that there remain at least three levels of constitution, and hence three levels of consciousness, at work for Husserl here. We must turn to his account of the relationship between passive and active syntheses to begin to make sense of why he can speak sometimes of a twofold and sometimes of a threefold consciousness without contradicting himself.

Husserl is adamant that it is only because of passive syntheses that the ego is able to actively direct its regard (Hua XI, 120). We saw earlier that the realm of passivity begins already with protention, which is characterized as a "passive intentionality" (76). Passivity there implied that protention occurs without the ego acting on it, that is, without consciously taking it up. The essential elements of passive constitution[5] are associative structure, affecting,[6] and attention.[7] Here attention refers to a tendency of the ego and not yet the explicit directing of the egoic regard by consciousness; it is a "tending of the ego toward an intentional object, toward a unity which 'appears' continually in the change of the modes of its givenness" (EU, 85). This tending-toward occurs because of affecting (*Affektion*), that is, "the peculiar pull that an object given to consciousness exercises on the ego" (Hua XI, 148), though again this pull (*Reiz*)[8] is different from, and in a sense prior to, the ego's attentively turning toward an object.[9]

The result of this tending-toward is an association, which itself enables the constitution of unity in multiplicities. But one must be careful to avoid conflating "association" in this context with psychologistic and empiricist uses of that term.[10] Rather than an active process of linking things together based on past experience, association in this context is a "purely immanent connection of 'this recalls that,' 'one calls attention to the other' " (EU, 78). If this association is possible only because of affecting, turning-toward, and tendency (*Tendenz*; Hua XI, §28), as we have already discussed, it is also the case that being affected can pass over into passive constitution only because of association, that is, only because what is currently affecting us "recalls"[11] something in the past.

Initially this process of passive association enables us to reproduce things from our past in the present: Seeing something now automatically calls to mind some previous experience. This calling to mind is most often done on the basis of similarity: That which is reproduced from the past is like that which is perceived in the present in some way.[12] This type of reproductive association—that the past is reproduced, re-presented (as past) in the present—is "an absolutely necessary lawful regularity . . . without which a subjectivity could not be" (Hua XI, 118–19; see also 124) because in it "the entire past-consciousness is co-awakened" (122). Reproductive association enables our present consciousness to be united to our past consciousness and thus makes possible the historicity of the subject.[13]

This passive association that makes possible the historicity of the subject must be kept distinct from internal time-consciousness.[14] While internal time-consciousness is a necessary presupposition of associative synthesis (cf. Hua XI, §27), the two are not the same. Association is needed to "awaken" the associated objects, as retention and (especially) protention are empty. Without association, Husserl claims, internal time-consciousness would be "meaningless" (125) because it abstracts from content and hence cannot give us "any idea of the necessary synthetic structures of the streaming present and of the unitary stream of the presents" (128). However, without internal time-consciousness and the temporalization of consciousness that it makes possible, the idea of association, and the historicization it makes possible, would of course be impossible. As Husserl puts it, "In the ABCs of the constitution of all objectivity given to consciousness and of subjectivity as existing for itself, [internal time-consciousness] is the 'A' " (125). Hence, association is founded upon, but distinct from, internal time-consciousness.

But association must also be kept distinct from the actively intentional acts of the ego. Association is a passive synthesis, as Husserl points out time and time again, and as such is distinct from active syntheses.[15] Indeed the "specific intentions" of active consciousness arise from, and hence presuppose, passive synthesis (Hua XI, 118).

We are left, then, with three distinct levels of constitution:

1. active syntheses (i.e., specific, egoically directed intentional acts)
2. passive syntheses (e.g., association)
3. internal time-consciousness

Recall now the three levels of constitution that I discussed earlier (from Hua X, 73):

1. the things of empirical experience in objective time
2. the constituting multiplicities of appearance belonging to different levels, the immanent unities in pre-empirical time
3. the absolute time-constituting flow of consciousness

We can see that there is an affinity between the two lists, a likeness. To what extent this likeness holds depends on the relationship, if any, between the active and passive syntheses under discussion in the first list and the "objective" "things" and "immanent unities" of the second list. For the time being, however, it is sufficient to show that the bifurcation of consciousness into passive and active levels is compatible with the three levels of constitution discussed above. One is not forced to choose between the two because they are not in conflict. In fact the appeal to a bifurcated consciousness can help us make rudimentary sense of the relationship between the three levels of consciousness: Two of them are passive, one is active.[16] And conversely, adding the third level to bifurcated consciousness helps us make sense of the transition from passive to active syntheses.

II. From Passive to Active Synthesis

To provide the account of the transition from absolute time-constituting consciousness to the active intentions of the thematizing ego that Husserl called for, we must return to the concept of association. Previously I discussed reproductive association, that is, the way something in the present recalls something in the past and hence ties together the historicity of the subject. I suggested there that the key aspects of association were affecting, turning-toward, and tendency (Hua XI, §28). The first two I have already discussed: Something in the environment exercises a pull or an allure on us, and this causes us to passively turn-toward that something, that is, constitute that thing. In this way, the very process of constituting things in the world is already discretionary: By exercising an alluring pull on our consciousness, the thing not only causes us to take it up (i.e., it rather than something else); it also causes us to take it up in a certain way (i.e., we take X up as X, not as Y or Z or A). This latter occurs because the affective allure of that something is associated with another, similar affection: "This recalls that" (to use Husserl's expression) because this and that are affectively similar in some way. This affective similarity entails that, at least at this stage of constitution, the affection is *felt* (*Gefühl*) rather than understood. At this point, what is constituted is called by Husserl an "empirical type"[17] and is the result of a concordance of tendencies: This affective pull tends to recall that (previously experienced) affective pull; also that (previously experienced) affective pull tends to produce a certain set of characteristics or consequences; the similarity between present affective pulls and relevantly similar previously experienced affective pulls tends to produce similar characteristics in the present as were experienced in the past; and so on. The result of this concordance is what we commonly refer to as a 'tendency.' For example, the thing in front of me affects me in a way that recalls earlier experiences when I have been similarly affected. These earlier experiences in turn share some common characteristics that I then infer will apply also to the situation before me. In the earlier experiences, the thing in front of me had a solid back, was able to hold weight, and so on, and so I infer that this thing in front of me now in the present will also have these characteristics. This in turn enables me to expect, with varying degrees of certainty, how the other sides of this thing could be perceived if I were to make those other sides available to me in a primary presentation (i.e., by walking around it so that I could see its back directly). That is, because of the tendencies produced in association, I am able to expect other, currently nonpresent sides of the thing, which allows me to apperceive what I see as a chair, a thing like other chairs.

Because they result from affection rather than understanding, these tendencies produce object-like formations (*Gegenstandlichkeit*), but not full-fledged objects, which come about only by passing through the tribunal of judgment (Hua XVII, 69). The former have epistemological value in terms of sense and help us constitute a world, while the latter have epistemological value in terms of meaning and take place in the realm of judgments and science, broadly speaking.

Let me use the following to illustrate this point. Let us assume, following a long line of philosophical tradition, that humanity is qualitatively different from other animals and that the main reason for this qualitative difference is the use of reason.[18] Let us further equate this reason with an ability to make judgments (as rudimentary as S is p). Would the fact that humans, alone among the animals of this world, possess this ability to make judgments mean that humans alone have a world? Of course not; animals too interact consistently with the world. This is not evidence of higher-order thought but is possible via tendencies and habits (which in animals we tend to call instincts).[19] Few of us would say that animals make judgments of the type: "This is a chair." Yet few of us would also disagree that domesticated animals tend to consistently use chairs as devices for sitting on and will do so even when presented with a new chair or type of chair. Placed in a room with a three-legged chair, for example, and assuming the animal (let's say a cat) has not had any previous experience with a three-legged chair, none of us would be surprised if the cat sat (or lay) in the chair. This is more than merely custom or habit, even if it is rooted in these things; it is an implicit recognition of the chair, part of the constitution of a world, but a recognition and constitution that do not require a judgment or higher-order thinking. Rather the cat makes use of habitual tendencies in order to bring about an association of "this recalls that" (EU, 78). The three-legged thing in front of the cat recalls other two- or four-legged chairs the cat has had previous experience with, and the cat then responds to the thing before her in ways that are habitually similar to the way she has previously interacted with those two- and four-legged chairs.

Similarly we too have an environment, or an environing world, in which we act and with which we interact, and we do so without need of recourse to active syntheses. So what is gained by active syntheses, that third level of consciousness? What does this third level of constitution provide us that is not provided to the animals in our scenario? Husserl would say meaning. The world, though crucially important and constitutively valued (i.e., things are not just constituted but have a certain sense; they are to be used in certain ways, embraced or avoided, eaten, attacked, or fled from, etc.), is, properly speaking, meaningless (*Bedeutung-los*) for the animals.[20] That it is meaningless does not mean it is without sense (*sinn-los*).[21] This distinction is parallel to the distinction between passive and active syntheses: We passively constitute sense and actively constitute meaning. Through sense we are given a world; through meaning we are given knowledge.

It is this step of constituting the object and its meaning that marks the move from passive to active synthesis. The gap between these two is a "quantum leap,"[22] a qualitative and not merely a quantitative difference. The difference is between the unthematized thing of experience and the object of thought characterized by judgment. What motivates the shift from passive to active synthesis is what Husserl calls "interest" (*Interesse*). Whereas the similarity between things is merely felt in the affective allure during association, in judgment these similarities are brought before the gaze of the ego and made thematic. The thing constituted in association is the individual taken as itself; in taking it as itself, it is implicitly recognized as being like other similar things, but these similarities are known latently and dormantly. When these similarities are themselves made the point of interest, we move beyond the sphere of passive association to that of active judgment. As long as I take my dog, Jack, only as Jack, that is, as that being which Jack is, I remain in the sphere of passive constitution. It is when I consider Jack as a dog, as one dog like other dogs, or as a black Lab (like other Labs, or like other black things), that I begin to move into the camp of active synthesis. In active synthesis, that which makes things similar— the unity that unites across the multiplicities—is seen and disclosed. This disclosing is made possible by judging (what lies dormant in passive constitution can be made thematic only by active judgment) and makes possible a certain exactness that is not possible within the realm of passive constitution alone. This exactness is indicative of the move to objectivity.

At issue in this move, then, is interest: To what interest does the ego direct itself? If my interest is on something else (say, performing a philosophical analysis), I will habitually use chairs as chairs (perhaps we could even say "recognize them as such") without ever actively comparing that which lies before me with other chairs or with the essence of chair-ness.[23] If, however, something occurs to bring my interest to the chair itself (e.g., the chair on which I am sitting while performing my philosophical analysis breaks), then the chair itself becomes the object of my interest rather than part of the system of support that enables the subject to function.

With the chair as object, I begin to consider whether the thing on which I had been sitting, and which now lies in pieces beneath me, was in fact a chair. To do this, I think of what makes something a chair: physical extension, being constructed of certain materials that can bear a minimum amount of weight, and so on. I then compare those characteristics with the thing before me (now beneath me). After such a comparison, I am able to decide whether the object on which I had been sitting was in fact a chair, or whether it was something else; that is, I can decide "X is a chair" or "X is not a chair."

We see, then, that the objectlike formations constituted in passive synthesis are the necessary ground on which active synthesis can be performed: Without the constituted unities of empirical types, I would have nothing on which to make judgments (Hua XXXI, 3–4). And the move from passive to active synthesis is undergone by an activation of interest:[24] In turning my egoic powers toward something, I begin to interact with that thing in a way that is entirely different from my previous, noninterested (though still affected) interactions.[25] Jack who sighs on the floor of my office while I write is experienced *and constituted* differently by me than is Jack when he coughs, for example. In the former situation, I have little interest in Jack's status as a dog (like or unlike other dogs) so much as Jack helps give sense to the world. In the latter situation, however, the fact that Jack is a Lab-shepherd cross, and therefore has genetic dispositions toward certain diseases, makes the things that make him like and unlike other dogs very important to me. I could not take such an active interest in Jack's status as a dog if I hadn't first constituted him as a "dog-like" thing, and I do this because of passive association.

However, this does not make the relationship between passive and active synthesis purely unidirectional.[26] Though passive constitution is necessary to provide the object-like formations to be judged in active synthesis, the results of these judgments can themselves become fodder for passive associations. Once I make judgments, these judgments are "sedimented" (Hua XI, 38) into my experience and become a "that" which can be taken up in an association of "this recalls that." Despite this counter-movement, however, passive constitution remains ultimately primary: Without a primal passive constitution, there would be no products of active constitution to be passively employed in association.

In clarifying the relationship between passive and active synthesis, I have made use almost exclusively of passive association. What about the "passive striving" of protention? What is its relation to active synthesis? Here we see the importance of the second level of constitution as an intermediary step between the first and the third levels. If the move from the flow of absolute consciousness to the acts occurring in objective time is too great to be immediately recognized, the mediation of passive constitution helps us make this step. As I have already discussed, internal time-consciousness makes it possible for the subject to have an experience by making possible the subject's temporality, that is to say, making possible the subject as temporality, as temporal. Protention reaches, strives toward a fulfillment in the future. But this striving remains empty, merely structural, without the content provided by particular fulfillment. Particular fulfillment applies to the givenness of the object rather than to the different (temporal) modes of givenness of that object to consciousness characteristic of general fulfillment. This givenness of the object in particular fulfillment is characterized by a relative fullness; the closer the object is to me—spatially and temporally—the more full is the intuition I am able to have of it. Corresponding to the fullness of this intuition is the strength of the allure or draw that the intuition is able to exercise on consciousness. The fuller the intuition, the greater the pull on consciousness it is able to exert. Consciousness, so affected, begins to organize what has been drawn to its (passive) attention. This organization happens by way of associative tendencies: Things are linked with things that tend to be similar to it, both in the present and in the past. These tendencies, built up from a horizon of retained experiences, allow us to perceive: We apperceive sides of the thing not immediately given to us, and we perceive that thing as within a *world*. This world, then, becomes the background or the basis of the constitution of objects and their meanings. This constitution of the object and its meaning is the realm of active synthesis.

III. Futurity and Passive Constitution: Expectation

We now have a picture of the movement from the flow of absolute consciousness to the acts of empirical time. What is not yet clear is the role of futurity in this movement. We know that protention plays a key role in the flow of absolute consciousness, but this is not the sum total of futurity's importance to phenomenology. In order to fully appreciate this importance, we must turn now to the role of futurity in passive constitution.

We have already seen the centrality of association to passive constitution; indeed the two are virtually synonymous. In the movement from reproductive association, in which the present recalls something past, to the constitution of a world via tendencies, a second, "higher level of association" (Hua XI, 119) emerges, what I will call expectations or expectative association. If the immanent association of the present recalling the past is able to help us constitute a world in the present, this is primarily because the tendencies produced in reproductive association simultaneously create a horizon of expectations that enables us to apperceive things in the world (119).

To return to the earlier example of the chair: I perceive the chair as a chair, though I perceive only one side of the chair at a time because I have a horizon of *expectations* that enables me to expect, with varying degrees of certainty, how the other sides of the chair could be perceived if I were to make those other sides available to me in a primary presentation (i.e., by walking around so that I could see the back of the chair directly). That is, because of my past-consciousness, I am able to expect other, currently nonpresent sides of the chair. This allows me to apperceive what I see as a chair, a thing like other chairs.

The movement of reproductive association described earlier is incomplete without the corresponding expectative association because reproductive association alone cannot expect anything of the thing present before me now. Though tendencies can be recalled and applied to the present thing, as described earlier, they become useful in and for apperception only when they can be used to expect certain characteristics of the present thing. It is through this expectative association that we are able to induce the thing in the world before us.[27] Further, this expectative association is done automatically, reflexively, that is to say, passively: We do not have to consciously call to mind past experiences and try to determine from them what will come next in order to experience a chair as a chair, the world as the world. Indeed if we had to "use experimentation to generate the example of what is to come, this surely shows a poor relation to the future" (PA, 19), as our normal relation to the future enables us to expect what is (to come), that is, to apperceive objects and perceive a world.

Yet surely there are cases in which my expectations are not met: the chair breaks, the wall on the other side of the house has been knocked down, the shape in the shadows turns out to be a shrub and not a person. Do these cases not prove that expectations are secondary to perception, that expectation is possible for but not necessary to the constitution of a world? Not at all, and for two reasons: First, expectations unfulfilled are still constitutive of that experience. For example, I am surprised that the chair on which I am sitting suddenly breaks. This surprise occurs precisely because it is not what I expect: I expect chairs to be stable and good for sitting on, and when this expectation is not met, I experience the expectation as unfulfilled, in the mode of disappointment. But this disappointment rests upon the "systems of rays of expectations" because "disappointment essentially presupposes partial fulfillment; without a certain measure of unity maintaining itself in the progression of apperceptions, the unity of the intentional lived-experience would crumble" (Hua XI, 26). If I did not expect the chair to maintain its structure and hold my weight, I would not be disappointed when it did not do so.[28] However, this disappointment does not lead me to think that the thing on which I had been sitting was not a chair, or at least it does not cause me to think that I had not just been sitting on something. There is always some level of continuity, and there has to be such for experience to continue.

And this continuity is the second reason that instances of disappointment (and other nonconfirming modes, such as negation, doubt, possibility, etc.) do not entail that expectations are not necessary for the constitution of a world. On the level of absolute consciousness, continuity occurs via protention and its retention in fulfillment; without this stream of protentions and retentions, the flow of consciousness would cease to be unified as a single flow and hence would cease to be identifiable as mine. On the level of passive synthesis, this continuity takes another form. Though no particular object remains continuous in my experience, there must be some level of continuity if the experience is to remain. Corresponding to my continuing experience of absolute consciousness, then, the correlate of all my experiences that provides unity or continuity at the level of passive synthesis, is the *world*. Though some particular expectations will be unfulfilled, and some states of affairs in the world will change, "there is a unity of synthesis in spite of such alterations running through the successive sequence of universal intendings of world—it is one and the same world, an enduring world, only, as we say, corrected in its particular details, which is to say, freed from 'false apprehensions'; it is in itself the same world" (Hua XI, 101).

And this world cannot be constituted without the vital role of expectation. Primarily, expectations help us prefigure and in doing so function as "an empty intuition . . . that provides its general framework of sense" (Hua XI, 22). That is, expectations help us begin to give sense to the apperceived thing before that thing is fulfilled in a confirming synthesis. This ability to clarify and prefigure the thing is a distinct mode of bringing to intuition that happens in the realm of futurity alone (80; see also chapter 1 above). Without this clarifying intuition, the confirming intuition of present perception would not constitute a fulfillment, in the full sense of that term discussed in the previous chapter; without a clarifying intuition that begins to give sense, we would not be able to experience the confirming intuition as the fulfillment of an earlier striving. This is what Husserl means when he says that "in the normal case of perception, all fulfillment progresses as the fulfillment of expectations" (26).

We have already seen that fulfillment is twofold, both general and particular, and that futurity is a necessary aspect of any fulfillment. Simply put, without futurity there would be no fulfillment. Without an experience of fulfillment in the realm of general fulfillment, the unity of the absolute flow of consciousness would be lost, as we saw in the previous chapter. Without an experience of fulfillment in the realm of particular fulfillment, the unity of experience that constitutes a world would be lost. Hence without expectation there is no clarifying intuition; without clarifying intuition there is no fulfillment in the confirming intuition; without fulfillment there is no unity of experience; without unity of experience there is no world.

IV. Protention and Expectation: Moving Husserl Past Kant

We see that many of the structures laid out in our discussion of a positive account of protention take on significance in the discussion of expectation. The forms and distinctions that were helpful in distinguishing between protention and retention gain their true weight only when the "particularity of content" that is abstracted from all discussions of internal time-consciousness (Hua XI, 128) is brought back into the picture. With the move to passive constitution, such content returned to the forefront of our analysis. This helps us see, for example, how the continual striving characteristic of protention, when applied via the distinction between clarifying and confirming modes of bringing to intuition in expectation to passive synthesis, enables the apperception of objects and hence the constitution of a world. Internal time-consciousness, then, provides a "universal, formal framework," "a synthetically constituted form in which all other possible syntheses must participate" (125), while expectation is distinguished from protention because expectation is tasked with bringing the future to intuition (129).

But despite this language, the distinction here between protention and expectation is not merely the Kantian distinction between forms of consciousness and their intuitive content. Kant is concerned only with the conditions of possibility for the constitution of objects that transcend consciousness, and hence "his question is only this: What kinds of syntheses must be carried out subjectively in order for things of nature to be able to appear, and thus a nature in general" (Hua XI, 126). Husserl, however, is concerned with something "lying deeper and essentially preceding" Kant's concerns about the constitution of transcendent objects, namely, "the constitution of the subject's stream of lived-experience as being for itself, as the field of all being proper to it as its very own" (126). For Husserl, the distinction is not (just) between form and content but between modes of givenness: Expectation functions in the mode of intuition, protention in the mode of nonintuitive differentiation.[29] Even more radically, perhaps, one could say the distinction is between the givenness *to* consciousness characteristic of intuition and the givenness *of* consciousness (to itself) characteristic of the absolute flow of consciousness. Husserl's radical departure from Kant therefore comes in the claim that subjectivity itself is not given a priori (in the Kantian sense, meaning with no reference to experience) but is also constituted. Hence, as constituted, the forms of subjectivity, the "universal, formal framework" (125) of consciousness, including that of the "transcendental synthesis of time" (126), are "only conceivable in genesis" (125).

Futurity, especially as it functions in the two passive levels of constituting consciousness, reveals to us a sense of constitution that moves beyond the traditional notion of constitution attributed to Kant. By leading constituting, transcendental consciousness necessarily to the issue of genesis, futurity shows that constitution is not some "closed" a priori system of subjectivity but is essentially open to issues of genesis. This openness, we will see in later chapters, will have significant consequences for our understanding of phenomenology, especially its doctrine of intentionality. But if the consequences of such openness for a theory of transcendental constitution are not immediately obvious, perhaps they will become so once our examination of constitution is complete. Let us turn, then, to the third level of constituting consciousness and the role that futurity must play there.

3

Experience and the Essential Possibility of Anticipation

Having now explained the distinct modes of relation to the future that are at work on the levels of absolute consciousness and passive association, the last aspect of our opening study on the role of futurity in phenomenology will be an explanation of the mode of futurity that applies to the level of active synthesis, that is, of active intentions of the ego. At this level, we find all of the acts that are consciously taken up by the ego and that are founded on passive syntheses of association. That is, on this level we find a world that is more or less already constituted, and we then set out to intentionally interact with that world. While we have so far been concerned with the role of futurity in constituting the world and the subject in (and of) that world, we now turn to the role of futurity in our purposive actions in the world. Here we must account for the ways we actively set the future as the object of our egoic consciousness. I will refer to this as our intending of the future[1] and the act that corresponds to it as anticipation. With protention and expectation, anticipation completes our account of futurity as it functions in constituting, transcendental subjectivity: For every distinct level of constituting consciousness, there is a distinct account of the mode of relation to the future for that level.

I. Why Speak of Anticipation at All?

Up to now we have been fortunate enough to rely mainly on Husserl's own words to help formulate an account of futurity in phenomenology.

However, Husserl does not offer an analysis of anticipation, and hence we cannot rely on him explicitly at this stage. But this sets up a problem before we can even begin our analysis of anticipation: If Husserl does not give an account of anticipation (at least not in any detail for what I mean by that term here), then by what right do we attribute this notion to his phenomenology? In phenomenology it is easy to pay too much homage to past masters of the discipline. We too easily allow ourselves to be caught up in the minutiae of their books and articles (and, increasingly, of lectures and notes that we have no reason to think were ever intended for publication) and do not allow ourselves to go beyond the letter of the text to the spirit of what is written. We are often hesitant to describe something as Husserlian, for example, unless we find Husserl explicitly endorsing it in one of his texts. While one must certainly be careful in ascribing positions to authors, there must also be room to account for applications of someone's thinking to areas they did not consider. In phenomenology especially, where we are supposed to be concerned with "the things themselves" and not "the texts written about the things themselves by previous phenomenologists," such room should exist for the expanding of phenomenological insights into new realms. This expansion, however, does not have to be at the expense of an appreciation of the masters. Here I will not only try to develop a phenomenological account of anticipation but will also try to show that such an account develops out of and is consistent with Husserl's reflections on time, futurity, and phenomenology more generally. As such, I believe it is consistent to describe this notion of anticipation as broadly Husserlian, even if the details are not provided by Husserl himself.

Initially the need for something like anticipation seems to arise out of a mathematical inconsistency. There are three levels of constituting consciousness in Husserl's descriptions, and accounts of futurity that correspond to only two of those levels; one level remains without a corresponding mode of futurity. Attempting to derive a third level of futurity solely on this basis, however, would seem to be more metaphysical than phenomenological. Fortunately there is more solidly phenomenological evidence for the need for anticipation as well. All of us have an experience of being egoically oriented to the future: I look forward to my wife's return home from work this evening, or I hope that the Toronto Maple Leafs will win the Stanley Cup. Both of these acts of the ego occur in the present (I am *now* looking forward to my wife's return; I am *now* hoping for a Stanley Cup victory), though what corresponds to these acts is not (even potentially) a present fulfillment. Rather these acts are necessarily oriented toward a future fulfillment, which means, at the least, that they cannot be fulfilled (neither confirmed nor disappointed) in the present; they both necessarily orient the subject to the future (and in the case of the Leafs winning the Stanley Cup, perhaps to the very distant future!).

Further, the Husserlian accounts of protention and expectation, though playing a role in these acts, are not in themselves enough to fully explain those acts. Protention, as a striving (into the future) that opens up the distinction between clarifying and confirming modes of intuition, is operative in my hoping and in my looking forward to some future event. But protention, you will recall, is an "empty" striving, in that it takes place on the level of abstraction (Hua XI, 128). This empty abstraction is supplemented by expectation as an aspect of passive association. Where protention opens up the distinction between clarifying and confirming modes of intuition, expectation begins to provide us with an actual clarifying intuition that can then be confirmed (or disappointed) in a fulfillment. Again, though this is at work in my hoping and my looking forward to a future event, it is not equivalent to those acts: Expectation is both passive, in that it requires no active involvement of the ego, and associative, in that it yields us a sense-filled world of object-like formations but no objects as such. But what I am hoping for or looking forward to is a distinct object (or an objectified state of affairs), and this hoping or looking forward is a distinct act that results from the turning of my egoic regard to some future object (or objectified state of affairs). This is different from protention and expectation.

Another way to establish the need for the distinction I am arguing for is to look at it from the other direction. If our orientation to the future (including both hope and looking forward to something) that we are calling anticipation requires both protention and expectation, this should not surprise us: Protention and expectation are necessary aspects of any act whatsoever. Perception, for example, would be impossible without protention (to allow us to perceive temporality; see chapter 1) and expectation (to apperceive objects as objects when we are presented with only one side of that object; see chapter 2). Perception, however, is very possible without anticipation; in fact perception, if taken as a presentifying act, cannot occur simultaneously with anticipation, which is, by necessity, oriented not toward a present but toward the future. Hence what I am referring to by the term "anticipation" is distinct from protention and expectation, and therefore any complete account of futurity in phenomenology must also provide an account of anticipation as distinct from protention and expectation.

II. Some Essential Aspects of Anticipation

If we now see the need for a discussion of anticipation in our account of futurity, we cannot turn directly to Husserl to help us in such a discussion.

Fortunately, though, we are not entirely alone in our search for anticipation. In an essay published in 2004, James K.A. Smith provides five essential aspects of hope (one particular mode of anticipating) that he thinks are in line with Husserlian phenomenology (though he admits that he is not aware of any "specific analysis of hope as a mode of intentional consciousness" performed by Husserl himself; DH, 205n.26). These aspects are a subject of hope, an object of hope, the act of hope, the ground of hope, and the mode of fulfillment proper to hope (205–10). Let us deal with these in turn to see how well they might apply to an account of anticipation.[2]

The first of these aspects seems to be valid for any anticipation whatsoever: For any orientation to the future, there must be a subject that is so oriented.[3] So I believe we can add this to our list of essential features of anticipation.

The next aspect, the object of hope, is slightly more complicated. I agree that anticipation is always anticipation of something, but where anticipation and hope differ is in the characterization of this object. Smith claims, I think accurately, that the object of hope must be good or else our orientation toward that object is not one of hope but of something else (e.g., fear; DH, 208). This seems true for hope, which is positively inflected, but need not be true for anticipation in general, in that I can anticipate, for example, that the United States is headed for trouble (say, if it continues its current practice of rabid deficit spending). Here I am anticipating a future event, but I do not hope that this will occur because I do not think the event itself is good. So there must be an object of anticipation, but not necessarily a good object; that is, I can anticipate something bad.

A further question in regard to the object of anticipation is the level of determinacy it must achieve. Here the Husserlian distinction between clarifying and confirming intuitions is helpful. The problem is not how strongly determined the confirmation of an object must be but how clarified an object must be in order to properly be the object of anticipation. In regard to hope, Smith says that the object must not be absolutely indeterminate (DH, 222), but it cannot be absolutely determined either (225). In terms of anticipation, the same seems to hold true. On the one hand, the object of anticipation cannot be absolutely indeterminate, that is, entirely unclarified; with no clarification, there could be no confirmation, no fulfillment, and hence no act at all. On the other hand, a wholly determined object would by necessity have to be present and hence unanticipatable: Any object that is not present would lack some determination. However, does this also entail that the object cannot be wholly clarified? This is difficult to answer, because I'm not sure what an entirely clarified object would be. I could in theory know all aspects of an object's size, shape, color, and so on, even know when it would appear in time; such an object would have a high level of clarification and hence would be easily confirmed when a corresponding intuition was made present. But it seems to me there must always remain a difference between the clarification and the confirmation: No matter how clarified the object is, this does not guarantee its confirmation, in that we must still "match" the confirmation to the clarification as referring to the same object. Given this, it is not clear that we can ever speak of a full clarification. At any rate, anticipation seems to allow for a higher degree of clarification than does hope: I can anticipate the outcome of a computer program that I run and in which I control all the variables and can do so with a 100 percent level of certainty—but I think this would still count as an anticipation (i.e., as my being oriented to a future object, even if it is an object that I know will come).[4] Such a situation does not apply to hope (cf. DH, 217).

Third, hope is an act, by which Smith means that it is intentional and that it therefore must be distinguished from acts done "out of" hope, "in" hope, and so on (DH, 208). The first of these two claims is true, even if it does not seem to add a great deal to our discussion, given that we have already established that anticipation requires both a subject and an object.[5] The second claim is helpful when applied to anticipation, in that it can help us differentiate between "true" acts of anticipation (i.e., I anticipate future troubles for the United States, given its economic policies) and acts based on that anticipation (i.e., I therefore choose to invest less in U.S. companies). The key difference between these acts is the temporal character of the object: Acts of anticipation are oriented toward an object that "is" in the future; there could, by necessity, be no present fulfillment (whether in confirmation, disappointment, or anywhere in between) of an anticipation. This is distinct from acts done "out of" or "because of" anticipation, which all have as their focus a present object (in the current example, the investment of my money).

The fourth element of Smith's phenomenology of hope is the ground of hope. Smith introduces this to distinguish hope from illusion and wishful thinking, which he claims are "modes of intending the future [that] are unsound because they either lack ground or are flawed in the character of their ground" (DH, 209). The ground, then, is what contributes to the confidence I have in my hope (209). I agree with the distinction Smith is trying to make between hope and illusion/wishful thinking, but I disagree with him that illusion and wishful thinking are distinct modes of intending the future. Rather I would argue that illusion does not intend its future object in an essentially different way than does hope; indeed this is what can make it so difficult to distinguish between hope and illusion. Illusion does not intend the future differently; it just makes a poor inference, if you will, from what is present to what can be expected in the future. The difference is epistemological (as Smith recognizes; DH, 209) rather than intentional. Hence the distinction between hope and illusion is not that they have different modes of intending the future but that they have different modes of understanding the present—specifically, perhaps, a difference in the validity accorded to the present as evidence from which to anticipate a future. I do not, then, actually hope that I will see a unicorn someday; rather I fantasize that I will. Rather than anticipation, this is wishful thinking. If I were to truly anticipate seeing a unicorn, I would have to have some level of confidence that this could occur. If I had such confidence, it would have to be based on something in the present or past (i.e., some expectational horizon). One could anticipate seeing a unicorn only if one understood the present in such a way as to include unicorns in one's horizon of expectation. From this we can conclude that anticipations are based on some interpretation of the present.[6] As such, we can see that anticipation must have a ground: It must be grounded in some way in our horizons of expectation, which are themselves related to our retentional and protentional horizons.[7]

Finally, we can speak about the role of fulfillment in anticipation. All anticipations strive for fulfillment. This point is true, but trivially so; chapter 1 has already shown us that *every* act strives for fulfillment. Indeed this striving is characteristic of protention, which is a structure of absolute consciousness. But how, then, do we distinguish, for example, between hope and fear, if not by distinguishing one as seeking fulfillment and the other as seeking to avoid fulfillment? I contend that the difference in our constitution of the object of these acts as good or bad, respectively, is sufficient to make the point that Smith tries to ground in fulfillment. It seems to me that we are afraid (or we dread or we do not look forward to something) not because of some difference in fulfillment vis-à-vis hope but because of how we constitute the object of each. We are afraid precisely because we think that the (feared) object will come to pass, that our fear will be fulfilled. The difference is in how we evaluate the object: whether we want it (good) or don't want it (bad). Describing this as a difference in fulfillment needlessly complicates the issue.

Using Smith's phenomenology of hope as our guide, we have come to see the following essential traits of anticipation:

1. a subject
2. an object that must be at least partially clarified but admits a very high—perhaps total—level of clarification

3. an orientation toward something that cannot be present (i.e., a future object)
4. a "grounding" in our horizons of expectation[8]

Smith's account, while helpful in distilling some essential features of anticipation, is not sufficient to complete our analysis of anticipation. He deals with only one mode of anticipating (hope) and not with anticipation itself; hence, though his analysis yields some essential features of anticipation, these are not explored in their full phenomenological depth. Specifically problematic is the question of how anticipation can simultaneously be oriented toward a nonpresent object and be "grounded" in our present horizons of expectation. What is the nature of the relationship between the present and the future at work in anticipation? Is it projection, some type of inference?

If so, it would not be qualitatively different from expectation but merely an active expectation rather than a passive one. While the active-passive distinction would be enough to make the acts distinct, such is not the only difference between expectation and anticipation. In order to understand why this is the case, we must turn to an analysis of the mode of givenness that is characteristic of anticipation itself. Then we will see what is unique about anticipation's relation of the future to the present.

III. The Givenness of Anticipation

Jean-Yves Lacoste begins "The Phenomenality of Anticipation" by offering a distinction between pre-experience and pre-givenness as the two essential phenomena in any analysis of anticipation (PA, 15). Pre-experience is analogous to what I earlier described as expectation: that which makes sense of the present by relating it to a past and then projecting it into the future. Pre-givenness is that which is "given to us inchoately, in the mode of a hint or promise" (15). Since the first of these is better discussed under the rubric of expectation, I will leave it aside for now and focus on pre-givenness. There is something distinctive in the manner in which anticipation gives itself to us, namely, that it gives itself to us in such a way as to give itself as already here, but not yet here. This eschatological[9] paradigm (the already but not yet) is borne out in every act of anticipation: What we anticipate (whether in hope or in fear, with happiness or trepidation) is not only yet to come (i.e., some future object or state of affairs) but is also already here in some sense, prefiguring what is to come. Analogous to our (pre-)experience of expectation, in which we begin to clarify the anticipated object as X, and hence begin to prefigure it and in this prefiguring make it in some sense already here, in pre-givenness the object offers itself as yet to come. In doing so, the object gives itself, in a certain sense, as yet to be given, as pre-given: given-before (it is given).

This pre-givenness is distinctive of our orientation to the future. Past objects are not pre-given but are given, and then repeated, given again differently, in a different mode (i.e., as past).[10] Repetition is then governed by an "axiom": "[T]he same might be given to us, but we will not be the same" (PA, 18). Even if I remember perfectly the event of walking my dog that I underwent yesterday, the fact that I have undergone the event already once does not pre-give the event to me today. Rather today, even if I remember the event perfectly, that is, absolutely identically to how it was experienced yesterday, I am different in my relation to the event: I now perceive it as *yesterday's* event, as something that already happened and that I am now remembering, rather than as something occurring now. The same situation applies for events that I can repeat in the present: Today I watch a movie that I also watched yesterday. The movie, of course, is not different today from what it was yesterday, but I am different: Today the phone rings and distracts me, or I worry about the safety of a friend and so am not taken up in the story of the movie in the same way. There are countless ways I am different today from what I was yesterday, but what is essential is that I am different: Though the same object is given to me, I am different, and hence the object is given to me differently. Therefore repeated events are not pre-given in the initial event but are given differently in the repetition (i.e., at the very least, they are given *as repeated*).

It is via the givenness to consciousness that we can come to see the centrality of anticipation to Husserlian phenomenology. The nature of the givenness of anticipation reveals to us something about phenomenology itself and the relation of intentionality to transcendental subjectivity. Our consciousness is "narrow," by which Husserl means that, though our consciousness can do many things—imagine, perceive, believe, hope, and so on—it can do only one of these at a time (at least actively). Though an object exists in multiple modes of being and hence gives itself to consciousness with multiple modes of givenness, it is received in consciousness by only one mode at a time. When I read a book, for example, I move through the printed words on the page, so to speak, to what is indicated by those words. However, I can also direct my gaze to particular features of the book's appearance as a book (i.e., its decorative cover, its classic script, etc.) or even as an object (e.g., its weight when I have to move it), but I cannot do all these things simultaneously: When I am reading the book, I am not paying overt attention to the script or the decoration, and surely not to the weight of the book; when I am enjoying the beauty of the script, I am not reading the words but looking at them; and so on. For this reason, every experience is bordered by what Lacoste calls "non-experience" (PA, 19), by that which is in some sense present in the object experienced but not overtly experienced.

For Lacoste, the "link between experience and non-experience, between what happened, the happening, and the non-happening, is the point of departure of any investigation into anticipation" (PA, 19). An experience that is fully satisfied with what is experienced, that does not point beyond itself to the domain of nonexperience, is an experience of enjoyment (*jouissance*) in the phenomenological sense.[11] And enjoyment—though it does not exclude protention, as even enjoyed experiences are temporal—excludes anticipation, as "the presence of enjoyment does not anticipate a future that will give us more joy" (22), and hence "[n]o enjoyment has as its function to give us a foretaste of an even greater enjoyment" (23).

If enjoyment excludes anticipation, this begins to help us delimit the sphere in which anticipation can occur: Only those experiences that are not experiences of enjoyment can count as potential anticipations. Alternatively phrased, the field of potential anticipations is limited to the field of nonenjoyed experiences,[12] those experiences in which I am not totally absorbed. In these experiences, something that is not in the experience, something that is absent, affects us. Absence is thereby given to consciousness (PA, 25), but given precisely as absent, that is, as pointing toward something that is not here but still affects us. This affection by the absent points us beyond the present and hence inhibits enjoyment: We cannot be totally absorbed in an experience that, in its essence, points beyond itself. "The experience of absence is, therefore, made present in a presence that is antithetical to the presence of enjoyment" (25), and this unique mode of presence makes possible an intention toward the future, that is, anticipation (be it in the mode of hope or waiting; see 25).

Anticipation, then, in its essence, cannot be fully closed (PA, 27). It must always be open to something that stretches beyond itself (i.e., the future object).[13] But such an essential openness does not seem to allow for fulfillment, for the realization of what is anticipated. This does not mean that there is no fulfillment whatsoever in anticipation, as this would lead to incoherence. Every anticipation exhibits at least general fulfillment; this is the only thing that allows an anticipation to stretch through time, which would seem to be an essential feature of anticipation. But the relation between anticipation and particular fulfillment can be explained only by way of the distinction between clarifying and confirming intuitions. The object of anticipation is fulfilled only via clarification; there is no confirming realization in anticipation. Such a realization would seem to be the end of anticipation. What is distinct about anticipations is that, rather than containing their own fulfillment, rather than being completed only when what is anticipated is realized, anticipation is antithetical to its realization (30) in such a confirming intuition.

But if there is no confirming intuition, how do we experience anticipation? There must be some such confirmation, it seems, if anticipation is to be an object of experience. Lacoste claims that anticipation "certainly has an experiential reality similar to anything else that is experienced in consciousness" (PA, 31). For him, the work of art provides an example of the unique mode of givenness of anticipation, the unique phenomenality "of what has not emptied its being in its being-present but which is given to us to anticipate a future presence that will be even fuller" (26). But that which makes the work of art a good example of anticipation is true also for any object whatsoever: "[T]he work of art is here completely . . . [but] this being here cannot be identified with a complete presence. A new interpretation, a new look, a new reading will let appear what has not yet appeared—even though it was 'here' " (26). The ability for any new look to yield something that has not yet appeared even though it was "here" in the given is not accidental but follows from our narrow consciousness, from the fact that our experience is essentially composed of presence and absence (a point that any analysis, no matter how rudimentary, will show to be constitutive of Husserlian phenomenology).[14] Because of this play of presence and absence,[15] of experience and nonexperience, what is given as present—and hence as fully here, as given in itself—can also hold the promise of being given yet more fully in the future, of offering something else of itself that is already 'here' but not yet experienced (see Hua XVII, §16c).[16] It is because of the multiple modes of being and the multiple modes of givenness of every object, every consciousness, and every experience that anticipation is possible. In other words, anticipation, or at least its possibility, is an essential feature of Husserlian phenomenology, and "[t]he logic of anticipation is calmly inscribed in the logic of experience" (PA, 31).

But where experience is characterized by fulfillment, anticipation seems to be characterized most strongly by its antithesis to confirming intuitions. We are now in a position to return to Lacoste's initial claim about anticipation: that it is both pre-experience and pre-givenness. We now understand, however, why this is better expressed as (pre-)experience and (pre-)givenness (cf. PA, 31): Anticipation is both experience (of the present) and pre-experience (of the future), both given and pre-given. If anticipation fits "calmly" within the logic of experience, it does so only by opening experience to its own logic, a logic that includes unrealization, openness, and absence (though not these alone, but also realization, confirmation, and presence). In revealing itself, anticipation "stumbles into the essentially unrealized character of existence" (31): That which is given is both fulfilled in the present and offers the promise of a future, greater fulfillment, and therefore the "problem of pre-givenness and pre-experience ends up being related to the problem of the promise" (33).

By evoking the promise as a means of understanding anticipation, we are now in a position to see how anticipation differs from expectation beyond the distinction between active and passive. Where expectation is based on inference, in anticipation something is "given to us inchoately, in the mode of a hint or promise" (PA, 15). When I make a promise, I am making claims about some future time, claims that therefore cannot be evaluated in the present.[17] However, the promise also is a present experience and hence bears a relation to the present not through its object but through its ground, to use the language we gained from Smith's phenomenology of hope. That is, when I promise to water your plants while you are gone, this promise cannot be verified when the promise is made; since you have not yet left, my promise to water your plants while you are gone can neither be confirmed nor disappointed but, as a promise, suspends its verification until the future time corresponding with its object. However, this does not mean that my promise does not also bear some relation to the present: I make the promise in the present moment, and it is therefore a present act. Specifically the promise relates to the present as the ground on which the promise is made; the present horizons of expectations, built up from a past, provide, in addition to the meaning or content of my promise, also the level of certainty that is accorded to my promise. We call this trustworthiness: If a person has proven herself trustworthy, we are likely to have confidence in the promise she makes us; if she has proven herself untrustworthy, we have little confidence in her promise; if she has proven herself neither trustworthy nor untrustworthy, then our confidence in her promise is premised on the confidence we accord to promises in general, which in turn is shaped by the trustworthiness of other people who have previously made promises to us.

This mode of relating the present to the future is different from that of expectation, where the relation is one of inference (see chapter 2). In inference, there is nothing analogous to trustworthiness. There is a validity of inference—am I justified in making inference A from the set of present evidence E?—but no trustworthiness; one would not say that E is trustworthy (or not trustworthy) as evidence. Where expectation is an inference concerning possible futures made through the lens of the past (i.e., the use of horizons of expectation that have been established from horizons of retention) in order to interpret the present, anticipation is a waiting[18] for the future based on our interpretation of the present *and* an interpreting of the present so as to make possible the arrival of the anticipated. Trustworthiness, in our standard use of that term, is not merely an indicator of the likelihood of future actions; it is also—and perhaps most important—an indicator of one's experience of (the present condition of) another person: that is, so-and-so is the type of person who can be trusted. Similarly anticipation is not merely directed toward a future object, but it also affects our experience of the present.

IV: Anticipation, Ethicality, and the Essential Futurity of Phenomenology

If trustworthiness moves us beyond the (largely epistemological) question of justification, then we are left to wonder what avenue it pushes us toward; if anticipation is not an epistemological endeavor, what is it? Because of the reference to trustworthiness, it would seem to be primarily an ethical or promissory act. Such a result would be surprising, given the banality of anticipation: Is my waiting for my wife to return home from work an ethical act? What would make it so?

But before we take up this problem of the potential ethicality of anticipation,[19] and hence of futurity, let me make explicit why such a question is of the utmost importance not just for our understanding of the theme of futurity but for phenomenology itself. The distinction protention opens up between clarifying and confirming modes of intuition allows fulfillment to step to the fore as a key moment in the functioning of consciousness, thereby allowing us to make sense of the double intentionality of absolute consciousness. By turning to fulfillment, we are able to move beyond the content-apprehension schema that is more appropriate to neo-Kantianism toward a more genuinely phenomenological account of consciousness as always already constituted. The passive striving toward the future characteristic of protention enables the general fulfillment that constitutes the self-relatedness—and self-constitution—of the stream of absolute consciousness, thereby enabling this phenomenological account of consciousness to avoid problems of infinite regress. But futurity also enables, via the distinction between clarifying and confirming modes of intuition opened by protention and enacted in expectation, the particular fulfillment that constitutes objects—and ultimately the world—alongside the self-constitution of the stream of absolute consciousness. This twofold notion of fulfillment in turn establishes the subject as not only constituting but as also in some way constituted.[20] This understanding of the world enables phenomenology to escape the subject-object dualism of Cartesian philosophy without abandoning the certainty of self-reflection that was Descartes's crucial advancement of the discipline of philosophy.

Because of the interplay between protentive self-constitution and expectative world constitution that establishes consciousness as simultaneously constituted and constituting, consciousness is not wholly present to itself. The narrowness of our consciousness entails that our experience always points to its limits, to what is beyond it. This pointing beyond, which is a necessary feature of our participation in a world, is the very phenomenality of anticipation. Properly understood, the unique relation between present and future opened up by anticipation is nothing less than our experience of being a subject in and with a world. Anticipation is not merely one thing we can do among others, one conscious act among others, but is in a sense determinative of conscious acts in general: That which makes possible active consciousness is simultaneously that which makes possible anticipation. The phenomenality of anticipation is, in a sense, nothing else than the phenomenality of conscious experience. Therefore if anticipation can be shown to be essentially ethical, this would lend all of phenomenology an ethical overtone. If ethicality is essentially not epistemological, discovering a fundamental ethicality in phenomenology would reorient phenomenology away from the epistemological and therefore, it would seem, away from constituting, transcendental subjectivity. In the possibility of an essentially ethical anticipation, then, an entire edifice of phenomenological understanding is at stake.

With the stakes now properly before us, let us investigate the possible ethicality of anticipation.

PART II

Futurity and the 'Openness' of the Intentional Subject

4

Phenomenology, Openness, and Ethics as First Philosophy

The suggestion that the constituting powers of the subject are in some way marked by the possibility of something fundamentally nonepistemological (provisionally called "ethics") may seem surprising, but it should not be, at least to anyone familiar with the work of Emmanuel Levinas. Levinas's invocation of ethics constitutes a reinvigoration of Husserlian phenomenology, a return to an ethical project already suggested, but not drawn out at length, in Husserl. This is the hypothesis that will serve as the foundation for part 2 of this work. In Levinas the ethical nature of the orientation to the future is shown to be at work not just in the active level of anticipation but even in the passive levels of expectation and protention, indeed in the "passivity more passive than all passivity" that is a major theme of Levinas's work. This in turn illustrates that the pure constituting subject is essentially opened to something outside itself: The subject is not only self-constituted but is also Other-constituted. This openness does not result from a choice made by the constituting subject but is instead the very condition of constituting subjectivity. In Levinas, then, we get a clarification of how the essential openness of futurity and constitution, mentioned in Husserl, constitutes a fundamentally nonepistemological—but still phenomenological—project that can be characterized as "ethics." Therefore not only *can* one appeal to Levinas to help clarify a phenomenological account of futurity, but ultimately one *must* do so if one is to accurately take account of the depth and significance of Husserl's work on futurity.

I. Levinas's Critique of Husserlian Phenomenology

Levinas's account of ethics as first philosophy is a reinterpretation of phenomenology, a reinterpretation that crystallizes around the issue of temporality and especially the future. His critique of Husserlian temporality is threefold. First, he criticizes the exclusively theoretical character of Husserl's analysis of time.[1] This is problematic for Levinas because it reduces everything and everyone to the conditions of the subject's own experience and reduces that experience exclusively to what can be reflected upon and objectified. That is, everything must appear to me within the conditions and horizons that I have established, the conditions and horizons of my theoretical, constituting consciousness. This critique is directed against what Rudolf Bernet will call "the appropriation of the presence of things and persons."[2]

This appropriation, which applies equally to Husserl's account of time and Heidegger's account of care, is similar to Levinas's second critique of phenomenology, which is again directed to both Husserl and Heidegger. On this critique, the problem is the reduction of all time to the present of the subject. That is, because of the horizons of retention and expectation, the account of time put forward by phenomenology reduces the novelty of time to the predictability of horizons. All of time becomes predicated on the possibilities of the (present) subject. This "subjective possibilization of the present and the future"[3] eliminates the chance of something totally new arriving and affecting consciousness.[4] Like the first objection, this one too reacts against making experiences of alterity conditional on subjective consciousness. By so reducing the other to the same, it claims, the phenomenologies of Husserl and Heidegger dismiss the possibility of real, genuine experience of the other.

The third prong of Levinas's critique of Husserl again has to do with reducing the alterity of the Other to the conditions of the subject. This third critique is directed to the past, and to its possible presentation, either as retained or as remembered. In both cases (i.e., as retained or as remembered), the past remains little more than a displaced present that can always be re-presented. Hence its character of alterity is lost, and it is reduced to the possibilities of subjective, present experience.

All three prongs of the critique can be summed up in the following quote from *Otherwise than Being*: "A subject would then be a power for re-presentation in the quasi-active sense of the word: it would draw up the temporal disparity into a present, into a simultaneousness" (OB, 133).[5]

II. The Immanent Nature of the Critique: Intentionality and Sense

Levinas's critique of phenomenology consistently hammers home the same point: Phenomenology, as conceived by Husserl and Heidegger, fails to do justice to alterity (and ultimately to the alterity of the Other person[6]). Recall that Husserl himself has ascribed a certain essential openness to the subject, for example in the centrality accorded to protention in internal time-consciousness, coupled with the way protention "leaves open" the status of what is coming (Hua X, 297). As such, Levinas's critique of phenomenology here can be understood as in continuity with at least some statements made by Husserl himself.

This would seem to suggest that Levinas's concerns remain tied to the phenomenological project rather than forcing him to go *beyond* phenomenology.[7] Rather, as I have already suggested, these concerns emerged already in Husserl, even if he did not himself pursue them,[8] and hence we can understand Levinas as developing the implications of several statements made by Husserl in ways that perhaps go beyond much of Husserl's explicit analyses but do so in light of other, less-developed aspects of those analyses.[9] I think Levinas himself says it best when he states that he is working within the "forgotten" horizons of phenomenology (OB, 183; see also RR, 130). Nor is this an isolated claim. He makes claims at several key junctures in his oeuvre, including in his most well-known texts, which suggest that he understood his work as operating within the phenomenological tradition, even if he did have to elaborate his own understanding of that tradition.[10] Most notable among these statements are perhaps his claims that "Husserlian phenomenology has made possible this passage from ethics to metaphysical exteriority" (TI, 29) and later that *Otherwise than Being* is "faithful to intentional analysis" (OB, 183).

But surely any reader of *Otherwise than Being* and *Logical Investigations* or *Ideas I* will acknowledge significant differences between these works, differences that are not merely stylistic but evidence of fundamentally different understandings of key phenomenological concepts. Since Levinas's claim is that he is "faithful to intentional analysis," let us turn now to see how he understands that term and how he understands his own usage of it as being "faithful" in some way to Husserl.

A. Intentionality as the "Essential Teaching of Husserl"

Intentionality is one of the central doctrines of phenomenology. That this is true does not, however, entail that it is a simple doctrine nor that its implications were fully understood. Indeed the term does not seem to be used univocally, even by Husserl himself.[11] This equivocation in part underlies the key thesis of this chapter, that *Levinas draws the impetus for his "radicalization" of phenomenology from within the bounds of Husserlian phenomenology*.[12] Specifically I will strive to show that Levinas's threefold critique of phenomenology evidences distinctly phenomenological concerns. In doing so, I hope to show that the recovery of the "lost horizons" within which Levinas claims to be working is essential to understanding his articulation of ethics as first philosophy and to a proper understanding of the role of futurity in phenomenology.

The three main points of Levinas's critique of Husserlian phenomenology are that it is overly theoretical, that it reduces all time to the possibilities of subjective horizons, and that it conceives of the past as always necessarily re-presentable; that is, in principle every past can be brought into the present for consideration (in memory or retention, depending on how far in the past). These three points are, of course, intimately interrelated: Because the past must, in principle, be re-presentable, time must be understood according to the possibilities of the present of the subject; because Husserl conceived phenomenology as primarily theoretical, it must be possible in principle to make of all experience, including our experience of the past, a theoretical object able to be reflected upon; and because the object of phenomenological study is the *Erlebnis* (lived experience) of the subject, every such experience can be thematized in the reflection of the subject that lived through it. If all of this flows in some way from the notion of *Erlebnis*, this notion itself is based on the fundamental theme of phenomenology: the intentionality of consciousness. Because consciousness is always consciousness of, we can study the acts of consciousness to help us make sense of our experience in the world: Given that my consciousness is always conscious of the world, in studying the specificity of my conscious apprehension of the world (e.g., in the act of perception) I can learn how the world is given to me and hence can come to understand better myself, the world, and my relation to it.[13]

For Husserl, this idea of intentional consciousness leads directly to his principle of principles: that "*every originary presentive intuition is a legitimizing source of cognition,* that *everything originarily* (so to speak, in its 'personal' authority) *offered* to us in '*intuition*' *is to be accepted simply as what it is presented as being,* but also *only within the limits in which it is presented there*" (Hua III, 43–44). Levinas, however, will employ this same notion of intentionality to overturn the privileging of the theoretical that resulted from Husserl's principle of principles. Over the course of several essays between 1940 and 1965, Levinas develops the implications of the phenom-

enological notion of intentionality in order to show that "not every transcendent intention has the noesis-noema structure" (TI, 29) of Husserl's
theoretical intentionality. For Levinas, intentionality necessarily puts us
into direct and immediate contact with something external to us, something
"concrete" (WEH, 66; TI, 28) or "sensible" (IS, *passim*).

The "external" here is an evidentiary, not an ontological, exterior. Following Husserl (via the notion of intentionality currently under discussion),
phenomenology has rejected the traditional conception of the relationship
between self and world as that between ontologically distinct realms: the
"inner" sphere of the psyche and the "outer" sphere of the material world
(which, as distinct from the psyche, may or may not exist). Rather in phenomenology interior and exterior become different modalities of evidence
abstracted from "the concrete fact of the mental life [*spiritualité*] that is
sense [*sens*]"[14] (WEH, 62, translation modified). Hence intentionality, as
the relation between consciousness and the world, is "nothing like the relations between objects" but is "essentially the act of bestowing a sense (the
Sinngebung)" (59, translation modified). For Husserl, since "[m]ental life is
the act of bestowing sense" (71, translation modified), this conception of
intentionality as the act of *Sinngebung* quickly leads to the conception of a
world constituted by thought (74).

However, Levinas is quick to point out that if one takes intentionality
at its word and without importing any other philosophical or metaphysical
ideals (as the principle of principles would seem to necessitate all good
phenomenology do), then this bestowal of meaning, this *Sinngebung*, is at
least as much received from the world as it is constituted by the subject.[15]
For, though mental life "is the act of bestowing sense," Levinas can still
question whether "I am not something besides this act" because I am a
human being and not just a consciousness (WEH, 71, translation modified). As I am a being in the world, "my thought as a constituted human
being is no longer the pure act of bestowing a sense; it is an operation accomplished on the world and in the world, an interaction with the real"
(71–72, translation modified).[16]

Hence intentionality, for Levinas, rather than being the act of the subject's bestowing meaning on the world, is actually the act of the subject's
being in relation with the concrete (TI, 28), with that basis on which the
intellectual rests, and which therefore prevents the intellectual from being
"taken for an absolute" (WEH, 66). The concrete is that which is experienced immediately, without the intervention of the active ego. It is therefore
that which I described in chapter 2 as the "world" of object-like formations
constituted in passive synthesis,[17] and it is accessed, Levinas claims, by
nontheoretical intentions. But this idea of nontheoretical intentions is not

a Levinasian innovation, for "it was Husserl who introduced into philosophy the idea that thought can have a sense, can intend something even when this something is absolutely undetermined, a quasi-absence of object" (61; see also LI, 575), and hence the idea "of a non-theoretical intentionality, straight-off irreducible to knowledge," is "a Husserlian possibility which can be developed beyond what Husserl himself said" (EI, 32).

The putting-into-relation of the subject and the world characterized by intentionality finds its initial mark in Husserl's analysis of internal time-consciousness. There the notion of the primal impression (*Ur-impression*), which functions as "the origin of every consciousness" (WEH, 77), initiates the flow of constituted, phenomenological time. However, as we will see shortly, it does so only by putting consciousness in contact with something that comes to it from outside of consciousness. For now, though, let us pause briefly to consider what Levinas's reinterpretation of intentionality tells us about the first prong of his critique of Husserlian phenomenology. The first point of contention, you will recall, was the overly theoretical character of Husserl's phenomenological analysis. This criticism, however, is firmly rooted in the work of Husserl himself,[18] specifically in the idea of passive synthesis: "What does it matter if in the Husserlian phenomenology taken literally these unsuspected horizons [of passive synthesis] are in their turn interpreted as thoughts aiming at objects! What counts is the idea of the overflowing of objectifying thought by a forgotten experience from which it lives." This idea is "the essential teaching of Husserl" (TI, 28).

B. Sensibility, Impression, and the Reversal of Sinngebung

The full weight of the tension in Husserl's notion of intentionality is highlighted in Levinas's analysis of sensibility and the primal impression. It is here that Levinas is able to bring the full weight of Husserl's insights to bear against some of the presuppositions that color Husserl's thought,[19] thereby continuing the self-critical character of phenomenology.[20] Through the analysis of the primal impression, Levinas is able to indicate a necessary passivity at the heart of Husserlian subjectivity, a passivity that not only puts us in contact with the exterior but also indicates that sense is bestowed from that exterior to the subject, thereby challenging the freedom and pure spontaneity of the Ego. This contact with the exterior—which we will again see arising from within Husserlian phenomenology—is the impetus behind the second and third aspects of Levinas's critique of Husserl. It will also place us on the threshold of the ethical relation, thereby beginning to return us to the question of the possible (nonepistemological) ethicality of anticipation.

Levinas's critique of Husserl's concept of time revolves around its being always a constituted temporality.[21] But, as Levinas is right to point out, this is only half of the picture of temporality that Husserl puts forward (even if it is the half that he devoted the majority of his research to, especially in the analyses of time in Hua X, Hua XXXIII, and the L manuscripts). His notion of the primal impression is that which puts consciousness in direct contact with the world and therefore that which forms the basis of the constituted temporality. Now I said in chapter 1 that the positive account of protention developed there can help us do away with the idea of a "primal impression" via the notion of fulfillment; what is retained is the earlier protention, and not the primal impression.[22] This is true especially in the horizontal intentionality characteristic of general fulfillment. However, the transverse intentionality (*Querintentionalität*) that characterizes particular fulfillment needs some relation to the world in order to ensure that consciousness is doubly intentional and hence can be aware both of itself and of the world at the same time and in the same act. The primal impression is the very relation between consciousness and world and hence enables the double intentionality of consciousness. We can therefore understand what motivates Husserl to say that "[c]onsciousness is nothing without impression" (Hua X, 100).

Levinas's insight is that impression, as the way consciousness and the world are related, precedes the constitutive power of the subject. Again, however, this is not a Levinasian innovation but rather a reinvigoration of an originally Husserlian insight: "The word 'impression' is appropriate only to original sensations; the word expresses well what is 'there' of itself, and indeed originally: namely what is pregiven [*vorgegeben*][23] to the Ego, presenting itself to the Ego in the manner of something *affecting it as foreign*. . . . This non-derived [impression] . . . breaks down into primal sensibility and into Ego-actions and Ego-affections" (Hua IV, 336). As this quote from *Ideas II* makes clear, impression—while containing some activity on the part of the Ego—is largely a matter of the relation to that which is exterior or "foreign" to the Ego, a matter of sensation. This originary relation to the exterior, occurring in the primal impression, is the "origin of all consciousness" and is "original passivity [which is] at the same time an initial spontaneity" (WEH, 77). This passive activity calls to mind the passive syntheses discussed in chapter 2 and their role in endowing the world with sense. But a key aspect of those passive associations was the ability of the world to affect consciousness, to arouse its attention so that consciousness could associate the present stimulus with something within the subject's horizons. These subjective horizons are a transcendental condition of intentional consciousness. But Levinas recovers another set of horizons, "forgotten horizons," that establish another transcendental condition of intentional consciousness: the horizon of sensation, conceived as "the *situation* of the subject" (RR, 117; see also IS, 150). That is, the "world is not only constituted but also constituting" (RR, 118), and therefore the intentional object "calls forth and as it were gives rise to the consciousness through which its being shines" (119). Association can be described as passive, then, not just because it is done without the active (i.e., egoically directed) involvement of the Ego, but more important because it is derived from a being-affected by something exterior to the subject, a being-impressed upon by the world in sensation, and hence by a passivity and a passion in the Thomistic sense. The world is therefore implicit in the bestowal of sense upon it by the subject. Hence *Sinngebung*, which characterizes the mental life of the Ego, does not proceed exclusively *from* the Ego but is in part given *to* the Ego. These other horizons—the external horizons of sensation—endow the thoughts of the Ego with sense, but with "a sense that is not predetermined as objectification" (TI, 188). "The sensibility we are describing . . . does not belong to the order of thought but to that of sentiment," that is, affectivity (TI, 135).[24]

The essential aspects of this stunning reversal of *Sinngebung* are twofold: first, that the subject is not sovereign in constituting its world but participates within that world in order to give it sense; second, that this world in which the subject participates is *foreign* and exterior to the subject, even as it is always in relation. What follows from this is that the subject is constituted by something that is exterior to it; there is alterity within the subject: "Essentially 'impressional,' is [consciousness] not possessed by the non-ego, by the other, by 'facticity'? Is sensation not the very negation of the transcendental work and of the evident presence that coincides with the origin? Through his theory of the sensible, Husserl restores to the impressional event its transcendental function" (IS, 150). This conclusion—which contradicts much of what Husserl says regarding the freedom of the Ego—is a distinctly Husserlian conclusion, arising from Husserl's analyses of intentionality, time-consciousness (especially the primal impression), passive syntheses, and sensation. It also provides the impetus for the final two of Levinas's critiques of Husserl: that everything in the world can be reduced to the (internal) horizons of the subject and that everything in the subject's past experience is capable of being re-presented. The first of these clearly contradicts the transcendental horizons of the subject's (exterior) situation, of which sensation makes the subject aware. The second conflicts with the exteriority and alterity of that of which sensation makes us aware: If the world plays a role in the constitution of its sense, then not everything in the subject's past experience (here, specifically, not all of the sense bestowed upon the world) can be re-presented to the subject (see TI, 28).[25] This ruining of re-presentation, of representation, *in* the work of Husserl is the logical extension *of* the work of Husserl, prepared already in *Logical Investigations*.[26]

III. From Phenomenological Critique to Ethics as First Philosophy

But it is not just Levinas's criticisms of Husserl that arise from within the phenomenological enterprise launched by Husserl. Indeed Levinas's positive contribution to phenomenology—the primacy of the ethical relation—cannot be divorced from his "long frequenting of Husserlian labors" (RR, 113, translation modified), since the reversal of sense bestowal occasioned by the transcendental horizons of sensation makes possible an essentially ethical sense bestowal, "a *Sinngebung* essentially respectful of the Other" (RR, 121). By attempting to demonstrate this now, I hope to show that Levinas's development of ethics as first philosophy provides a useful—indeed perhaps an essential—step in our attempt to discover an ethical understanding of Husserl's account of futurity (and most especially of anticipation), not in the least because Levinas's conception of ethics is thoroughly influenced by Husserl, though perhaps not the Husserl of *Ideas I*. This section will, I hope, help justify the turn to Levinas at this juncture of our analysis of futurity in phenomenology, in addition to helping to clarify just what "ethical" might mean for us in this situation.

Early in *Totality and Infinity*, Levinas describes ethics as the "calling into question of my spontaneity by the presence of the Other" (TI, 43), where the Other refers specifically to the human Other (*l'autrui*). But we have already seen that the relation to exteriority manifest in sensation challenges the freedom and spontaneity of the subject. Is exteriority, then, enough for ethics, as Simon Critchley seems to suggest?[27] In some small degree, perhaps, this claim could be defended. It is more likely, however, that one should see the exteriority of sensation as analogous to—even derivative of or the condition of[28]—the true exteriority encapsulated by the face of the Other. What Levinas provides us with in his analysis of the face-to-face encounter is not merely a description of an empirical event or even of a lived experience; he uses such a lived experience to "deduce" (TI, 28) the radical reversal of *Sinngebung* initiated in impressional sensation. Whereas impression remains a mixture of passive and active, in the face-to-face encounter the role of the subject will be radically changed, activity removed, leaving only a "passivity more passive than any passivity"[29] that takes the logic of the reversal of sense bestowal to its extreme conclusion.

What sets the face-to-face encounter with the Other person apart from our encounter with the exteriority of the horizons of sensation is the height of the Other. The face of the Other,[30] which remains a modality of sensation, expresses the "eminence" of the Other, "the dimension of height and divinity from which he descends" (TI, 262). From this height, "the face speaks to me and thereby invites me to a relation incommensurate with a power exercised, be it enjoyment[31] or knowledge" (198). What the face expresses to me through this dimension of height, then, is a relation with something which I neither live from (enjoyment) nor move toward (knowledge), that is, a relation with something that does not affect me as a constituting power: It is not the basis from which I constitute nor that which I seek to constitute. This relation is the relation of separation: a relation with that which will always remain distinct from me, not constituted by me. In so challenging my sovereignty as constituting agent, the face, via the dimension of height, proves more extreme in its critique of the Ego's freedom than did the impressional sensation of the world indicated earlier (though, of course, the face is encountered within the world via sensation). In awakening me to a relation that bears no relation whatsoever to my constituting powers, the face also opens me to my nonconstituting "capabilities," exemplified most clearly in the passivity of sensation.

But this is not the extent of the face's effect on me. In separation, the I is awakened to the total primacy of the Other over the same. This primacy is a primacy of *Sinngebung*: The Other gives me my sense before I am there to receive or constitute it. This is because the uniqueness or ipseity of the subject is not rooted in its being one thing like and unlike others, in the way that my dog Jack is like other dogs (in the sense of being a dog with dog-like qualities) but is unlike other dogs (in the sense of being this dog that he is, with a distinct spatiotemporal place, etc., and not other dogs). Rather the "ipseity of the I consists in remaining outside the distinction between the individual and the general" (TI, 118). The refusal to be aligned under a general concept is not one aspect of the I but "its whole content; it is interiority" (118).[32] This interiority is called into being by the supreme exteriority of the face of the Other, which, by refusing to be contained (194), gives us a concrete, sensible instantiation of the idea of a thought that is wholly exceeded by its object, that is, of the Cartesian idea of the Infinite: "a relation with a being that maintains its total exteriority with respect to him who thinks it" (50). The Infinite is not merely an excess of manifestation but an affirmation of a relation with that which immediately "absolves itself from the relation in which it presents itself" (50). This absolution, this asymmetry strikes us as a moral command: "[Y]ou shall not commit murder" (199), which is to say, you shall not renounce comprehension altogether, you shall not remove yourself from relation (198). That is, the face of the Other commands me to maintain a relation with it, even as it absolves itself from that relation. This is the weight of its asymmetry.

But this command to maintain a relation is the very creation (TI, 293) of the subject. The interiority of the subject, as stated earlier, comes in its refusal to be aligned under a general concept. Instead the interiority comes from *responsibility*: Called to relation with a being that immediately absolves itself from this relation, it is only I who may maintain this relation. I receive myself—that is, I receive my unique *sense*—from the Other who transcends me in the relation of separation. The "facing position, opposition par excellence, can be only as a moral summons. This movement proceeds from the Other" (TI), and again: "In the face-to-face, the I has neither the privileged position of the subject nor the position of a thing defined by its place in the system; it is apology, discourse *pro dono*, but discourse of justification before the Other" (293). Hence "[t]ranscendence is not a vision of the Other—but a primordial donation" (174). And donation, givenness, as we know from phenomenology, is the production of sense.[33] It is, then, not just the sense of the world that is given to the subject but the very sense of the subject itself—the ipseity of the subject itself— that is the first thing given. In this sense, the subject cannot be said to be present in this first encounter with the Other. Rather the subject is subjected to, held hostage by (in the language of *Otherwise than Being*) the Other, which is to say, the subject is subject-ed, is given its status as subject, by the Other. In the face-to-face, we see the alterity of the Other bestowing its sense otherwise, "in the positive modality of the unique and incomparable,"[34] thereby showing that "[s]ubjectivity is structured as the other in the same, but in a way different from that of consciousness" (OB, 25).

The inversion of *Sinngebung* inspired by Husserl's notions of intentionality, sensation, and primal impression is at the core of Levinas's account of the ethical: "[T]he essential of ethics is in its *transcendent intention*" (TI, 29). The possibility of an ethical *Sinngebung* alluded to at the end of "The Ruin of Representation" (RR, 121) finds its ultimate fulfillment—and radicalization—in the face-to-face encounter of ethics.

But that the essential of ethics is in its account of the bestowal of sense should give us reason to consider the precise nature of what ethics means for Levinas. First, he is clearly speaking of ethics in terms of subjectivity, not intersubjectivity (see TI, 26). Second, ethics is best understood in terms of the ethical relation. This point does not contradict the first only if the ethical relation in its primordiality is not an intersubjective relation but a relation that endows sense and subjectivity, endows the sense of subjectivity from the height of infinity (though it is true that only another human can have the absolute foreignness necessary for height; TI, 73)[35] to something that is not yet a subject.[36] Hence the ethical relation is primordially subject-ive, that is, primordially about the constitution of the subject; it is not primordially about the relationship between two subjects.

From Eschatology to Awaiting

Futurity in Levinas

We have seen that Levinas's "ethical" philosophy can be considered a continuation of Husserl's comments on the openness of futurity and constitution. While this may increase the acceptability of talk of "ethics" in phenomenology, it does not yet speak directly to our problem of the possibility of an essentially ethical aspect of phenomenology introduced by the notion of futurity. That is, while we have now come to understand a bit better the relationship between phenomenology and ethics, we do not yet understand the fundamental relationship between this "ethics" and futurity and to what extent this "ethics" is fundamentally nonepistemological[1] and hence can function as an elaboration of anticipation.

An examination of the role that futurity plays in Levinas's thought will enable us to evaluate more precisely the nature of the openness of futurity and constitution, first noted by Husserl and expanded by Levinas, and its implications for futurity and phenomenology. But it can do so only if we see the essential role played by futurity throughout Levinas's thought and not just in the early works. There is a dominant reading in Levinas scholarship that the early centrality of futurity reaches its zenith in the evocation of eschatology in *Totality and Infinity* (TI 22–26). The analysis of the trace that begins with "The Trace of the Other" (1963) inaugurates a new analysis of temporality, one that finds its expression most clearly in the "prehistory of the I" (GDT, 175) of *God, Death and Time*, where we are told that, though this prehistory can be found in *Totality and Infinity*, it is in

Otherwise than Being that Levinas undertakes "to write [it] at length" (GDT, 278n.12).

A closer examination of the function of futurity, however, shows that there is no major shift at work here. For example, Levinas says in 1948 that time "is the very relationship of the subject with the Other" (TO, 39) and in 1976 that time is "the very relation with the Infinite" (GDT, 110; see also 17, 19). In the intervening years, of course, he has been at pains to show that it is the Other through whom the self encounters the infinite, and hence there is a continuity that persists here through a certain change in language. Given the essential connection between futurity and the ethical relation for Levinas, this continuity in his account of futurity—despite the change in language—should have a parallel in a continuity in his account of ethics, despite the change in language (and imagery) found in, for example, *Totality and Infinity* and *Otherwise than Being*. Properly understanding the role of futurity, then, will help us read Levinas anew, aligning him more closely not only with Husserl but also with himself.

I. The Future as the Relation to the Other

Levinas's account of futurity, like so much else in his philosophy, is intimately tied to his account of the subject's relation to the Other. If the relation to alterity is therefore a central trope of Levinasian philosophy, futurity must occupy a central place in that philosophy, given the intimate connection between futurity and the subject's relation to the Other. In explicating Levinas's account of futurity, therefore, we must necessarily pay attention not just to his account of temporality but also to his accounts of the constitution of the subject, as well as the relation of that subject to the Other. All of these themes coalesce in Levinas's conception of futurity.

A. From Solitude to the Other: Levinas's Early Account of Subjectivity

Levinas begins *Time and the Other* with the following remark: "The aim of these lectures is to show that time is not the achievement of an isolated and lone subject, but that it is the very relationship of the subject with the Other" (TO, 39). Through a series of "ontological" analyses, Levinas hopes to show both "the place of solitude in the general economy of being" (39) and "wherein this solitude can be exceeded" (41). Solitude is defined here not as "factual isolation" or as "the incommunicability of a content of consciousness" but as "the indissoluble unity between the existent and its work of existing" (43). Existents emerge out of the "anonymous" (47) existence that occurs without subjects (45).[2] Levinas characterizes this anonymous existence as the *il y a*, the "there is." It is a "verbal" form of existence, the "very work of being" that cannot be denied but lurks behind every negation as the "field of every affirmation and negation" (48).[3] The *il y a* is the "ultimate horizon for all experiences in the usual sense of the world,"[4] and as such is always "on," so to speak, always working, always in action; it is always assumed in every experience, always already at work. In fact Levinas will characterize it precisely by this constant action, this inability to rest (48–49). This inability to rest comes from its lack of self, which thereby removes from it the possibility of "withdrawing into sleep as into a private domain" (49). It is in this anonymous *il y a* that an existent will "contract its existing" in what Levinas calls "hypostasis" (43).

In contracting its existing, the existent gains the ability to tear itself away from the constant vigilance of anonymous existence. This ability to tear itself away is consciousness, "the power to sleep" (TO, 51). By stepping out of the *il y a*, the existing of the existent is characterized as a privacy, an internal domain from which the existent can depart in work and into which the existent can again withdraw. This movement of departing from and returning to the self is the work of identity, and in its identification "the existent is already closed upon itself; it is a monad and a solitude" (52). In existing, the existent is solitude. This event of gaining its existing, this departure from the self, *hypostasis*, is the present, not as a point in linear time but as the very "event of existing through which something comes to start out from itself" (52). For this event, that is, for the existing of an existent to be possible, solitude is necessary (55). In its solitude, the subject masters existing by stepping out of the anonymity of the *il y a*. Solitude therefore is "not only a despair and an abandonment, but also a virility, a pride and a sovereignty" (55).

But this sovereignty has a price, for the subject's identity is not only the departure from self characteristic of mastery but also the return to the self. The present consists in this inevitable return to the self. The existent is "occupied with itself" via its "materiality" (TO, 55). The very *hypostasis* that makes the subject free simultaneously enchains the subject to itself in responsibility: The subject is both Ego and Self, both sovereign and enchained, free and responsible. This is the tragedy of solitude, to be "shut up within the captivity of its identity" (57), always chained to itself.

Salvation from this enchainment begins with the subject's being nourished by a world, by its very materiality. Materiality, then, enchains the existent to itself but also opens "an interval between the ego and the self" (TO, 62) via the world as "an ensemble of nourishments" (63). In nourishment, we seek nothing else *save the object that nourishes*; contrary to

Heidegger's insistence on the world being a system of tools that ultimately refer back to our own projects and care,[5] Levinas insists that "human life in the world does not go beyond the objects that fulfill it" (63).[6] It is in these very objects that the existent begins to escape from its enchainment to itself by losing itself in its *enjoyment* of these nourishing objects. As such, enjoyment is a "departure from self" (64n.38) that counts as the "first morality," a morality that will be overcome but is necessary nonetheless (64).[7]

This morality of "earthly nourishments" must be overcome because it does not truly escape the self. Rather it is characterized by light and reason, which seem to give the subject the ability to "take distance with regard to its materiality" (TO, 65) but are in fact only "that through which something is other than myself, but already as if it came from me" (64).[8] Reason and light enable us to separate the ego from things and thereby make us "master of the exterior world." But they are "incapable of discovering a peer for us there," and hence they never find "any other reason to speak" (65).

From out of this situation of the immediate enjoyment of nourishment, the ego begins to work, to cross the space that separates us from ourselves by taking hold of the object (TO, 68). By so reducing the distance, however—by making external objects mine through my work[9]—I ultimately return to myself and remain enchained. Work, then, is effort, but ultimately pain and sorrow, "the phenomena to which the solitude of the existent is finally reduced" (68). Pain, physical suffering, reveals the "impossibility of detaching oneself from the instant of existence": "[S]uffering is the impossibility of nothingness" (69). This impossibility of escape from the weight of existence—the inevitability of enchainment to itself of every existent—is challenged finally by death, which places the subject "in relationship with what does not come from itself" (70). Death is therefore "an experience of the passivity of the subject" (70), but an experience that is foreign to all light and all reason, to all knowability. Indeed this is "the principal trait of our relationship with death," namely that it is the "situation where something absolutely unknowable appears" (71). As such, death "marks the end of the subject's virility and heroism" (72); it marks the end of the sovereignty of the Ego—but it also marks the end of the ego's solitude.

Contrary to Heidegger's analysis of death as that which is most proper to the self,[10] Levinas here shows that "death indicates that we are in relation with something that is absolutely other . . . something whose very existence is made of alterity" (TO, 74). Solitude is therefore "not confirmed by death, but broken by it" (74). Plurality is thereby introduced into the heart of existing. This is not a plurality of existents (contra Heidegger's *Mitsein, Mitda-sein,* or *Miteinandersein*)[11] but a plurality insinuated "into the very existing of the existent" in a relationship with an Other that is not a relationship of communion or sympathy, but of Mystery (75).

But how, then, can the existent encounter this mysterious Other—this death—without merely reducing it to light, reason, possibility, that is, to itself? Levinas says that one must "welcome the event" of this relationship with the Other that is revealed to us in death, but not as "one welcomes a thing or object" (TO, 78). One must simultaneously let the event happen and face up to the event (78), be both passive and, to a certain degree, active. This occurs in the event of the face-to-face encounter with the Other.

B. Futurity and the Relation to the Other

The face-to-face encounter is widely known as the center of Levinas's ethical phenomenology. However, it also crystallizes his first attempt to elaborate a theory of the future. In seeking to explain how the existent encounters the Other in the face-to-face, Levinas appeals to the future: "The relationship with the Other is the absence of the other; not absence pure and simple, not the absence of pure nothingness, but absence *in a horizon of the future*, an absence that is time" (TO, 90, emphasis added). The appearance of the future at this critical juncture in the argument is not sudden but has been well prepared throughout *Time and the Other*. Already in the discussion concerning death, Levinas has made the association between the relationship with death and the relationship with the future (71). This is predicated on two distinct but interrelated moments: the relationship between the present and hypostasis and the understanding of the future as absolute surprise. Levinas describes the present, as I have said, not as a single point in linear time but as the upsurge of the existing of the existent from out of the anonymous existence of the *il y a* (55 ff.), that is, as hypostasis (43). Given this relationship between the present and hypostasis, it is not surprising that he claims that the "now is the fact that I am master" (72). The present is the very establishment of the existent, of its sovereignty, its self-possession in identity. Contrasted with this, Levinas defines the future as "what is not grasped" (76, 77). This immediately puts it at odds with the identifying powers of the solitude of the existent and the powers of light and reason that it manifests in its enchainment to itself. If the future is what is not grasped, that is, is not the "taking hold of an object" characteristic of work or the return to the self characteristic of reason and light, then the future must be other than what has been analyzed so far. Since Levinas has so far discussed only the solitude of the existent, this suggests that the future must be otherwise than solitude, otherwise than the existent.

This is in fact the case, as Levinas defines the future as "absolutely surprising" (TO, 76). In keeping with our common understanding of time, this makes sense: While the present is currently here, and the past has already happened, the future alone is that which is not-yet and hence that which we cannot know. The future defies understanding, is of a different order than knowledge. It is surprise, come from elsewhere, not the product of ourselves and our history.[12] It is, in other words, the mystery of the other, and as such, it parallels our relation to the Other. But in order to make use of this justification, the future must be put into relationship with the present. It is only when compared to the present, which is already here, that the future presents us with the possibility for surprise: As it is not here *now*, the future could come as something other than what is here now. The future as absolute surprise gains its status as time only when put into relationship with the present (79).

But putting such a notion of the future in contact with the present will be difficult. Unlike our common understanding of time, for Levinas the present and the future are not points on a continuum but are defined in opposition to each other: one as the very solitude of the subject, the other as the relationship with alterity. These two "have between them the whole interval" (TO 79) and hence are not contiguous. The future of absolute surprise, "the future that death gives, the future of the event" is "nobody's" and cannot be assumed by a human being (79).[13] Hence our relation with the future is not simple but is a relation to mystery—to the other: "[T]he very relationship with the other is the relationship with the future" (77).

This returns us to the question of how we can be in relationship with the other without compromising the alterity of the other or the solitude of the subject. The problem is that of the very possibility of ethics and has taken us to the problem of time, especially the problem of the future. The resolution to both problems lies, for Levinas, in the relationship between people. For ethics, this occurs in the face-to-face, as we have already discussed. But similarly for time, "the encroachment of the present on the future is not the feat of the subject alone, but the intersubjective relationship. The condition of time lies in the relationship between humans" (TO, 79). Not just any relationship between humans will do (for we often reduce others to our own projects and needs), but specifically an erotic relationship, a relationship of "voluptuousness" (89). In the caress, the subject touches, has sensation, but this does not exhaust the caress, for "what is caressed is not touched, properly speaking" (89). Indeed the "seeking of the caress constitutes its essence by the fact that the caress does not know what it seeks," cannot know it, for what it seeks constantly slips away, is "always inaccessible" (89). Rather than frustrating the caress, though, or rendering what is sought entirely absent, this constant slipping away "feeds" the caress, enriches it, in fact constitutes it: The caress results from Desire, which always exceeds what is sought and is constituted by that excess rather than need, which seeks to be fulfilled, as in nourishment (cf. TI, 33–35; TA, 350).[14] The withdrawing of what is sought in the caress therefore offers "ever richer promises" to the caress; that which is sought cannot "become ours or us" but is "always still to come. The caress is the anticipation of this pure future without content" (TO, 89).[15]

This constant aiming (but an aiming that seeks what, by necessity, it cannot have and is enriched by this seeking and not having) is the "intentionality of the voluptuous" (TO, 89). It is also "the sole intentionality of the future itself, and not an expectation of some future fact" (89).[16] Futurity therefore is characterized by being the "object" (so to speak) of Desire: that which is sought but can by necessity never be grasped, that which enriches in its slipping away. It is in this sense that the absence of the Other in the ethical relation can be described as occurring in "a horizon of the future" (90), and it is this slipping away of the Desired "that is time" (90). Stated otherwise, and to repeat Levinas's earlier claims which are perhaps now clarified as to their meaning and depth, "[T]he very relationship with the other is the relationship with the future" (77), and time "is the very relationship of the subject with the Other" (39).

C. The Ambiguity of Totality and Infinity

Time and the Other thus establishes an order that is otherwise than knowing that characterizes futurity and/as the relation to the Other. It is able to do this by revealing the fundamentality of the parallel distinctions of futurity and the relationship to the Other from the present and the solitude of the existent, respectively. In so doing, Levinas's account of the future, as his account of the relationship to alterity, seems to be premised on certain sharp dichotomies: self/Other, present/future, and so on.

But this understanding of the future will be problematized in *Totality and Infinity* through a reconception of materiality. The analyses in *Time and the Other* open the door for this later reading but do not go far down the path thereby opened onto. In *Time and the Other*, as we have already said, Levinas claims that, in addition to enchaining the existent to itself, materiality also opens "an interval between the ego and the self" (TO, 62) via the world as "an ensemble of nourishments" (63). This notion of materiality is expanded in *Totality and Infinity* with Levinas's introduction of the *elemental* as the "non-possessable which envelops or contains [what we enjoy] without being able to be contained or enveloped" (TI, 131). The elemental is therefore the "background from which [the things that are enjoyed] emerge and to which they return in the enjoyment we have of them" (130). As seeking things, as seeking to represent things as things, enjoyment is a return to solitude. But enjoyment never fully reaches the things we enjoy as things (130), because it always opens onto "the medium [milieu] in which we take hold of them," namely, the elemental (130). And in opening onto the elemental, enjoyment opens us onto our own condition: "One does not approach [the elemental] . . . one is steeped in it; I am always within the element" (131).

Enjoyment therefore seems to open us onto the "forgotten horizons" of Husserlian phenomenology discussed in chapter 4. However, this insight does not yet appear fully to Levinas in *Totality and Infinity* but is constantly interrupted there: Levinas will say, "In enjoyment I am absolutely for myself" (TI, 134), and that "sensibility is enjoyment" (136), but then say shortly thereafter that "sensibility enacts the very separation of being" (138) and that "enjoyment seems to be in touch with an 'other'" (137).

Such a seemingly simultaneous ability to establish the solitude of the self and still be in contact with the Other is impossible, according to the stark dichotomies of *Time and the Other*. It is the invocation of the future within the present (or presence) of solitude that enables this seemingly impossible move, but it can do so only by reevaluating the relationship between futurity and the present.

Enjoyment is able to be in touch with an 'other,' then, only because "a future is announced within the element and menaces it with insecurity" (TI, 137).[17] This futurity repeats much of the analysis of futurity in *Time and the Other*: It comes from "nowhere," is "coming always," is "indeterminate" (141). But the futurity of enjoyment "opens up an abyss within enjoyment itself" (141); enjoyment and sensibility are "separated from thought" and are "not of the order of experience" (137), because, in enjoyment, I do not represent the world, I enjoy it. Hence I cannot encounter the Other in enjoyment—but I can escape totalizing thought there. In this way, enjoyment and sensibility serve as a kind of precursor to the face-to-face but are distinct from it: "[E]njoyment does not refer to an infinity beyond what nourishes it, but to the virtual vanishing of what presents itself. . . . This ambivalence of nourishment, which on the one hand offers itself and contents, but which already withdraws . . . is to be distinguished from the presence of the infinite in the finite and from the structure of the thing" (TI, 141). What this futurity of the elemental reveals is not, then, the Other of *Time and the Other*. Rather this concept of futurity "is lived concretely as the mythical divinity of the element" (142). This "mythical divinity" manifests itself in a certain "nothingness that bounds the egoism of enjoyment," and through this nothingness "enjoyment accomplishes separation" (142). But what is separated from me in this mythical, elemental "night" of nothingness "is not a 'something' susceptible of being revealed, but an ever-new depth of absence, an existence without existent, the impersonal par excellence" (142).

We are beginning to return to a familiar scene now, with the futurity of enjoyment, a scene that we were so at pains to leave earlier in this chapter. Elsewhere, Levinas has characterized "this nocturnal dimension of the future under the title *il y a*. The element extends into the *il y a*" (TI, 142, translation modified).[18] Surprisingly the analysis of sensibility and enjoyment in *Totality and Infinity* returns us to that ultimate horizon out of which the existent must continually raise itself in its hypostasis (cf. EE, 23). What is perhaps the most surprising in this is that the very thing that put us in contact with the Other (i.e., futurity) here puts us in the realm of the impersonal *il y a*, yet the accounts of futurity given in the two analyses are remarkably similar; the always still to come, the indeterminacy of the future that comes from nowhere and is nobody's—these remain consistent through the two discussions of futurity. How can "the very relationship with the other [be] the relationship with the future" (TO, 77) if that future puts us in contact not with the "infinite in the finite" that is the face-to-face but rather with the anonymous existence of the *il y a*?

The beginning of an answer to this question has already been sketched out in the previous chapter. There we saw that Levinas—after a series of sustained studies of Husserl's phenomenology—changed his conception of materiality and sensibility, during the late 1940s and the 1950s. This is what enabled him to recover a positive use of phenomenology in *Totality and Infinity* vis-à-vis the ontological analyses of *Time and the Other*. In this reevaluation of materiality (and the subsequent change to his understandings of sensibility and proximity), Levinas will use the notion of futurity at work here to tie the Other, and the "relation" to the Other, to the primal horizon *before* and out of which the subject emerges in its subjectivity. The apparent contradiction at work in the use of futurity in *Totality and Infinity* will be resolved only by a fundamental reevaluation of temporality, and with it a reevaluation of the relationship with alterity and the solitude of the subject, since time is "the very relationship of the subject with the Other" (TO, 39).

II. The Trace of Prehistory

A major problem remains in Levinas's account of time and futurity as discussed so far. This problem is significant in that it conflicts with his later development of the notion of intentionality and its correlates (materiality, sensation, impression, etc.). The problem is that the novelty of the future must be distinguished from the novelty, the newness, of the upsurge of every instant (cf. EE, 7).

Stated interrogatively: What differentiates the "absolute surprise" of the future from hypostasis, from the move from anonymous existence to the existent? Levinas's invocation of materiality in solitude (or of sensibility in enjoyment in *Totality and Infinity*) has already undermined that solitude, because materiality, as Levinas will later discover in his readings of Husserlian intentionality, already puts us in contact with the other and already reveals the passivity of the subject that Levinas, in *Time and the Other*, wants to reserve for death and the relation to the other. If materiality is solitude, how do we encounter alterity?

What is needed for this encounter is the "absolute surprise" that defines the future in *Time and the Other*. But Levinas will eventually come to acknowledge that this absolute surprise has always already happened. If absolute surprise is the temporality of futurity, then the subject will find itself "always too late" not just in relation to its past (to something already happened) but also in relation to its future (to that which is to-come, that which will surprise). What makes this temporality absolutely surprising is that, though futural as absolute surprise, the surprise has already happened: Futurity not only puts me in contact with the Other in the face-to-face; it also opens up an abyss within enjoyment itself, an abyss that makes possible separation. In the face-to-face encounter, the surprise is in the encounter with the face that opens up the dimension of height, alterity, ethics, and so on. But what makes this surprise *absolute* is that the self discovers in the face-to-face that it has already been opened up; alterity has already stricken it, riven it in two. This is alluded to already in *Time and the Other*, when Levinas says that plurality is within the very existing of the existent, and in *Totality and Infinity*, when futurity leads us to the anonymous existence of the *il y a*. But the depth of this statement emerges only after the analysis of materiality considered in the previous chapter.

In that analysis, we showed that Levinas came to understand materiality and sensibility itself as that which puts us in immediate contact with alterity (if not yet with the pure alterity of the Other person), before signification and thought. This enabled a radicalization of intentionality and sense bestowal (*Sinngebung*) such that we could now understand sense as bestowed from the world to the subject rather than from the subject onto the world, as Husserl had conceived of it. This reversal of *Sinngebung* meets its radical extreme in the situation of obsession or hostage: The Other gives the subject its very sense of subjectivity and self, in the mode of responsibility.

The task that lies before us now is to explore the temporality of such a situation. What does it mean, temporally speaking, that the subject receives its subjectivity from the Other? More important for our current purposes, can we still understand such a situation on the basis of futurity, as *Time and the Other* suggests, or does this situation occur in some other 'time'? I have already shown that there are hints in *Totality and Infinity* that futurity no longer places us in contact with the Other but in fact is constitutive of the anonymous existence of the *il y a* from which the subject must take up its existing by its hypostasis. Hence futurity has been, so to speak, pushed back to a time *before* the existing of the existent, to before the subject exists as subject.

Levinas begins his elaboration of the temporality of the Other's bestowing sense on the subject most notably in his important essay "The Trace of the Other" (1963).[19] At the beginning of that essay, he equates the primacy of the future with "knowledge as comprehension of being," with "light and obscurity, disclosure and veiling, truth and nontruth" (TA, 346), thereby seeming to signal a move away from the future as the temporal site of the encounter with alterity. Focusing on the passivity of the subject that we have already seen characterizes the heart of Levinas's reversal of Husserlian *Sinngebung*, he speaks of the need for a "heteronomous experience" that would not reduce the Other to the same (348), an experience that cannot be recuperated into the light of the self and its presence (347). It is because light (as the condition of reason and consciousness) is the condition of all experience that we need a "heteronomous" experience or a "work," but not the work of taking objects in my hand described in *Time and the Other*. Rather what is needed is a "work conceived radically [as] a movement of the same unto the other which never returns to the same" (348), but which is not, for all that, pure loss (349). A work so conceived is "a relationship with the other who is reached without showing himself touched"; it is a "being-for-beyond-my-death" (349). To be for beyond my death is to be for "a future beyond the celebrated 'being-for-death'" (349).[20] To do this is not to stretch out the time of the present subject forward; this would be to reduce the alterity of the future to the sameness of the present. Rather to be for beyond my death is to "let the future and the most far-off things be the rule for all the present days" (349). In other words, it is to move beyond my time to the time of the Other.

Levinas calls this being-for-beyond-my-death "eschatology" (TA, 349) or "liturgy" (350). But the talk of futurity is soon abandoned for discussion of the trace of "an utterly bygone past . . . which cannot be discovered in the self by an introspection," a past, therefore, that cannot be remembered, "an immemorial past" (355). The trace "occurs by overprinting. . . . He who left traces in wiping out his traces did not mean to say or do anything by the traces he left" (357).[21] In other words, the trace signifies as if by accident; it "signifies outside of every intention of signaling and outside of every project of which it would be the aim" (356–57), and signifies to the subject a past that cannot be remembered by the subject because it was never present for the subject (358).

This appeal to an "immemorial past" will become a major focus in *Otherwise than Being.* There Levinas begins to describe the encounter with the other primarily by words such as "hostage," "obsession," and "substitution."[22] At stake in this work is the "irreducible diachrony whose sense [*Otherwise than Being*] aims to bring to light" (OB, 34). This notion of diachrony is the key development in Levinas's reconception of time. In contrast to the time of subjectivity, which is the present as "the promise of the graspable," of knowledge (DR, 98), the 'time' of the sense-bestowing encounter with the Other that is characterized as "obsession" or hostage must be such that it cannot be synthesized, that is, united or made synchronous with the intentions and knowledge of the subject, existing always in the present. To avoid this synchronization, it is not enough to place this encounter in the past or the future, as these can both be reduced to the constituted time of the Ego, and hence reduced to the presence of the present (in the past-present or the future-present). What is needed is a notion of time that defies all recourse to synchronization, all attempts to be unified in the project of the Ego. This radically nonsynchronous time is diachrony, "the dia-chrony of a past that does not gather into re-presentation" (112), "a lapse of time that does not return . . . [that is] refractory to all synchronization," "a past more ancient than every representable origin, a pre-original and anarchical *passed*" (OB, 9), "a past that is on the hither side of every present" (10). The anarchical past cannot be recuperated, not "because of its remoteness, but because of its incommensurability with the present": Where the present is "assembled in a thematizable conjunction," diachrony is "the refusal of conjunction, the non-totalizable" (11).

This radically nonrecuperable, nonsynthesizable time is diachrony, and it introduces a radical alterity into the subjectivity of the subject.[23] Diachrony is not part of the play of intentional thought, of noeses aiming at noemas. This "non-intentional participation in the history of humanity" (DR, 112) is possible only by realizing the horizons in which the self always already finds itself: horizons of nature and the world but also of language (cf. OB, 34–37) and of sociality (DR, 109–11), that is, of relations to other people. These relations, as discussed in chapter 4, are constitutive of the sense of subjectivity bestowed on the subject; they condition the subject before the subject is there to take them up purposively. This puts the subject always in the position of "hostage" or "substitution": I am always "for-the-other" in responsibility but in a responsibility that "is an assignation of me by the other" (OB, 100). The Other, who is always on the scene before the self (11), gives the self its very sense and uniqueness—and does so by putting the onus of maintaining the relationship with the Other on to the self. It is this responsibility that makes the self "for-the-other" because the self is always responsible for the relationship with the Other, indeed for the very life (and hence the death) of the Other.

What moves this analysis of the subject's being "for-the-other" beyond the earlier analyses of *Totality and Infinity* is the making explicit of the fact that "responsibility for the other can not have begun in my commitment, in my decision" (OB, 10). Rather the "unlimited responsibility in which I find myself comes from the hither side of my freedom, from a 'prior to every memory,' an 'ulterior to every accomplishment,' from the non-present par excellence, the non-original, the an-archical" time of diachrony (10). It is the Other who commands the self to responsibility, and in this responsibility the self finds its very uniqueness as a self (106). But the self finds its uniqueness passively; it "cannot form itself" (104) but is, rather, called into being, or better "created," by one who simultaneously creates it in relation and withdraws from that relation. The self is therefore "a creature, but an orphan by birth" (105). It is held responsible for the other, in the place of the other—and therefore is "hostage" (11) of the other, in the sense of both being held hostage by the Other as persecutor and in being hostage for the other, that is, the ransom held in place of the other as hostage (110–12).

This conception of ethics as hostage or substitution relies necessarily on diachrony for its sense: It is because we can conceive of a time that is irreducible to the time of (constituting) consciousness, that is, a time irreducible to the time of the self, a time that is necessarily other than my time, a time of the Other, the Other's time, that we can conceive of the self as constituted by this relation with the Other *before* the self is there to be in relation. If the self met the Other as an established self, and hence in the time of the Self, the self would be primarily free and would then choose to be responsible (or not) for the Other. Such a self would be freedom, not responsibility. In order to find the sense of self as for-the-Other, the self must be understood as being constituted by an alterity within the self such that "I am an Other" (OB, 118). In the self, then, alterity and identity are united in the figure of "expiation," but "the ego is not an entity 'capable' of expiating for the others: it is this original expiation" (118).[24]

This "original expiation" is possible only because the Other encounters the self before the self is a self (at least, before the self is an ego).[25] The self then gains its sense from this encounter which happened before the history of the self had begun, that is, in the "pre-history of the I" (GDT, 175).

III. The Futurity of Diachrony

The use of phrases such as "responsibility anterior to representation" (DR, 111), "an-archic responsibility" (111; see also OB, 99–102), "senescence" (OB, 52), and the "immemorial past" (DR, 113) abound in Levinas's descriptions of diachronic time and seem to bear out a certain necessity, namely, the need for the self's encounter with the Other to be *before* the self is on the scene. This in turn would seem to suggest a certain privileging of the past, of an irrecuperable past that escapes the Husserlian attempts to constitute time in knowledge and consciousness. This irrecuperable past is diachronic in that it does not begin from the self and does not return to the self. It is due to this very alterity and diachronicity, we will see, that the "pre-history of the I" bears an essentially *futural* element, a conclusion that may seem surprising, given its situation in the past/passed. But this futural element must be brought to the fore if we are to properly understand Levinas's conception of ethics, and with it what is entailed in "ethics as first philosophy," that is, in a fundamentally nonepistemological phenomenology.

Diachrony is manifest most clearly in the trace of a past that comes before recuperable egoic experience. Such a past is of a different order than that of the past-present. In other words, it is not enough that this an-archic past occurs before the empirical "arche" of a particular subject. The year 1867, for example, can still be recuperated by me in my experience via the notion of history.[26] In history we use language to present past experience as constitutive of our present experience by tracing a narrative arc from that past experience to the present. Though I was not alive in 1867, I do know that that was the year of Canadian confederation; I can trace an entire history from that moment of Confederation (or even before that) to my current situation as a Canadian citizen. As such, I am able, in some way, to incorporate 1867 as a moment in my experience, even though I never had a direct experience of it.

The an-archic past of diachrony, then, is a past of a different order than the past-present. This, however, opens the door for a possible return of the future in and by this an-archic past: In empirical, constituted time, past and future are mutually exclusive, because they both refer (in opposite ways) to the present. Diachronic time, however, is of an entirely different order than that of the present. Shifting away from the present of the subject to the diachronic time of the Other, diachrony recovers a futurity at the heart of diachronic time. This futurity is first introduced via the notion of a future beyond my death (cf. TA 349; DR, 115). This future beyond my death is the very meaning of responsibility for the death of the Other (DR, 116), a responsibility that remains consistent from *Time and the Other* (1947) to "Diachrony and Representation" (1982). In other words, we can truly understand our responsibility for the Other only when we realize that there is a "*future* beyond what happens to me, beyond what, for an ego, is to-come" (DR, 116). This "nonencompassable future" is the very "concreteness of responsibility" (117), that is, the immediateness of our being responsible before the self's active constituting. This shows itself in the "non-in-difference and concordance that are no longer founded on the unity of transcendental apperception," that is, in the self's responsibility for the Other (118).

The immediateness of our relation to the Other manifests itself, Levinas claims, in a particular relation to the future that he calls the "futuration of the future" (DR, 115). This "futuration of the future" is not "given in the to-come [*à-venir*], where the grasp of an anticipation—or a protention— would come to obscure the dia-chrony of time" (113). Rather we are introduced to a new concept of futurity, one that does not follow from the Husserlian analyses of protention and expectation (which is what Levinas means by "anticipation" here) precisely because it does not come back to the transcendental unity of apperception, that is, the unity of the "I think." The "futuration of the future is . . . 'the fall of God into meaning,'" where God is the signification of the absolute that commands us with an imperative that is beyond "the natural order of being" (115). This "*imperative* signification of the future . . . concerns me as a non-in-difference to the other person, as my responsibility for the stranger" (115), and concerns me beyond the standard understanding of relationship as that in which the terms are already simultaneous (116). This is what enables Levinas to change his definition of time from "the very relationship of the subject with the Other" (TO, 39) to time as the "way of being avowed—or devotion" (DR, 115) that characterizes the subject as obsessed, hostage, and substitute of the Other. This is not a move away from the earlier definition of time as relationship to the Other but is rather a clarification of that relationship that seeks to maintain the otherness of the Other (115).

The futuration of the future is, according to Levinas, marked by awaiting, "an awaiting without something being awaited" (GDT, 115).[27] This "awaiting" relies on the essential passivity of the subject that characterizes its relation to the Other, "a passivity more passive than any passivity, that is . . . a nonassumable passivity" (115). We passively await by not awaiting something in particular. But any act of anticipation, that is, any egoically directed act that has the future as its object, must have an object and therefore must await *something*, even if it is a highly unclarified something, in the sense of the clarifying mode of intuition made possible in protention. Therefore, whatever Levinas is describing here cannot be an egoically directed act.

But we do not need our analysis of anticipation to reveal that to us. Rather it emerges already from Levinas's account of diachronic temporality and its distinctive account of futurity. With diachrony, Levinas goes beyond Husserl's conception of the future, significantly altering it by moving beyond the totality of the subject enclosed on itself, the totality of the constituting subject, to the alterity opened up within the self, the self as always already opened up to the other. Unlike the temporality of subjective constitution, which moves in a continuous line (or flow) from past, through present, to the future, diachronic time is interruptive rather than uniting, disquieting rather than cohering.[28] As such, the possibility of an an-archic past that is essentially futural remains. In this regard, Levinas never abandons his early characterization of the future as having the character of absolute surprise. Instead he works this absolute surprise into the upsurge of each instant, that is, the upsurge of exist*ing* vis-à-vis the anonymous scene of exist*ence*.

It is this futurity, understood as absolute surprise, that can help us make sense of the awaiting without something being awaited, an awaiting without horizons (of constitution), by inserting the relationship with the Other into the very heart of the existing of the subject itself. In its passivity as hostage-to-and-for-the-Other, the self exists in and as "deference to what cannot be represented and which, thus, cannot be expressed as *this*" (GDT, 115–16). This deference does not manifest itself in a Heideggerian "letting-be" but is marked by a non-indifference that is, for the self, "a way of being disquieted, disquieted in a passivity with no taking charge" (116). The self cannot rest comfortably in itself, then, but is constantly interrupted by an alterity that is found already within itself. The Same contains more than it can contain[29]—the Same is the Other-within-the-Same—and hence the Same is Desire (116), is inspired by what is other than the self, and can thereby never be reduced to the self. In Desire, the self always awaits the appearance of the Desired, while knowing that the Desired is that which cannot appear in the light or reason of the self.[30]

The role of futurity, then, seems to help us show how the very subjectivity of the subject can also be the relation to the Other. Absolute surprise is one and the same thing as an awaiting without something being awaited because what is absolutely surprising is something that does not come from us (and our horizons of expectation and protention) but comes from an infinite Other, and what comes from the Other most primarily is our very uniqueness or sense of self. Here we have the most extreme radicalization of the reversal of *Sinngebung* that Levinas proposes: The subject itself, rather than being the Ego-pole of all intentions, is actually from the Other and hence for-the-Other. The I is given from the Other.

Subjectivity itself, then, is futural for Levinas, as we have seen it also was for Husserl. But whereas Husserl understood futurity largely (though, as we have seen, not exclusively) on the basis of knowledge and the subjective constitutive correlation between noema and noesis (and Heidegger understood futurity on the basis of the mineness of one's own death), Levinas understands futurity on the basis of the absolutely surprising revelation of that which cannot appear: the Other as withdrawing in its appearance, the Other as Face and as trace. Where Husserl's subject constitutes itself in its consciousness of/as time, and Heidegger's subject is concerned with the projects suggested by the possibility of its own death, Levinas's subject is responsible for the Other who constitutes it as responsibility in the diachronic time of a beyond-my-death. In this move, not *beyond* but *within* the subject, a move that manifests itself in the move from horizons of constitution to Desire and responsibility, we begin to see more clearly the possibility of a nonepistemological understanding of the role of the future in shaping our understanding of the present, that is, an "ethical" understanding that will enable us to differentiate anticipation from expectation and may challenge an entire edifice of phenomenological understanding.

6

Levinas's Unique Contribution to Futurity in Phenomenology

At the end of part 1, our analysis of anticipation revealed that a sharp distinction of it from expectation—and thereby the preservation of the three levels of constituting consciousness that are necessary to establish phenomenology as a unique science—was possible only if we could find a way for the present to be affected by the future other than that of subjective horizons of constitution. Doing so would suggest the possibility of a fundamentally nonepistemological account of phenomenology, which we provisionally deemed "ethics." Levinas's account of futurity, properly understood, helps clarify the issue of ethicality, but we are left to determine how this affects the limit, scope, and role of phenomenology itself.

I. The Levels of Constituting Consciousness and Consciousness as Constituted

Levinas's unique contributions to a discussion of phenomenological futurity show us that the self-constitution of the subject (in its most basic level of constituting consciousness) is possible only because the subject is first and foremost constituted by an Other. We have already seen that Husserl admits of alterity in the second and third levels of constituting consciousness, but this is not where Levinas asserts his account of constitution by alterity. In characterizing futurity, the relation to the Other, as an "awaiting," Levinas seems to align himself with the active level of consciousness, whose distinct mode of futurity—anticipation—was characterized in some ways similar to awaiting, as discussed in chapter 5. However, in addition to the lack of an object, placing Levinasian futurity—and therefore the ethical relation—as this level is further contradicted by the characterization of futurity as not an active aiming at something but a patience, a passivity, a waiting to be impressed upon by the other. The importance of this passivity in Levinas's account of futurity cannot be overstated: The future is absolute surprise because it arrives from somewhere outside the subject and comes *to* the subject, that is, impresses itself upon the subject, in a way other than the horizons of expectation and protention (DR, 113). Nor can Levinasian futurity be equated with the level of passive association, since this is a mix of passive and "active" (not egoically directed but still constituted by the Ego), while Levinas is after the purely passive—a passivity more passive than any passivity—where there is no active involvement of the Ego. Indeed there cannot be, as the encounter with the Other in diachronic time that is constitutive of the Ego occurs prior to the Ego's being on the scene (OB, 114), and hence the Ego can have no active involvement whatsoever at this level.

This leaves us with the level of absolute consciousness as the only remaining level for the account that Levinas describes. This level is outside of what can be easily talked about and is metaphorically described as flow by Husserl (Hua X, 75). Absolute consciousness is beyond (or beneath) the acts of the Ego, though it is, at the same time, not entirely distinct from those acts. Absolute consciousness is the temporality of the subject—the subject as temporal. It is therefore made up of retained primal impressions and the protentive striving of these retentions for fulfillment in the next instant. For Husserl, the focus is on the work of protention and retention. By focusing on the primal impression, however, Levinas opens absolute consciousness onto something other-than-constituting-consciousness and thereby moves beyond even absolute consciousness, which remains, at least in its Husserlian explanation, a constituting consciousness.

Levinasian futurity, then, introduces another level of consciousness into the subject: constituted consciousness. "Constituted" here, though, does not refer to consciousness as a product or totalization of the levels of constituting. It refers to the fact that consciousness, in its most basic level (and in this sense, Levinasian futurity could be said to refer to absolute consciousness, understood now in a quasi-Anselmian, rather than distinctly Husserlian, way: that level of consciousness than which nothing more basic can be conceived), results not from the constituting work of the Ego but from the sense bestowed upon it by the Other.[1] Before it constitutes, consciousness is constituted. Before it bestows sense, consciousness is endowed with its own sense. Since it is bestowed upon consciousness, this most basic level of consciousness is purely passive (received from the Other, impressed upon by the world)[2] and hence lies outside any level of constituting consciousness.

Levinas's account of futurity, then, as distinct from protention, expectation, or anticipation, reveals yet another level of constituting consciousness: consciousness as constituted or, as Levinas will call it, the ipseity of the I.[3] Levinas maintains that ipseity is more basic to subjectivity than is absolute consciousness conceived as internal time-consciousness. This radical ipseity is bestowed upon the I from elsewhere, bestowed as responsibility. The responsible subject, then, is constituted/constituting rather than the purely free, constituting Ego of Husserl's internal time-consciousness.

II. Reconceiving Consciousness as Constituted/Constituting

However, this does not make Levinas's responsible subject wholly other than Husserl's time-constituting subject. Rather the passivity of the subject as constituted makes its appearance in the subject as time-constituting via the notion of primal impression. The discovery of a fourth level of constituting consciousness therefore does not merely add to the multiplicity of levels but splits each level from within, as our earlier, purely Husserlian analysis has already suggested: Absolute consciousness has the primal impression; passive association has the passive being-affected by the world; active constitution requires the previous achievements of passive association and is *always open to the promise of further discovery*. Every actively constituted experience is (pre-)experience, and this not because of some teleological drive to pure totalization[4] but because of the insertion of diachrony into constituted time at every level.[5] Ipseity therefore is not (merely) a distinct level of constituting consciousness but is also a passive-ication of each level of constituting consciousness.

And if it is Levinas's account of futurity that has brought us to the realization of ipseity, which affects every level of constituting consciousness, then it stands to reason that that account of futurity would itself affect every mode of futurity corresponding to those levels of constituting consciousness. This begins already with Levinas's attempts to define or characterize futurity: Futurity is awaiting (without something being awaited), it is absolute surprise, and it is the impersonal par excellence. I ended chapter 5 by trying to show the interrelation between these three characterizations of futurity. Now let us turn instead to the interrelation between these three characterizations of futurity and the threefold account of futurity we developed from Husserl. The purpose of this is to show how Levinasian futurity, like his phenomenology in general, can be conceived of as a rein-vigoration and reimagination of Husserl's account.

A. Similarities between Husserl and Levinas on Futurity

Aspects of each distinct mode of Husserlian futurity remain present in Levinas's account. The essentially striving character of Husserlian proten-tion, for example, seems to find its correlate in the ceaseless striving of the *il y a*. This incessant pushing of existence—the "impossibility of nothing-ness" (TO, 69)—is strikingly similar to Husserl's later talk of protention as the instinct or drive for self-preservation.[6] The ceaseless striving of proten-tion made possible the distinction between clarifying and confirming modes of intuition. This is because, for Husserl, the striving was conceived of as purely auto-affective.[7] This made sense in the realms of horizontal inten-tionality and general fulfillment but was more difficult to analyze in trans-verse intentionality and particular fulfillment. No such distinction follows from the ceaseless striving of the futurity of the *il y a* because this striving, for Levinas, is not subjective but precedes the hypostasis of the subject.

The distinction between clarifying and confirming intuitions set the stage for expectation, which is a clarificational mode of futurity that allows us to apperceive objects and hence constitute a world. Part of this expecta-tive association was the ability of the world to affect me. In Levinas, this affection by the world occurs in sensibility and ultimately sets the stage for the reversal of *Sinngebung*. Hence part of what we have characterized as expectation is captured in Levinas's conception of futurity as absolute sur-prise, as the arrival of what comes from beyond or outside the self. Of course, this is but a small part of the expectative association, and other parts of that association (e.g., the use of retentional horizons to expect and apper-ceive objects) do not occur in Levinas's account of futurity. But there remain some similarities between the two accounts, some points of contact.[8]

Finally, as I have already mentioned, the awaiting that characterizes anticipation finds its most extreme fulfillment in the awaiting of Levinas's patient Desire, an awaiting that is never fulfilled but awaits that which necessarily withdraws itself in its appearing.[9] Levinasian awaiting, then, shares both similarities (e.g., awaiting) to and differences (e.g., the lack of an object, activity vs. passivity) from anticipation.

B. Differences between Husserl and Levinas on Futurity

There are seeds of similarity, then, between Levinas's different attempts to define futurity and Husserl's threefold account of futurity. As important to our understanding of Levinas's innovation of futurity in phenomenology, however, are the differences between these accounts. Levinasian awaiting, though somewhat similar to anticipation, remains totally distinct from it in both object (or lack thereof) and level of intentionality (purely passive vs. egoically directed and active). By folding passivity back into awaiting, Levinas has established passivity in all constitution, even active constitution; even where we purposively direct our egoic gaze toward an object, there is still passivity at work. In one regard, there is the passivity of the world's impressing itself upon us that distinguishes phenomenological constitution from idealism.[10] In another regard, there is Levinas's insistence on the primacy of responsibility over freedom: The self is not the sovereign agent of constitution but reacts to the world with a sense that is already bestowed upon it.

But what are the concrete repercussions of this responsibility? Alternatively phrased, this returns us to an earlier problematic: How is the act of waiting for my wife to return home from work essentially ethical? Levinas's account of futurity has helped us to see how the notion of (pre-)experience, drawn from Lacoste, helps manifest the essential ethicality of every act: Every constituting act is both experience of what is present and a pre-experience of the potential for greater fulfillment yet to come. Levinas's account of futurity as patient Desire (awaiting without something being awaited) allows us to see that the greater fulfillment to come is not a confirming fulfillment but a clarifying one: What is to come will itself be also a (pre-)experience—an experience that both gives itself and suggests something more—and therefore will act not as a confirmation of a previous intention but as further clarification for a future intention. In this regard, every experience, as (pre-)experience, is an experience that gives more than it can contain.[11] This process of being ever clarified but never confirmed reveals that some things lie outside our powers of constitution but not outside the realm of our experience. How is this possible? Because, though every experience is a constituted experience, not all of my experiences are constituted *by me*. This is the conclusion of Levinas's inversion of *Sinngebung*: Sometimes sense is bestowed to me or on me, not by me.

This conclusion is confirmed also in the reworking of passive association offered by Levinasian futurity. Rather than basing our sense of the world on our ability to expect certain things of the world (a point that focuses on the constituting side of passive constitution), Levinas's account of the future as absolute surprise reminds us that we are stricken by something that comes from beyond or outside of ourselves. In being so stricken, we are not only surprised to discover that which is different from us and hence resistant to our powers of constitution (i.e., the world will not let us constitute it in whatever way we please), but we are *absolutely* surprised to discover this alterity within our very selves: There is much in myself, in the most basic aspects of myself, that resists my constitution; I am not free to constitute myself in whatever way I please but am condemned to my uniqueness. For better or worse, I am myself, and not in isolation but in relation to others.

This relation to others as constitutive of the self reaches its zenith in absolute consciousness. By conceiving the ceaseless striving of protention according to the restlessness of the *il y a*, Levinas suggests that the ceaseless striving is not of our own accord. Rather the ceaseless striving precedes our existence as a subject (an existent); in fact it is the very thing that causes us to recoil into ourselves, thereby establishing our existence as a single subject, in solitude and separation. This striving is internalized by the subject in a *synopsia* (GDT, 116), which is a "virtual synonym for 'synthesis' " (259n.5) but derived from synesthetic disorders rather than from the power of the sovereign Ego. In deriving this synthesis from a displacement of one sense into the other (the hearing of colors, the seeing of sounds, etc.), Levinas indicates that the internal time of the subject, the internalization of time that is the subject—absolute consciousness[12]—is a displacement of sense: The sense of the Other becomes the sense of the self.[13] In temporality so understood, the very flow of consciousness is an experience (as is any synesthetic scenario), but an experience that is not optimal, or that leaves room for continued optimalization: We can get to know the thing experienced better; there could be future experiences that will yield us new information about the thing experienced.[14]

Levinas does not think that the internalization of time as synopsia is a human failing; rather "it is a matter of an essential ambiguity in this patience we are describing, that is, of an impatience with this patience within this very patience" (GDT, 116). Some of the otherness of the sense bestowed upon me—the otherness of the bestowed sense that I am—must be lost in order for this sense to constitute "a unity of a person in an inhabited world" (116). Ipseity, the very uniqueness of the I bestowed by the other, is simultaneously I and other. The experience of ipseity is the experience of one sense (the sense of the Other) displaced into another sense (the sense of the self). Ipseity is experienced as synopsia; the subject is a hostage.

And it is this lost "sense of the Other" that stirs ceaselessly in the striving of futurity on the most basic level of constituting consciousness. This is Levinas's radical redefinition of protention in the anonymous striving of the *il y a*. This anonymity is recognized as coming from the Other only in the absolutely surprising encounter with the face of the other, where the surprise is not just the encounter with the height and separation of the

Other but with the fact that this Other already stirs ceaselessly within me. Ultimately I can begin to see that all of my experiences reveal something of this sense of the other (though not always the Other) in that, in all of my experiences, sense is bestowed on me or to me as much as sense is bestowed by me.[15]

What is revealed by Levinas's account of futurity is that futurity shows to us the essential openness of the subject. This essential openness is our ipseity, our very uniqueness. In other words, we are not first a subject and then open to others (in community, multiplicity, etc.); rather our very subjectivity, our very mode of existing as a subject, is already pluralized, already opened onto alterity. By reemphasizing the passivity that was present but dormant in Husserl's analyses of futurity, Levinas has reconceived futurity and done so in a manner that has reconceived the subject of phenomenology. Not only is the subject, as studied by phenomenology, essentially opened onto alterity but the discipline of phenomenology is essentially altered: Phenomenology must now study not only constituting acts but also the "acts," or perhaps the "passed,"s, the being pass-ed, the passiveness, of being constituted. Levinas has further demonstrated the need for this passed to be studied by way of futurity: Futurity opens us onto what is essential in phenomenology.

III. Ethics and the Promise

Levinas's development of futurity has revealed an essential openness at the heart of phenomenology and phenomenological futurity, an openness that he deems ethicality. This ethicality is an ethical *Sinngebung*, a bestowal of sense to the subject by the Other. But we must pause here, for we still have not answered a question raised earlier: How does this ethicality manifest itself concretely in anticipation? What, in the act of waiting for my wife to arrive home from work, is essentially *ethical*?

This question has been partially answered by a clarification of what is meant by ethical in this situation: ethical here implies the inversion of *Sinngebung*, not some code of conduct for intersubjective relations. In this sense, there is perhaps nothing overly contentious about suggesting that anticipation is essentially ethical; this would mean only that anticipation reveals to us that we do not constitute everything; some things come to us from beyond us and outside our control; some things we must encounter, we cannot constitute (or we constitute by encountering). The futural orientation of anticipation seems to admirably lead to this conclusion.

But if there is nothing contentious about saying that anticipation is essentially ethical in this sense, this is because there is perhaps nothing overtly provocative about such a claim either; it seems to say nothing beyond that the subject is intentional. What stirs us about the claim that anticipation is essentially ethical is the idea that something in the act of anticipating—and perhaps in futurity more generally, as Levinas has blurred the lines of demarcation between the functioning of anticipation, expectation, and protention, if not their roles—commits us or in some way makes us responsible to other people. But this latter claim has only been suggested and has not yet been proven (or disproven) by our study to this point.

However, the conclusion of Levinas's innovation of futurity leads us to the doorstep of just such a problem. If the subject is essentially opened onto alterity, and especially onto the other person, and if this openness onto the other person manifests itself in the ceaseless striving of futurity, then futurity leads us inexorably to the question of responsibility to other people. However, the person to whom we are ethically bound is not necessarily the person we are anticipating. In waiting for my wife to arrive home from work, the ethicality of this act would not be due to the relation with my wife; the fact that it is my wife that I am waiting for is but a contingent factor of this particular act of anticipation and reveals to us nothing about anticipation *qua* anticipation. I can, after all, also anticipate the Toronto Maple Leafs winning the Stanley Cup, or even the arrival in the mail of a book I've ordered online. In neither of these last two cases do I have any kind of relationship, let alone an ethical one, with the object of my anticipation.[16]

So what would form the basis of any potential essential ethicality of anticipation? In futurity, we are returned here to the question of the promise.[17] I have said that anticipation is characterized by the promise: What is experienced now *promises* also a future experience. What remains to be shown is that the use of "promise" in this situation is more than just a trick of language. We must establish the agent of the promise (who is promising?), the recipient of the promise (to whom is something promised?), and the content of the promise (what exactly is promised?).

Levinas's account of futurity seems to provide us with at least the beginning of an answer to these issues. Since it is the Other who is active in futurity, the Other would seem to be the agent of the promise; since it is the self who is passive in futurity, the self would seem to be the recipient of the promise; and since what we Desire in futurity is an experience of what is to-come, this object or experience to-come would seem to be the content of the promise.

Though this would seem to be the answer suggested by Levinas's ethical account of futurity, this is not in fact the case. First, that which is to-come is also that which will never arrive. As diachronic, the futuration of the future can never become a re-presentation in synchronic time; it can never become a present experience of the Ego. It is the withdrawal of what is given in experience that awakens the self to futurity, that is, to its relation to the Other through patient awaiting and Desire. However, it is constitutive of this Desire that what is desired always and necessarily withdraws itself and can never be presented (cf. TI, 33–35). If the object of the ethical promise in anticipation is the experience to-come, then the promise is always necessarily broken, for that which is to-come will never arrive.

Second, the relation between self and Other in diachrony is such that the self cannot be the recipient of the promise because the self is not present at the time of the encounter. Rather the self is created by this encounter with the Other and comes to be a self only because of this encounter. Such a nonpresent nonself could not be the recipient of a promise.

For these reasons, it would seem that the theme of the promise does not apply to Levinas's account of futurity, and his explicit statements seem to support this thesis (see DR, 120). But perhaps something of the promise can be saved here. First of all, though the experience to-come will never arrive, we have already shown that, for Levinas, the experience of the Infinite that withdraws in its appearing—the experience of a thought that thinks more than it can contain—is the experience of an ever-clarifying intuition with no corresponding confirmation.[18] As such, the experience of what is to-come can appear as trace—not as present, or re-presentable, but as the trace of diachronic time.

Second, and more significantly, because the subject is created by the relationship with the Other in diachronic time, perhaps we can conceive of it not as the recipient of the promise but as the promise itself.[19] By being constituted as responsibility, the very ipseity of the self is constituted by its being-in-the-place of the Other. As such, the subjectivity of the subject is itself a promise to stand in for the Other, to take responsibility for the Other and the death of the Other. In the radical reversal of *Sinngebung* described by Levinas, the self is neither agent nor recipient of the promise; the self becomes the content of the promise: The self is that which is promised.[20]

Levinas's account of futurity, then, suggests that the self is promised before it can make the promise, that the self's existence is to exist as a promise (of responsibility). Does such a claim move us toward a more commonsense notion of ethics, or does it merely create an idiosyncratic understanding of the promise? Has the door finally been opened through which we may evaluate the possible ethicality of anticipating something in the future? Or have we merely discovered a pathway into another hallway of mirrors that will distract us from the real issue?

The only way to answer these questions is to push forward. It is only by evaluating the relationship between phenomenological futurity and the promise that we will be able to determine whether pursuing the question of the promise will yield a new essential insight into futurity (as did our analysis of ethicality and/as openness) or into ethics (as our analysis of ethicality failed to do, at least in regard to our commonsense intuitions about ethics), thereby helping us to determine once and for all what it might mean that not just anticipation but, following Levinas, futurity itself is essentially ethical. At stake is not just a clarification of our understanding of futurity but also a clarification of the method and content of phenomenology itself: What could it mean for phenomenology that it is essentially ethical? Whether an analysis of the promise will reveal a more traditional account of ethics at the basis of phenomenological futurity, thereby saving ethics at the expense of a certain account of phenomenology, or will show that ethics, traditionally conceived, has nothing to do with phenomenology, thereby saving a certain account of phenomenology at the expense of the primacy of ethics, we are not yet in position to say.

But even if a traditional conception of ethics cannot be recovered, the problem of the possible ethicality of phenomenology remains pressing; at stake for phenomenology is the place of intentionality in its methodology. If the openness of Levinasian ethics can be understood along the lines of the openness of the subject onto the world constitutive of intentionality, then the issue of "saving" phenomenology or ethics takes on a more specifically phenomenological theme. If "ethicality" has problematized constituting subjectivity, and ethicality means little more than the openness onto the world, then how can phenomenology possibly hold together openness and constitution? How, in other words, can phenomenology be understood as both intentional and transcendental?

PART III

Futurity and Intentionality—The Promise of Relationship

7

Genesis, Beginnings, and Futurity

The purpose of this final section is to clarify the relationship between phenomenological futurity and the promise, and through this to clarify the other analogous parallel relationships that we have been discussing: between phenomenology and ethics, between constituting subjectivity and openness, between constituting futurity and futurity as surprise. In order to properly understand the centrality of the promise to phenomenology, we must first reveal the origin of this discussion in a phenomenological wrestling with the question of time. Arguing that both Levinas's and Husserl's phenomenological analyses fail to adequately account for the centrality of genesis (though in very different ways), Derrida offers his notion of *différance* as his positive attempt to remedy the problem of genesis, a remedy that cannot be understood apart from its lineage in phenomenological accounts of futurity. The analysis of the phenomenological problem of genesis is not only the first major project undertaken by Derrida, but it is a problem that continued to guide Derrida's work—both in his critiques of other major figures in phenomenology and in his own positive contributions to a phenomenological philosophy—throughout his life.[1]

I. The Problem of Genesis in (Husserl's) Phenomenology

In 1953–54 a young Jacques Derrida set out on an ambitious attempt to demonstrate that Husserlian phenomenology was severely compromised by a problem that it itself introduced: the problem of genesis. Genesis constitutes a problem because it has what seems to be an inherently contradictory nature. Genesis, Derrida writes,

> brings together two contradictory meanings in its concept: one of origin, one of becoming. On the one hand, indeed, genesis is birth, absolute emergence of an instant, or of an 'instance' that cannot be reduced to the preceding instance, radicalness, creation, autonomy in relation to something other than itself; in brief, there is no genesis without absolute origin. . . . But at the same stage, there is no genesis except within a temporal and ontological totality that encloses it; every genetic product is produced by something other than itself; it is carried by a past, called forth and oriented by a future. It only is, it only has its meaning, when it is inscribed in a context which on the one hand is its own, that is to say, to which it belongs and in which it participates . . . but which, on the other hand, goes beyond, which envelopes it from all sides. Genesis is also an inclusion, an immanence. (PG, xxi)[2]

This contradiction will emerge in various guises, depending on where and how the genetic movement is deployed, throughout Husserl's writings. *The Problem of Genesis in Husserl's Philosophy* will trace the various aspects of this emergence through all of Husserl's major published works (and a significant number of unpublished manuscripts as well), showing that genesis is a problem that Husserl postponed dealing with, though it constantly undermined his analyses. For our purposes here, it is not necessary to retrace all of these movements through the entirety of Husserl's thought.[3] Instead, and in keeping with our main line of argumentation, let us focus on the temporal aspect of genesis, its "essential" makeup and the problems it poses for Husserl's analyses of internal time-consciousness.

A. *The Temporal Nature of Genesis*

In the quote above, Derrida claims that every genetic product is "called forth and oriented by a future." Further on he will complement this by stating that "a certain anticipation is thus faithful to the sense of every genesis" (PG, xxiii). Though he equates this anticipation with protention (184n.16), thereby revealing that he is not working within the same analysis or vocabulary of Husserlian futurity as am I in the present work, this does not entail that there is nothing for us to learn about futurity from *The Problem of Genesis*. A few pages later, for example, Derrida claims that "it is always through an 'anticipation' which is at least formal, that any signification, founded on an *a priori* synthesis, appears, and appears to itself originarily" and this enables "the absolute sense of genesis [to] be at once 'originary' and 'anticipated'" (xxv). Thus anticipation "is always indispensable for the appearance of every possible meaning, whatever may be its sense" (xxvi). Derrida recognizes here the centrality of futurity to all of Husserl's thought, and not just his thought specifically on time-consciousness. But from this Derrida distills a claim whose radicality will perhaps become clear only with time: "Indeed, if some anticipation is always necessary, if the future in some way always precedes present and past, hence if some implication always remains hidden,[4] then the intelligibility and significance that depend on it essentially . . . run the risk of being definitively compromised by this. A phenomenological philosophy must be genetic if it wishes to respect the temporality of the originary lived experience" (xxvi). The integrality of futurity to phenomenology threatens the very project of phenomenology[5] unless one conceives of phenomenology along genetic lines.

The necessity of genesis is imposed on philosophy by the temporality of lived experience, that is, by the temporality of the object of phenomenological inquiry. The phenomenological principle of principles (see Hua III, §24) is premised on the self-givenness (*Selbstgegebenheit*) of lived experience (*Erlebnis*), and this lived experience gives itself in and as time. Hence any phenomenology must account for the temporalization of lived experience by matching that temporalization with an analogous temporalization in (phenomenological) analysis. This temporal analysis is genesis, that is, genetic phenomenological analysis.

Husserl himself, of course, recognized the need for genetic analysis.[6] However, Derrida claims that even Husserl's genetic accounts are insufficient, and are so because they fail to fully challenge the appeal to eidetics. By constantly looking for essences, Husserl confines himself to searching for that which is already constituted,[7] ideal essences, instead of that which is constituting. But it is precisely the purpose of phenomenology to search for the constituting transcendental subject.[8]

The disjunction between constituting and constituted reinserts us into a problem that has cropped up at several key junctions of our earlier analyses: How do we make sense of the relationship between constituting and constituted, that is, of intentionality? In Husserl, this is the very problem of time, of absolute time-consciousness, as posed in Hua X (cf. PG, 77). It lies at the heart of the distinction between horizontal and transverse intentionality, between general and particular fulfillment, and especially in the debate concerning the distinction between the second (i.e., immanent unities) and third (i.e., absolute time-constituting flow) levels of constituting consciousness.[9] It emerged again, and more explicitly, in Levinas's reworking of Husserlian phenomenology, with the addition of the subject as constituted into the discussion of the levels of constituting consciousness, which occasioned a fundamental rethinking of Husserl's notions of time, futurity, and phenomenology itself. The phenomenological subject and the phenomenological world must both be, as Levinas pointed out, "not only constituted but also constituting" (RR, 118). This in fact is a key presupposition of intentionality, that most basic of phenomenological presuppositions: It is only because the subject and the world are always already in contact, constituting and constituted, that consciousness can be intentional (rather than intentionality merely being a modification or "character" of consciousness, as it was in Brentano; cf. PG, 1).

Derrida's claim is that in order to take full account of the coincidence of constituting and constituted that is called for by intentionality, phenomenology must take full account of genesis. Any static account will necessarily privilege one of the two poles at the expense of the other: If we focus solely on the constituting power of the subject, we are led ultimately to psychologism, in either its mundane (Mill, Sigwart) or its transcendental (Kant) variations; if, however, we focus solely on meanings or idealities as constituted, we fall back into logicism. As Derrida shows, it was precisely the purpose of phenomenology to overcome this neo-Kantian stalemate between psychologism and logicism, because in "both cases, the origin and becoming of logic was missed, in a word, its genesis" (PG, 48).

That this genesis cannot be purely empirical is obvious, given Husserl's adamant rejection of psychologism in volume 1 of *Logical Investigations*. But the possibility of "transcendental" genesis—that is, the essential becoming of sense and meaning, sense and meaning as an essential becoming, as simultaneously constituted and constituting, as constituting itself—is problematized by its own genetic sense: as an essential becoming, as essentially genetic, "transcendental" genesis must not take place within the realm of what is already constituted (if it is to be originary and transcendental) and hence cannot appeal to universal essences or constituted subjects. For this reason, a transcendental sense of genesis must not reduce historical and factual existence to some universalized essence, which would be "no more than a concept in disguise" (PG, xxxviii). Indeed transcendental genesis "must not be the object of a reduction," for if it is to be *originary* becoming, "what subject will absolute meaning appear for? How can absolute and monadic transcendental subjectivity be at the same time a becoming that is constituting itself? In this radical autonomy of time, is not absolute subjectivity 'constituted' and no longer constituting?" (xxxix). This leads Derrida to the following conclusion: "Far from being reduced or, on the contrary, revealed by the phenomenological reduction, is not transcendental genesis something which, originarily, makes possible the reduction itself?" (xxxix). In order to accurately account for transcendental genesis, then, empirical and factual existence cannot be reduced. Yet simultaneously (and this is the paradox, the problem, the seemingly contradictory double necessity) they *must* be reduced, for it is only after the reduction that something can be rigorously and properly transcendental, that is to say, phenomenological.[10]

This dilemma is necessitated in part by the temporality of absolute consciousness, that is, the temporality of retention-impression-protention. If the impression is in part constituted by horizons of expectation, as we discussed in chapter 2, and these expectational horizons require retentional horizons as the basis for their expectations, then these horizons, horizons of the world, cannot be reduced without losing the temporality constitutive of absolute consciousness. Hence "the absolute of sense would appear to itself as such only in alienating itself and in putting itself in relation with what is not it; better, this alienation would be the condition of possibility of its appearance. It is not an accident that the themes of transcendental genesis and of transcendental intersubjectivity appeared at about the same moment in Husserl's meditation" (PG, xl). Because of this necessary temporality and alterity that is constitutive of the subject, "existence is at the very heart of the transcendental 'I' " (xl), and the theme of temporality is "the only foundation of a transcendental genesis of logic" (128).

B. The (Temporal) Insufficiency of Husserl's Analyses

If we have now understood the necessarily temporal aspect at the root of genesis, it remains for us to see the significance of this for our analysis of temporality. Why should the necessarily genetic nature of transcendental analysis affect the phenomenological conceptions of futurity that we have discussed so far? We have already seen, in Levinas's critical reworking of Husserl, that the latter does not sufficiently account for the passive aspects of phenomenological time, that is, the fact that the phenomenological subject is not purely constituting but is also constituted. Derrida will echo this critique, though with a slightly different tenor. By focusing on the region of prepredicative existence that passivity implies, Derrida establishes a fundamental "dialectic"[11] at the heart of phenomenology, a dialectic that is ontological in nature. "This ontology," he claims, "will show, by deepening the phenomenology of temporality, that at the level of the originary temporal existence, fact and essence, the empirical and the transcendental, are inseparable and dialectically of a piece" (PG, 159).

Husserl, Derrida contends, fails to adequately represent this situation. Husserl's eidetic analyses, as I have said, ensure that he remains always in the realm of the already constituted, thereby maintaining the sharp distinction between constituting and constituted, fact and essence, empirical and transcendental, and so on. By always choosing for one side (constituted, essence, transcendental) over the other, Husserl fails to maintain the dialectical tension between the two sides. As a result, phenomenology continues to slide back and forth between empiricism and logicism without being able to maintain a stable (if somewhat tense) position between the two.[12]

Let us turn again to the example of temporality to highlight this difficulty. Husserl's temporal scheme of retention-impression-protention shows us, as I have already remarked, that "every constituting moment . . . brings with it a constituted moment in the intimacy of its foundation" (PG, 134), in that every "living present" of time-consciousness is made up, not just of retentions and protentions, but of impressions as well. As such, the very absolute of time-constituting consciousness is itself always already composed of constituted moments. "This essential intrusion of constituted time into constituting time does not allow us to make the distinction rigorously between" pure, transcendental constitution and the facticity of existence (134). Indeed the "passive synthesis of time, which always precedes the active synthesis, is an *a priori synthesis* of fact and intention, of being and sense" (134). But Husserl, as we have already seen, and as Levinas also highlighted, constantly fails to appreciate the true sense of the passivity that he himself inserts into the living present and hence into the phenomenological subject as such. Husserl speaks only of the time-constitut*ing* function of the subject and not of its constituted aspects. Even in his later works, where his analyses appear to take on their most genetic character, he continues to maintain a rigorous distinction between "transcendental intentionality"[13] and "empirical existence"[14] and decides stridently for the former. This opens up a host of problems, as Derrida shows, not the least of which is the very possibility of the "crisis" itself: If the task of philosophy is transcendental, then how can an empirical event cover up this transcendental teleology and make its being "forgotten" possible? How can the "crisis" be anything more than an empirical accident, stripped of any transcendental significance? Conversely, if the task is empirical, how can it be infinite? How can it be ideal?

What Derrida is calling for is a fundamental reorientation of phenomenology that would "put us in contact with the existent as such" (PG, 106). This is because he claims that the "originarily synthetic identification of consciousness and time is equivalent to confusing the pure subject with an originarily historical existence that is . . . the very 'existence' of the subject.

This existence, as originarily temporal and finite, is 'in the world'" (PG, 128). Hence the problem of genesis, the problem of identifying the relationship between constituting and constituted, the problem of the passage between "primitive existence" and "originary sense" (xl),[15] arises precisely because of Husserl's temporal analyses. It is the purpose of genetic phenomenology to speak to this problem, to "retrace the absolute itinerary that leads from prepredicative evidence to predicative evidence" (106. translation modified[16]), to explain, in other words, the passage from primitive existence to sense. We can now understand the claim already cited that a "phenomenological philosophy must be genetic if it wishes to respect the temporality of the originary lived experience" (xxvi).

II. Phenomenology and Metaphysics: Holding Together Husserl and Levinas

Derrida's genetic critique of Husserl, premised as it was on the valuation of prepredicative existence and passivity, would seem to set Derrida on a Levinasian path. Such thinking would not be incorrect, provided it is properly supplemented. Though Derrida maintains certain aspects of Levinas's critique of Husserl (especially the critique of the overly theoretical and overly active characteristics of Husserl's analyses), he is also at pains to show that Levinas repeats a fundamental Husserlian problem, even if he does so in an essentially different way: While Husserl emphasizes the active and Levinas the passive aspects of phenomenology, neither, Derrida will claim, adequately accounts for the fundamentally dialectical (or ambiguous or tense) nature of the phenomenological origin.

A. Derrida on Levinas (Reading Husserl)

Derrida's early encounter with Levinas in "Violence and Metaphysics" is significant in that the critique Derrida raises there relies on a more positive elaboration of Husserl than is found in *The Problem of Genesis*, the *Introduction*, or *Speech and Phenomena*. It is from this work that one can really begin to devise the "two Husserls" that Derrida will set against each other in the deconstructive moves of *Speech and Phenomena*. Worthy of note especially for our larger purposes here, this positive elaboration of Husserl—this valuation of Husserl against Levinas, which follows on the heels of a valuation of Levinas (or at least Levinasian themes) against Husserl in *The Problem of Genesis*—occurs in the section titled "Difference and Eschatology," that is, on the section whose title calls to mind one of the strongest elaborations of Levinas's account of futurity that was available at the time,[17] an account that, it will be recalled, cannot be separated from his account of alterity and of ethics.[18]

Where Derrida had criticized Husserl for not taking adequate account of the passive elements of phenomenology, in "Violence and Metaphysics" he seems to try to get Levinas to take account of the necessity of a certain activity in phenomenology as well. For example, let us take Derrida's response to Levinas's critique of Husserl's Fifth Cartesian Meditation. There Husserl posits a relation of "analogical appresentation" as constitutive of the relation between the subject (as *ego*) and the other person (as *alter ego*). Levinas responds that such a relationship loses the alterity of the other person, reducing it to the same. "To make the other an alter ego, Levinas says frequently, is to neutralize its absolute alterity" (VM, 123). But, Derrida claims, the "encounter" with the Other that defines Levinas's account of futurity is possible only if that Other in some way appears to an ego (123).[19] This is a necessity not just of phenomenological evidence (though surely of that too) but, more important, of the lived experience (*Erlebnis*) of any and every subject, for "egological life has as its irreducible and absolutely universal form the living present. There is no experience which can be lived other than in the present" (132). If the other person is to be encountered by the ego, even encountered as Wholly Other, it must in some way appear to, that is, become a phenomenon for, the ego.

But the nature of this phenomenality is not that of the object. In this regard, Levinas is right to question Husserl's overly theoretical attitude, and Derrida does not challenge the legitimacy of this putting into question (VM, 133). Rather Derrida seeks to show that "Levinas's metaphysics in a sense presupposes . . . the transcendental phenomenology that it seeks to put into question" (133). It is only because the Other can be discovered as another source of transcendental constitution (i.e., as an other transcendental ego, a *transcendental* alter ego) that the true, metaphysical separation between Same and Other can be safeguarded. This shows itself in "an essential, absolute and definitive self-evidence": Because "the other as transcendental other (other absolute origin and other zero point in the orientation of the world) can never be given to me in an original way and in person," but only mediately, that is, in Husserl through analogical appresentation, the "necessary reference to analogical appresentation . . . confirms and respects separation" (124). Because, and only because, the Other is another transcendental origin and not (merely) a thing in the world, my experience of it must be mediated through another act, an act that views it "as it is," that is, as another transcendental origin as my ego also is,[20] and "the theme of appresentative transposition [therefore] translates the recognition of the radical separation of absolute origins, the relationship of absolved absolutes and nonviolent respect for the secret" (124).

If metaphysical separation—the true alterity of the Other—is to be safeguarded, an appeal to transcendental phenomenology is necessary. Such an appeal is explained in Husserl (if somewhat unsatisfactorily), who strives to make sense of the "phenomenal system of nonphenomenality" that is transcendental phenomenology (VM, 125). Levinas, however, does not describe this system—in fact explicitly criticizes this system—and hence is not able to justify his call to speak to the Wholly Other, that is, to relate to the Other via a Saying that is irreducible to the Said. The only reason he can appeal to discourse with the other, it would seem, is if he has presupposed something that would make this possible (presupposed because he has done nothing to explicitly argue for its validity). This is why Derrida maintains that Levinas's metaphysical system presupposes the transcendental phenomenology that it seeks to overcome.

B. Double Necessities

At stake here is something more fundamental than Levinas's reception of Husserl. What Levinas's simultaneous presupposition and (legitimate) criticism of Husserl shows is a double necessity: On the one hand, alterity must be "without relation to the same [*sans rapport au même*]" (VM, 151);[21] this is what guarantees its infinite otherness. On the other hand, alterity is defined by discourse with the Other, by this ' "saying to the other'—this relationship to the other as interlocutor, this relation with an *existent*" that ensures that the ethical relation precedes ontology and therefore that ethics can be first philosophy (98; see also TI, 47–48). This double necessity not only haunts Levinas but repeats the double necessity that Derrida showed in *The Problem of Genesis* to have haunted Husserl: Since the relation of metaphysical separation is guaranteed only by appeal to the transcendental, the double necessity is that of transcendental and empirical, of constituting and constituted, of sense and being; it is, in other words, the repetition of the same "dialectic" that Derrida put at the heart of genesis and therefore at the heart of any genuine phenomenology.

This is possible only because of a second double necessity: If Levinas must necessarily presuppose transcendental phenomenology in his metaphysics, then conversely, transcendental phenomenology must presuppose Levinasian metaphysics. It was this second presupposition that enabled Levinas to develop his metaphysics from out of his "long frequenting of Husserlian labours" (RR, 113, translation modified), and it manifests itself most clearly in the notion of intentionality. Intentionality, as the simultaneity

(without union) of constituting and constituted in transcendental constitution, guarantees separation, both metaphysical and concrete, in Levinas's
sense (see TI, 28);[22] hence, paradoxically, it is the Husserlian understanding of intentionality (as opposed to its Brentanonian predecessor) that enables Derrida to save Husserl from the Levinasian charge that he employed
intentionality to repress infinity.

Levinas claims that Husserl, via the themes of vision and theoretical
intuition, equates intentionality primarily with adequation, which would
remove the possibility of distance, true alterity, and separation. Adequation would therefore lead to the one-sided *Sinngebung* against which Levinas reacts in developing his own version of phenomenology (cf. VM, 118).
But Derrida maintains that an understanding of Husserlian intentionality
as purely adequation is incorrect. It is "the *Idea in the Kantian sense* [that]
designates the infinite overflowing of a horizon which, by reason of an
absolute and essential necessity which itself is absolutely principled and
irreducible, *never* can become an object itself, or be completed, *equaled*, by
the intuition of an object. Even by God's intuition" (120).

The Idea in the Kantian sense manifests itself in myriad ways, and at
times, especially in the later Husserl, quite explicitly.[23] In relation to our
earlier analyses of futurity, the most relevant manifestation of this Idea is
in the notion of horizons. Horizons are not themselves objects because
they are the "unobjectifiable wellspring of every object in general" (VM,
120). By way of these horizons, every constitutive act can itself become an
object of phenomenological inquiry. So while in phenomenology "there is
never a constitution of horizons, but horizons of constitution," this is in
part because "horizons [open] the work of objectification to infinity" (120).
This indefinite opening of horizons onto the infinite prevents horizons,
and by extension intentional phenomenology and phenomenological intentionality, from closing into a totality that would preclude infinity.
Therefore, if "a consciousness of infinite adequation to the infinite (and
even to the finite) distinguishes a body of thought careful to respect exteriority, it is difficult to see how Levinas can depart from Husserl, on this point
at least. Is not intentionality respect itself? . . . In this sense, phenomenology
is respect itself" (121). If, therefore, ethics presupposes phenomenology (121),
this is only because phenomenology, via the notion of intentionality, has
already presupposed ethics.

This double presupposition opens us onto yet another double necessity,
both sides of which have already been mentioned but whose apparent conflict has up to now not yet been thematized. On the one hand, there is the
absolute necessity that experience takes the form of the living present:
"[E]gological life has as its *irreducible and absolutely universal form* the

living present. . . . The *absolute impossibility* of living other than in the present, this eternal impossibility defines the unthinkable as the limit of reason" (VM, 132, my emphasis). Yet how can experience take the form of the living present if, "by reason of an absolute and essential necessity which itself is absolutely principled and irreducible" (120), there must be a non-objectifiable overflowing of the horizons (i.e., the horizons of present experience)? To begin to answer this question, or perhaps more accurately, to begin to explore this question in its depth and significance, Derrida turns to an examination of what exactly is meant by the idea of presence. For "in order to speak, as we have just spoken, of the present as the absolute form of experience, one *already* must understand *what time is*, must understand the *ens of praes-ens*, and the proximity of the *Being of this ens*. The present of presence and the presence of the present suppose the horizon, the pre-comprehending anticipation of Being as time" (134). In this quote we see a number of disparate themes that have alternately occupied us in this sustained meditation on futurity: the absolutely primal character of time-consciousness, the ontological and metaphysical presuppositions of the supposedly "presuppositionless"[24] phenomenology, and the necessarily futural character of horizonality (albeit here described as anticipation rather than in my terminology of expectation). What we see, then, is that the significance of the dilemma of double necessity, of the "dialectical" movement at the beginning of ontology, lies precisely in an understanding of temporality and, more precisely, in a necessarily futural temporality that sets the subject in a world of horizons.

That this futurity is "precomprehending" shows its continuity with the passivity of prepredicative experience. But that the infinite opening of horizons embodied in the Idea in the Kantian sense entails, by necessity and in principle, an overflowing of adequation such that they can never be entirely fulfilled not only ensures the possibility of subjective activity; it also ensures a certain openness within that activity. What is (pre-)given in the horizons, that which enables expectation which in turn enables presence, is a situation in which what is experienced can always, by necessity and in principle, be exceeded, so that every fulfillment can be complete without being totalized. Stated otherwise, what is (pre-) given is experience as (pre-)experience.[25] This remains true not only on the level of active synthesis but also at deeper levels. If "phenomenology, in general, as the passageway to essentiality, presupposes an anticipation of the *esse* of essence, the unity of the *esse* prior to its distribution into essence and existence" (VM, 134), this "anticipation" is reduced in Husserl by another anticipation: "Via another route, one could probably show that Husserl silently presupposes a metaphysical anticipation or decision when, for example, he affirms Being as the nonreality of the ideal. . . . Without a presupposed access to a meaning of Being not exhausted by reality, the entire Husserlian theory of ideality would collapse, and with it all of transcendental phenomenology" (134). If this quote announces the entire project of *Speech and Phenomena*,[26] it is only because it is premised on, presupposes, the former quote, which contains implicitly the entire trajectory of Derrida's thought, from *The Problem of Genesis* on. As these quotes reveal, the tension between the "two Husserls" that will animate *Speech and Phenomena* is a tension between two anticipations, two futurities, perhaps two senses of futurity. It would not be incorrect to describe these two senses of futurity in shorthand as a Levinasian (which remains broadly Husserlian) and a more narrowly Husserlian futurity (though elements of both are present in the work of each of these figures). That these two, though distinct, are intertwined "dialectically" is the hypothesis that the entirety of Derrida's thought will seek to prove.

III. The Life of Economy: From Dialectics to *Différance*

But we must not proceed too quickly here. We balance on the precipice of not one but two major misconceptions. On the one hand, the appeal to anticipation and horizons of expectation could, if not properly qualified, lead us into a metaphysics of presence (VM, 117) that Derrida would be loath to identify himself with univocally. However, some kind of equivocal identification—an identification that is at once also a distancing—would perhaps be amenable to him, if only because of the "dialectic" he describes at the heart of phenomenology. However, this line of thinking is dangerous if pursued too quickly, and here we come up against our second potential major misconception: Does Derrida's use of the terminology of dialectic not risk identifying his thought with that of Hegel, that master of totalization? Derrida's relationship to Hegel is difficult at best to clarify in any meaningful way, and I will not pretend to do so in a brief subsection, almost as an aside. Rather I would like to show how the language of "dialectic"—startling, no doubt, for those readers of Derrida's later works— changes into a vocabulary with which those readers are doubtless more familiar: that of economy.

In his preface to the 1990 edition of *The Problem of Genesis*, an older (and perhaps wiser and more cautious) Derrida explains that the "law of differential contamination" that "imposes its logic from one end of [*The Problem of Genesis*] to the other," received in 1953–54 a "philosophical name that I have had to give up: *dialectic*, an 'originary dialectic'" (PG, xv). Though, as early as 1967, and while still pursuing the reading of Husserl begun in *The Problem of Genesis* (e.g., in *Speech and Phenomena*), the word "dialectic" begins to disappear from Derrida's discourse or has come to designate "that *without which* or *separate from which* difference, originary supplement, and trace had to be thought" (xv), this does not mean that *The Problem of Genesis* hides a latent Hegelianism that is later surpassed or moved beyond. Rather already in *The Problem of Genesis*, the dialectic of which Derrida speaks "claims to go farther than dialectical materialism (that of Trân Duc Thao, for example . . .), or further than the dialectic that Cavaillès thinks he should invoke against Husserl," and is instead a kind of "hyperdialecticism" (xv). This movement going beyond dialectic "in the course of a very respectful critique" (xv) will never cease to function in Derrida's work.

The word "dialectic," however, Derrida deems insufficient. He seems to attribute its inclusion in *The Problem of Genesis* to "the philosophical and *political* map according to which a student of philosophy tried to find his bearings in 1950s France" (PG, xvi). But if the word "dialectic" is something of a historical accident, the movement or concept that it was meant to invoke is not, at least not to the same degree. Already in the preface to the 1953–54 version of *The Problem of Genesis*, Derrida speaks of "unperceived entailment or of dissimulated contamination" (xl). This theme of contamination emerges more forcefully in Derrida's lexicon; indeed, as Derrida says, "the very word 'contamination' has not stopped imposing itself on me from thence [i.e., 1953–54] forward" (xv).

The theme of contamination seeks to show that two things that we take to be essentially separate (e.g., the subject and the other) are in fact always already intertwined (the other is "in" me, to use the phrase of *A Taste for the Secret*).[27] This preaccomplished intertwining repeats the "originary dialectic" but without as much metaphysical baggage. But this is not to say that "contamination" has no metaphysical baggage; there are a few problems with the language of "contamination" that will appear not just throughout Derrida's work but throughout his varied receptions across numerous disciplines and countries. The first (and perhaps largely unavowed) problem with a language of "contamination" is that it seems to presuppose a logic of purity.[28] This has led some to wonder whether Derrida is not in fact merely a classical metaphysician, a sheep hiding in the clothes of a postmodern wolf.

The question of whether or not Derrida is "haunted by the ghost of full presence,"[29] as a presupposition of purity might contend, is not simple to resolve. On the one hand, one cannot dispute a certain modern, even Enlightenment strain in his thought.[30] Even in *The Problem of Genesis*, he espouses the "inescapable idealism of any philosophy" that is "at once a temporal and ontological necessity" (PG, 140). There is, then, a classical and idealist strain in Derrida's thought, and this, I think, is uncontestable: "[O]ne must, in a certain way, become classical once more" (VM, 151).

But the classical strain of thought in Derrida results from precisely the original dialectic or contamination that he is at pains to show in *The Problem of Genesis*: "*[A]lways and essentially*, eidetic reflection [i.e., idealism] will presuppose an already constituted ontology" (VM, 151). If there is a logic of purity in Derrida, it is because he holds to the highest standards of philosophical rigor (contrary to the opinion of certain Cambridge doctors of philosophy). This rigor inspires in him the drive to analysis, to essential truths, a drive that is, alas, both made possible and severely compromised by the lack of "pure" origin described by the logic of contamination.

This drive for purity seems to indicate that Derrida would prefer simplicity and origins and that contamination is therefore a disappointment.[31] This results, I think, from another difficulty in the language of contamination, namely, what it prescribes for the "contaminated" situation. Contamination suggests not only a presupposed logic of purity but also a negative valuation of the situation of contamination and a desire to do away with contamination to return to purity. Contamination, in other words, is but a temporary problem to be overcome. This does not give enough weight to the fundamental *necessity* of the "contamination," the "dialectic," to its productive aspect, and it does not adequately account for the phrase in the quote above, almost an aside, that we must become classical "in a certain way." In this regard, the language of economy, which emerges in "Violence and Metaphysics" (e.g., VM 128–29), proves useful. In an economy, there is a reduction to a symbolic valuation (currency) that opens the door to Baudrillardian hyperrealism,[32] but also, and more important for Derrida, to the possibility of exchange, "commerce," or "discourse" between the interested parties. Such symbolic valuation and exchange enables not just the passing on of information but also the passing on of tradition (and hence the progress of science, including philosophy),[33] and even, as Derrida is at pains to show, the very possibility of discourse with the Other that characterizes Levinas's ethics,[34] which themselves both presuppose and are presupposed by phenomenology. Derrida says of this "transcendental origin," that is, of the condition of Levinasian ethics and phenomenology, that "it is an *economy*. And it is this economy which, by this opening, will permit access to the other to be determined, in ethical freedom, as moral violence or nonviolence" (VM, 128–29). Indeed this mutual presupposition, this "inter-contamination" is the product of such an economy, a necessary economy that enables the Greek and the Jew to have productive exchange (see 152–53).

But surely I am equivocating here. If the economy refers to the (productive) exchange between the two intercontaminated poles, it surely cannot refer also to the (ontological? transcendental?) condition that necessitates and makes possible that exchange. We must distinguish, then, between these levels of economy, between the essentially necessary intercontamination and its productive force of economy. This distinction must be kept firm, even as what it distinguishes can have no real difference; it is, like the distinction between the "parallels" of the transcendental and the empirical ego in Husserl, an irreal distinction that separates (via) nothing. "But the strange unity of these two parallels, that which refers the one to the other . . . by dividing itself, finally joins the transcendental to its other; this unity is *life*" (SP, 14).[35] This life is nothing other than "self-relationship" (14), though clearly one in which the ipseity of the self is not equivalent to an identity,[36] since life "is its own division and its own opposition to its other" (15). "Life" here clearly does not refer to "day to day life or biological science" but is rather an "ultratranscendental concept of life" that "requires another name" (15). This idea of that which "produces sameness as self-relation within self-difference," which "produces sameness as the nonidentical," and for which, in order to understand, "it was necessary to pass through the transcendental reduction" will come to take the name *différance* (82; see also VM, 129).

"Violence and Metaphysics," then, sets the stage for some key avenues of argumentation that will appear in *Speech and Phenomena* and that will ultimately set the stage for Derrida's development of *différance*. First, the development of the notion of economy, and the symbolic valuation that it enables, sets the stage for Derrida's exploration of language, and more specifically, the problem of the sign. As stated in "Violence and Metaphysics," "[T]he phenomenon supposes originary contamination by the sign" (VM, 129). If the phenomenon supposes an economy of symbolic valuation, then the phenomenon supposes the sign, which is to say, a symbolic valuation. Second, and more significantly, "Violence and Metaphysics" clarifies the original dialectic or contamination at the heart of phenomenology in *The Problem of Genesis* as economy, as both transcendental and empirical (for the latter, see VM, 151–53), hence setting the stage for Derrida's notion of *différance*.

But in our rush to pursue *différance*, we must not forget to turn our attention back to another grave misconception on whose ledge we earlier found ourselves treading so precariously. If Derrida's appeal to anticipation and horizons of expectation (themselves key to the development of the contamination or economy whose (ultra)transcendental condition will be called *différance*) in his critique of Levinas are equivalent to those of Husserl, in whose name he issues his critique of Levinas, we run the risk of falling back into the "metaphysics of presence" whose name is so often invoked by Derrida. We cannot argue that Derrida avoids presence altogether, nor that he wishes to. He has already said too much about the "necessity" of presence for experience to have any hope (or any wish) of disavowing presence in its entirety. It is precisely the *economy* of presence and absence that will be of interest to Derrida, the movement and exchange between these, that will concern him moving forward. And, significantly for our current analyses, this economic movement, "the movement of differance" (SP, 82), will not be between Husserl, on the side of presence, and Levinas, on the side of absence, but rather, as we have already seen, will cut through the work of both of these figures.

Derrida will continue the line of questioning begun in *The Problem of Genesis* and modified in "Violence and Metaphysics" into *Speech and Phenomena*, where he will try to show again the tension within Husserl between presence and absence, between the "superficial" Husserl of naïve idealism and the "deep" Husserl of phenomenological temporality.[37] What will be significant for us in that analysis will be the way that, out of the analysis of the originary tension between presence and absence, constituting and constituted, meaning and sense, is produced, not only *différance*, as we have already seen, but the beginning of a Derridean account of futurity, an account that draws its roots from (a certain) Husserl and hence is still phenomenological, faithful to a certain phenomenology. If *différance* is the (ultra)transcendental condition of necessary intercontamination or originary dialectic, then it must speak to the tension between the two senses of futurity noted earlier. This Derridean account of futurity will develop over the course of Derrida's life, gaining increasing ethical, political, and religious significance as it becomes tied ever more closely to the issue of the promise. But the promise is not added to Derrida's account of the future from without or after the fact. The promise is a motivating force of Derridean futurity from the beginning, from before the beginning, to the extent that one might be tempted to say that, for Derrida, futurity is the promise. But let us not get ahead of ourselves.

8

From Deferring to Waiting (for the Messiah)

Derrida's Account of Futurity

Derrida's notion of *différance* emerges from his study of phenomenological temporality. In regard to Husserl, this engagement seems, at least explicitly, to be premised mainly on the retentional aspects of time (cf. SP, 64–67). If this is true, then Derrida's later emphasis on the *avenir* (future) as *à-venir* (to-come) would mark an odd though perhaps interesting departure from his earlier work. But in this chapter I hope to show that no such departure exists and that the messianic *à-venir* develops in continuity not just with Derrida's early work on *différance* but also with a broadly Husserlian phenomenological heritage.

At the heart of all the paradoxes or problems under discussion here is a fundamental tension that Derrida describes in "Violence and Metaphysics" as a tension between anticipations, that is, between futurities or senses of the future. Husserl (especially his explicit writings on time-consciousness) embodies one side of this tension; Levinas (whose work on the future arose from a broadly Husserlian critique of the narrower, explicit Husserl) embodies the other. But if *différance* is Derrida's response to this problem, it will not be a matter of resolving the tensions between the two but rather of describing that which underlies both of them, that makes each of them possible, but also impossible, that which necessitates the double necessities described in the previous chapter. We have already seen *that différance* is to function in this manner. It remains to be shown *how*; in doing so, we come to see the essential role played by the promise.

I. Différantial Future and Futural *Différance*

Différance first emerges in Derrida's work as his name for that movement which comes closest to describing the paradoxical genesis at the heart of subjectivity that he has been arguing for from *The Problem of Genesis* on. In the sentence immediately following its introduction as a term in *Speech and Phenomena*, Derrida states that the "movement of *différance* is not something that happens to a transcendental subject; it produces a subject" (SP, 82). In producing this subject, it does not produce an identical subject in the sense of *idem* identity; rather, by way of a "pure difference," it "produces sameness as self-relation within self-difference; it produces sameness as the nonidentical" (82). This pure difference constitutes the living present in its self-presence and thereby constitutes the self of the living present as a trace (85). This trace, by way of the temporality from which it can never be fully distinguished, that is, by way of retentional and protentional traces, is always involved in sense, sense that is therefore "always already engaged in the 'movement' of the trace" (85).[1] Since the trace is the relation of the living present with its 'outside,' that is, the "self-relation within self-difference" quoted above, the trace is always an "openness upon exteriority in general, upon the sphere of what is not 'one's own'" (86). As such an openness onto exteriority, the trace ensures that "*the temporalization of sense is, from the outset, a 'spacing,'*" and therefore we can conclude that "space is 'in' time; it is time's pure leaving-itself" (86).

This connecting of space and time is the fundamental premise of *différance* itself.[2] *Différance*, as a neologism, is meant to invoke simultaneously two senses of the French *différence*: "deferring as delay and differing as the active work of difference" (SP, 88). *Différance*, then, stands in as the namesake of an originary supplementation,[3] "which at one and the same time both fissures and retards presence, submitting it simultaneously to primordial division and delay" (88). Such a fissured and retarded presence cannot be thought on the basis of consciousness (which is always consciousness as presence, as the living present) or nonconsciousness. It must instead be described on the basis of a presubjective (but subject-constituting) "time" and "place," an ultratranscendental genetic movement that always holds in relation "an inside and an outside in general, an existent and a nonexistent in general, a constituting and a constituted in general" (86). *Différance*, in other words, is the very "originary dialectic" described in *The Problem of Genesis*, the (ultra)transcendental counterpart of the economy of "Violence and Metaphysics." And it is necessarily temporal.

But to describe it as broadly temporal is to miss a key component of *différance*. Its temporalization is essentially futural. This is true despite the fact that Derrida seems to refer primarily to retentional traces when discussing *différance* (see SP, 64–67, 85–86). If it was the concept of retention that led him to think *différance*, it is protention that gives *différance* sense. The concept of primordial supplementation that is *différance* implies the nonplenitude of presence which Derrida calls, "in Husserl's language, the nonfulfillment of intuition" (88). Recall that it is futurity that is, by essential necessity, nonfulfilled intuition; as bearing on an object that is, by definition, not present, futurity remains ever unfulfilled. It is in fact this very striving, the ever-striving, that characterizes protention, while retention bears on the mode of fulfillment. The nonplenitude of presence, then, is tied necessarily to futurity. The temporal nonplenitude of presence is a futural temporality: it is deferral.[4]

This deferral does not come to the scene of a subject in the living present. Rather this deferral breaks up the very idea of the living present itself. It is the living present itself that is deferred, and is so *"ad infinitum"* (SP, 99). But how to think this infinity here? On the one hand, there is the strict formal infinity of Husserlian ideality: As omnitemporal, ideal objects are infinitely repeatable.[5] This is the infinity of iterability.[6] The originary supplementation of *différance* designates the very possibility of supplementation itself, "the 'in the place of' (*für etwas*) structure which belongs to every sign in general" (88). The infinite deferral of the living present, then, is a deferral by way of supplementation, the "in the place of" that characterizes not only language but ideality in general. It is the formal infinite.

There is a second notion of infinity also at work here, though implicitly. The formal infinity bears a certain relationship to death (as opposed to the "life" of the living present, the life that is another name for *différance*; see SP 14–15, 82); that is, ideal objects must be able to function in the absence of the ego thinking those objects, of any ego thinking those objects. It is surviving the death of the subject that language makes possible and hence opens the possibility of ideality (see 92–97). But given this essential possibility, this ideal formality, sense—which cannot be separated from ideality—must also bear some relation to the death of the subject; any sense bestowed on the world must function apart from the ego that so bestows that sense. It must function, at least in part, ideally. As such, sense goes beyond merely the relationship between the ego and the object; it goes also, simultaneously, to the other (person), the other "absolute origin and zero point of the world" (VM, 124), the other who shares in the project of transcendental constitution by sharing in ideality.[7]

This Other is also an infinity, different from formal infinity. As a transcendental other, this Other is Infinite, as Levinas has already shown us.

This second infinity highlights the differential aspect of *différance*: *différance* opens the distance between self and Other.[8] But *différance* also, via language (and the formal infinity), entails the possibility of crossing that distance. And the relation to the Other is not only a differentiating relationship; it is also a deferring relationship: The relationship to the Other is, for Levinas, the relationship to the future (the impossibility of fulfillment, the ceaseless striving, etc.). *Différance* therefore not only opens the double necessity that the Other must appear in intuitive presence while simultaneously exceeding that intuitive presence,[9] but it also entails the necessarily ethical aspects of this double necessity: Phenomenology is ethical, and ethics is phenomenological (cf., e.g., VM, 121–22). This economy or dialectic of ethics and phenomenology becomes, because of the futural temporalization of *différance*, "hauntology" (SM, 10).

II. From Ghosts to the Messiah

Any account of futurity in phenomenology must take seriously Derrida's unique contributions to that discussion. We have already discussed the first such contribution: *différance*. The second contribution, the messianic, is often viewed as part and parcel of the "theological turn" in phenomenology, and as such of suspect phenomenological value.[10] If this term were to be proven to be nonphenomenological, it would, of course, merit no consideration in the current discussion. As such, our explication of the messianic in Derrida will function simultaneously as an elaboration of futurity in phenomenology and a justification for the inclusion of the messianic in this discussion.

A. A Tension between Futurities

The notion of hauntology is the "logic of haunting" (SM, 10) as manifest most clearly in Hamlet's encounter with the ghost of his father at the beginning of Shakespeare's play. This logic is contradictory: The ghost or specter "is always a *revenant*," which is to say that it *"begins by coming back"* (SM, 11). This idea of already-having-begun, of the beginning as a return (again), seems to establish hauntology as a retentional phenomena, but Derrida is clear that hauntology is in essence futural: "Here again what seems to be out front, the future, comes back in advance: from the past, from the back" (10). This embedding of the future in the past is indicative of a particular notion of futurity in which "the past [is] absolute future" (17), in which everything futural is contained already in the present (as inheritance of the past), and hence in which the future is never anything but the "future present" (17). This sense of futurity is the futurity of horizons, of a future that grows out of the past: teleology.[11]

But hauntology "harbors within itself . . . eschatology and teleology themselves" (SM, 10). These two figures of futurity—eschatology and teleology—invoke Levinas and Husserl, respectively (see the preface to *Totality and Infinity* and the "Origin of Geometry" or the Vienna Lecture, respectively). It is not clear, however, that they call to mind the same "specters" for Derrida that they do for us. Derrida seems at times to equate eschatology with teleology (e.g., SM, 60–61). But I mean to show here not only the disjunction between eschatology and teleology (highlighted already by the invocation of Levinas and Husserl) but also the way these two, as distinguished, are both present within the originary dialectic that is *différance*, that is hauntology.

I have begun already to show the connection between hauntology and the first form of futurity: teleology. By this I mean that the future is nothing more than the outgrowth of the past, and hence everything futural is, in essence, nothing more than a repetition of the past, "the past as absolute future" (SM, 17). But Derrida is at pains in this work to begin to show another form of temporality as well (90), one that does not unite past and future together in the present (the past-present and the future-present) but rather one in which time is disjuncted, disjointed: in which "time is out of joint" (*Hamlet*, Act I, scene v; see also SM, 1). In the prefatory "Exordium," Derrida claims that the purpose of *Specters of Marx* is to learn to live (finally), which, for Derrida, is to learn to live "*with* ghosts, in the upkeep, the conversation, the companionship" of ghosts, which is to say, to learn to live within a "*politics* of memory, of inheritance, and of generations" that is characteristic of our finite existence (xviii–xix). In invoking "ghosts" as his trope of inheritance, Derrida is intending to call forth the personal element of inheritance: We always inherit from someone, and hence our inheritance (cultural, economic, etc.) is always a response *to* someone. This is why, for Derrida, this is a matter of justice, of responsibility (xix).

But this seat of justice is located "within that which disjoins the living present," that is, within the "*non-contemporaneity with itself of the living present*" (xix). This marks a shift in emphasis from Derrida's earlier discussions of the noncontemporaneity with itself of the living present; in *différance* as discussed earlier, for example, that which divides the present from itself is primarily a *what* (*différance*, supplement, originary dialectic, khora, etc.), whereas now this division is a *who* (SM, 169).[12] This turn to the "who" opens up the question of responsibility for Derrida, a responsibility that is also and always a response-ability, the ability to respond to the Other who has already called to us.[13] As response to the other, the question becomes that of arrival: From where does the call arise? From whom? As such, it becomes, for Derrida, a question of the future, of "the regard to what will come in the future-to-come [*l'à-venir*]" (xix). In the subtle change from *l'avenir* (future) to *l'à-venir* (future-to-come),[14] Derrida highlights the infinitive form of the future but also its personal element of address to (*à*) another.[15] By opening up this infinitive and intersubjective element, he is able to reconceive of futurity itself: "Turned toward the future, going toward it, it also comes from it, it proceeds *from* [*provientde*] the future" (xix). In this Derrida has made explicit that which was implicit in *différance*: The noncontemporaneity with itself of the living present is essentially futural.

However, this essential futurity does not remove the force of the bind of double necessity that characterizes *différance*. That it is essentially futural does not remove from it the need and importance of inheritance, of the past, that is, of the reception into the living present: "Even if the future is [the call's] provenance, it must be, like any provenance, absolutely and irreversibly past" (SM, xix). The double necessity, the originary dialectic of *différance* remains, but we can now see more clearly its relationship to two conceptions of futurity: first, the future as absolute past, as growing out of the past: teleology; second, the future as relation to the address of the other, as coming from the future, as to-come (*l'à-venir*): eschatology.[16] These two senses of the future are captured most succinctly in Derrida's "umbrella" term: the messianic.

B. The Messianic

I call the messianic an umbrella term because it contains within it a distinction and bifurcation into two moments of the messianic: messianicity on the one hand[17] and messianism on the other. In making this distinction, it is Derrida's express intention to distinguish a "structure of experience" from "a religion" (SM, 168). This structure of experience, messianicity, "belongs properly to a universal structure, to that irreducible movement of the historical opening to the future, therefore to experience itself and to its language" (167). Messianism, on the other hand, is linked explicitly with Abraham (167) and through him, seemingly, to an entire socio-politico-ethno-religious history, or histories, history especially of theology, and of a certain relation to a certain God. Of course, it is not true that all messianisms are Abrahamic in character: Marxism itself is a messianism (59), one of many, and not necessarily all theological (168). But linking messianisms explicitly with Abraham helps illustrate the point, and hence the distinct difference, of messianisms: They are explicitly linked to some particular figure, or group, or whatever is the root of the messianism.

As the umbrella term, then, the messianic contains within itself both messianicity and messianism in the same way that *différance* contains within itself both sides of the double necessity: phenomenology and ethics, presence and nonpresence, and so on. Without relating these immediately to Husserl and Levinas (a project I undertake in section III), it is still possible to show that these two moments within the messianic map onto two distinct accounts of futurity, two accounts that Derrida, via the general notion of the messianic, seeks to hold together in tension, that is, without resolving either into the other. This, precisely, is a key problematic of the fifth chapter of *Specters of Marx*: "How to relate, but also how to dissociate the two messianic spaces we are talking about here under the same name?" (SM, 167). This "under the same name" will present some problems, ones that may force us at times to go against Derrida's explicit statements. There are times—especially in *Specters of Marx*, where the messianic is introduced systematically for the first time—when Derrida conflates messianicity and the messianic and when he therefore sets the messianic as the universal structure that is in opposition to messianism (see. e.g., 167–68). This will also lead to problems in his use of the language of universality; we will have to question whether the universality of the "structure of experience," in its relation to hospitality, is universal in the sense of Husserlian ideality, or whether it is not in fact the "determinate" messianisms that equate to the universality of ideality, whereas the universality of hospitality will relate to a new Derridean notion of universality, the "universalizable culture of singularities" (FK, 56).[18] In time, we will see how this distinction in universality maps onto the two notions of infinity at work in the "infinite" deferral of *différance* and therefore how this problem in universality arises from Derrida's attempt to relate—while dissociating—messianicity and messianisms under the "same name" of the messianic.

It is my contention that messianicity accords with the eschatological notion of futurity, and messianism with the teleological one. The beginnings of this can be seen in the "predicates" that Derrida says comprise messianicity: "annunciation of an unpredictable future, relation to the other, affirmation, promise, revolution, justice" (NM, 33). These predicates are fleshed out in *Specters of Marx* in passages such as the following:

> Ascesis strips the messianic hope [i.e., messianicity] of all biblical forms, and even all determinable figures of the wait or expectation; it thus denudes itself in view of responding to that which must be absolute hospitality, the 'yes' to the *arrivant(e)*, the 'come' to the

future that cannot be anticipated. . . . Open, waiting for the event *as justice*, this hospitality is absolute only if its [*sic*] keeps watch over its own universality. (SM, 168)

Fortuitously, the quotation begins with a word that harkens back to the phenomenological heritage that Derrida has inherited and that "haunts" his exploration of the messianic.[19] The ascesis that "strips the messianic hope of all biblical forms, and even all determinable figures of the wait or expectation" and thereby "denudes itself" (SM, 168) would be the rigorous self-discipline of the phenomenologist employing the reduction. The lack of content in messianicity, then, is not, contrary to some commentators, the result of a Kantian quest for formal universality; it is the result of the *epokhē* which Derrida holds to be "essential" to messianicity and to "the messianic in general, as thinking of the other and of the event to come" (59). If messianicity is, then, to a certain extent structural or formal (59), this is only as it relates to a futurity (event to come) that is intersubjective (thinking of the other), that is, a futurity that puts it in relation with the Other who calls me. This is what makes messianicity responsible/response-able ("it thus denudes itself in view of *responding*"; emphasis added) to the Other who must come, who will come, and who must be treated with hospitality.[20] But this Other, of course, must come as an "event" and not as the outgrowth of the past into a future (present). This aspect of messianicity is marked by the term "waiting" above. This sense of "open" "waiting" entails a difference from teleological futurity: "[I]f one could *count* on what is coming, hope would be but the calculation of a program. One would have the prospect but one would no longer wait for anything or anyone" (169). A nonteleological futurity that waits, open, for the arrival of the Other: What is this but eschatological futurity?[21]

But this, of course, is only one side of the messianic. On the other side we have the concrete histories of the determinate messianisms. While Derrida says that one may see messianicity as "the condition of the religions of the Book," one may also, and equally, consider the Abrahamic messianisms as "the only events on the basis of which we approach and first of all name the messianic in general" (SM, 168).[22] Messianisms, then, are the "other ghost which we cannot and ought not do without" (168). They would seem to be the historical "material" of our horizons, the very horizonality that makes experience possible. As such, they operate within the teleological conception of futurity, that conception which makes the past into an "absolute future."

Messianisms, then, provide concretion and a certain urgency to the open waiting of messianicity. While messianicity awaits the future to-come, messianisms keep us connected with the past (present) and hence give weight to the future (as future present): what comes in the future is urgently important because soon, imminently in fact, the future will be the present, that is, will be *my* living present, *my* experience. The messianic in general, then, "would be urgency, imminence but, irreducible paradox, a waiting without horizon of expectation" (SM, 168). Stated otherwise, the paradox is that the messianic is a "historical opening to the future" (167). As historical (messianism), the messianic must be not only rooted in the past but also essentially empirical; but as opening to the future (messianicity), the messianic must be universal, essential, ideal, that is, philosophical. It is the task of the messianic (in general) to hold together these two poles without collapsing either into the other. This is the paradoxical condition of the messianic. It is also the doubly necessary condition of *différance* and the originarily dialectical character of phenomenological temporality.

III. The Heritages of Derrida: The Universality of the Promise

If we now understand better the futural character of Derrida's work as it manifests itself from *différance* to the messianic, two tasks yet remain to be completed: first, the elaboration of the connection between the messianic and the phenomenological heritage we have been discussing up to now; second, the exploration of the essentially promissory nature of the messianic. These two are not unrelated.

The connections between the teleological conception of futurity and Husserl and the eschatological conception of futurity and Levinas are, at first, quite apparent. The very terms used as "names" for the different positions are themselves drawn from the work of the respective thinkers. In addition the horizonality characteristic of a teleological conception of futurity accords directly with the horizons of experience as developed by Husserl. The relationship-beyond-my-death that defines eschatology for Levinas in "Trace of the Other" is perhaps not as immediately identifiable with the messianicity that I am claiming shares that orientation. However, the appeal to the Other in messianicity, the waiting for the arrival of the other, and the personal quality opened up by the invocative *à-venir* (like the *à-dieu*),[23] all bear strong resonances with the Levinasian analysis of futurity.

A. Bolstering Derrida's Relation to the Phenomenological Tradition

A problem arises, however, with Derrida's ascription of universality to messianicity and the seemingly empirical (and hence nonuniversal) nature of messianisms. These would seem to reverse the previous order: It is Husserl whom Derrida considers as privileging the universal/ideal at the expense of the empirical, and Levinas whom Derrida considers to be a sort of "empiricism" (see the closing pages of VM). Does this align messianicity with Husserlian ideality and messianisms with Levinasian ethics? Though no one, as far as I know, strongly pushes the latter theory (though one could, I suppose, try to argue for the association of messianisms with Levinas because of the distinctly Jewish character of some of his work), the former theory is a popular if ultimately misguided conception of messianicity among Derrida commentators.[24] Indeed some will even take the structural universality of messianicity beyond Husserl, equating it with that of Kant.[25] I, however, would like to suggest that Derrida's messianicity is not structural in the sense of Husserlian ideality but rather that the universality (and the "structures") that it calls for are given a unique and ultimately non-Kantian spin.[26] Hence I will try to further bolster the equation of messianicity and messianisms with two distinct accounts of futurity (broadly Levinasian and Husserlian, respectively) held in tension, a tension called the messianic (in general).

Now it cannot be denied that there would seem to be good ground to associate Derrida's messianicity with a structural formalism of a Kantian type. In the discussion of the role of the *epokhē* in the messianic cited earlier, Derrida talks of "the formality of a structural messianism, a messianism without religion, even a messianic without messianism" (SM, 59). Of course, the messianic without messianism would seem to leave messianicity, and this, then, would be equated with a formal structure. Or Derrida will speak of "the necessarily undetermined, empty, abstract and dry form" of the messianic and the eschatological that he claims to be privileging in *Specters of Marx* (166–67). The language of formal abstraction here also seems to push in a Kantian direction. Combine this with the subtitle of one of Derrida's more in-depth discussion of the messianic (i.e., "Faith and Knowledge: The Two Sources of 'Religion' within the Bounds of Reason Alone"), and it becomes difficult to deny an inherent Kantianism at work in Derrida's discussion of the messianic.

However, two things emerge—quietly—to unsettle this conclusion. First, the formal structure of the quote above is ascribed first to messianisms, before the passage moves on to (seem to) allude to messianicity. This would suggest two things: first, the possibility of the structuralism of messianisms; second, that such structural messianisms, if they exist, are not the concern of messianicity, which instead is concerned with the "universalizable culture of singularities" (FK, 56). If one could abstract from out of the concrete messianisms a human structure of religiosity—as Kant perhaps tries to do and people like Eliade claim to do[27]—such an abstraction would remain within the realm of the constituted and would remain, to use the language of the early Husserl and Derrida, an empiricism (if perhaps a transcendental empiricism, à la Kant). Hence if Derrida *is* suggesting some type of abstraction—and it remains possible that he is—such a suggestion would be within the realm of messianisms and would not, I contend, be that of messianicity (though it could still be that of a certain Husserl, who Derrida has shown does not always escape the empiricism or the logicism that he is at pains to critique).[28]

The second quiet disrupting force emerges within "Faith and Knowledge." There, in the midst of the discussion of the messianic as one of the names for the "duplicity of origins" (FK, 55), Derrida introduces the invincible desire for justice—which belongs, from the beginning, to every experience of faith, belief, trust, and a credit irreducible to knowing ("à l'expérience de la foi, du croire ou d'un credit irréductible au savoir et d'une fiabilité")[29] and not just to that of religious faith alone—that "alone allows the hope, beyond all 'messianisms' of a universalizable culture of singularities" (FK, 56). This universalizable culture of singularities, though linked with a certain "abstraction," is not, however, tied to the empirical abstractions of structural messianisms. Rather the "structure of experience" that is messianicity is linked to the "abstract possibility of the impossible," that is, to the justice that "inscribes itself in advance in the promise, in the act of faith or in the appeal to faith that inhabits every act of language and every address to the other" (56). The universality at stake here is still that of certain "rationality" (56–57), but by way of "singularity" (especially the singularity of the Other), this rationality is allied to faith by way of a "mystical foundation of authority" that enables a particular faith, a particular performativity, a "technoscientific or tele-technological performance" (57).[30] The allying of reason and faith that is characterized most sharply perhaps in the phrase "Religion within the bounds of Reason alone" is, then, the *result*, not the *cause*, of a choice already made, a choice that Derrida has been speaking of since *The Problem of Genesis*, the choice that covers over the abyss, over the movement of *différance*; a choice moreover that is historical and empirical, with transcendental consequences, but one that cannot affect the (ultra)transcendental because it presupposes it: the choice for presence.[31]

Nothing can disrupt this choice absolutely. This choice is the possibility of faith, promise, future, and relation to the singularity of the Other (FK, 57). As we saw in his reading of Husserl, Derrida maintains that we cannot do without presence. This is precisely the need for the teleological conception of futurity. However, there is simultaneously the need for the decision of the Other that always disrupts the horizons of presence, that is, for the opening onto singularity "that can take the apparently passive form of the *other's decision* . . . which does not exonerate me of responsibility" (56). It is precisely this opening onto the singularity of the Other that is made possible in messianicity, and hence messianicity remains eschatological in its futural orientation, while messianisms are always teleological.

B. The Promise

If messianicity makes possible the opening onto singularity, it does so by way of the promise. It is the "formal structure" of the promise that enables us to distinguish messianicity from messianisms (FK, 59). Messianisms are, in essence, about (empirical) inheritance: the reception and transmission of a set of knowledge or beliefs from the past into the present and, hopefully, into the future (present). It is on the basis of this inheritance that one can define orthodoxies and heterodoxies. But messianicity is not about this aspect of inheritance; it is, as I have said, about waiting for the Other, about opening onto the future. And this waiting and opening are inscribed within a transcendental promise.

In chapter 3 I distinguished the promise from expectation on the basis of trustworthiness. Trustworthiness is the ground of a promise that occurs in the present (though its object is in the future) and is distinct from inference.[32] Trustworthiness, then, is another name for that nonepistemological movement by which the future is able to affect our understanding of the present and is therefore opposed to the epistemological movement to the same effect known as expectation. The distinction between these lies in what "holds" the ground: The ground (or justification) of an inference is in the available evidence and in the proper functioning of the rational capacities of the one making the inference.[33] The ground of a promise, on the other hand, is nothing other than the *person making the promise*: Though I can try to give reasons for why I trust one promise and not another, in truth the only valid reason is that I find one person making a promise to be trustworthy and another person making another promise not trustworthy. In other words, the ground of an inference is in the object of the inference, whereas the ground of a promise is in the subject making the promise.

By shifting the ground from what to who, from object to subject, Derrida, via the notion of hauntology and ultimately the messianic, places the centrality of the phenomenological subject outside of itself or, correlatively, places the outside of the subject within the center of the subject itself. If phenomenological temporality is essentially eschatological (without thereby giving up its essentially teleological nature), which is to say, is a time of the promise, than the promise made is made by another. Further, this promise is not made to us, but *is* us: [34] We are promised by the other, and it is our responsibility, like that of Hamlet, to respond to a call or promise that, in a certain sense, was made before we were on the scene. In *Hamlet* the promise of vengeance is not entailed by the conversation with the ghost but by the act of murder, which promises the son of the murdered to take vengeance on the murderer; the ghost must merely make Hamlet aware of a promise he is responsible for, a sense in which he has already been promised to a certain task, whether he knows it or not. And Hamlet, in swearing to the ghost, is making a promise to the other, but this promise has in fact already been made. Hamlet is only promising to live up to the promise, live up to himself as promised, taking on the promise that was given him, thrust upon him, by another.

When Derrida says, "For a promise to be assumed, someone must be there who is sensitive to the promise, who is able to say 'I am the promise, I'm the one to promise, I'm the one who is promising'" (NM, 30), the three clauses are not equivalent; they are a progression, a progression of responsibility as that which exceeds my experience (the Infinite, the Other) is slowly taken up in and as my experience. First, I acknowledge that I, myself, am promised; I "assume" the promise by taking it up as myself, the way one assumes a position.[35] From this being-promised I gain my subjectivity, my ability to make promises.[36] Only at this point can I make the promise that I am also the object of a promise that I make. I can now (try to) live up to the promise that is my inheritance from the other.[37]

Taking up this promise as my own is a process of affirmation, of saying yes. But the affirmation is always a doubleaffirmation because it is always a reply, a "reply in the form of a promise": "From the moment that the 'yes' is a reply, it must be addressed to the other, from the moment that it is a promise, it pledges to confirm what has been said. If I say yes to you I've already repeated it the first time, since the first 'yes' is also a promise of this 'yes' being repeated. . . . So the 'yes' is immediately double, immediately 'yes-yes'" (NM, 54–55). This saying yes, of course, need not be verbal.[38] Taking up my life as a promise, I affirm myself as promised and hence reaffirm not only a past but also an opening onto a future, a future in which the 'yes' is repeated, in which the promise is taken up again and again.

Derrida frames this relation between promise and inheritance as the work of mourning.[39] The work of mourning is to remember the one who has died without this remembrance preventing us from moving on and acknowledging that the one we remember is no longer alive.[40] This work of mourning is central to the task of inheritance (haunting), and its twofold focus mirrors the past and future orientations of time: Remember the past, but do so "without killing the future" (SM, 169). In taking up the promise that each of us is, we are not only living (in the present) out of the past (i.e., teleologically), but we are maintaining the openness to the future that defines eschatological futurity, that enables, Levinas has shown, the relation to the other, and therefore that enables ethics. The promise, then, is not added to Derrida's account of the future but is central to it. The structure of the promise (the moving of the ground of the act to the subject making the act, a subject who is not me but is "in" me) is the very structure of the future. Though it is ascribed to messianicity alone, a brief elaboration of the promise shows its twofold futural sense: Living up to a past in order to keep open a future, the promise contains both teleology and eschatology, empirical inheritance and personal inheritance, messianism and messianicity. The messianic, as the umbrella term, is explicated by this structure of the promise, a structure that holds together both sides of the double necessity of futurity, and a promise therefore that comes to be equated with the phenomenological conception of futurity.

9

The Promise of the Future

Seeing our explanation of the phenomenological notion of futurity culminate in the promise, it is tempting to move quickly to equate phenomenology with ethics: If futurity is an essential part of temporality (as I have tried to show), and promising is an essentially ethical act requiring trust between two or more people, then phenomenological temporality would seem to have as one of its essential components an ethical act, and therefore phenomenology could be conceived of as itself essentially ethical. But we must not move too quickly here. There are three major assumptions that have yet to be proven: first, that the promise is an essential aspect of phenomenological temporality and is not merely a convenient metaphor for the ideas of one particular thinker; second, that temporality is an integral part of phenomenology and not merely one set of issues to be elaborated phenomenologically; and third, that promising is an essentially ethical act, in a univocal sense of both of those terms. Let us take these in turn to see whether or not one is justified in considering phenomenological temporality, and ultimately phenomenology itself, as essentially ethical.

I. The Promise and the Future

We have seen that Derrida's contribution to a phenomenological conception of the future is twofold: *différance* and the messianic. With these Derrida tries to hold together (without collapsing either into the other or synthesizing them into some new third term) the horizontal, constituting futurity of Husserlian expectation and the open, constituted futurity of Levinasian eschatology. In doing so, Derrida has tried to show the double necessity at work in futurity: It must both take place within horizons (which is to say, grow continuously out of a past) and be an unexpected opening to the arrival of the Other (which is to say, function irruptively, discontinuously, eschatologically). I have tried to show that, running slightly against some of Derrida's explicit statements, the structure of the promise is integral not just to the second of these two futural movements but to the very twofold movement of futurity itself. It is this point that remains to be explored. As it stands, one could argue that the promise is merely a convenient metaphor for Derrida. I will try to show, however, that it is both more than a metaphor and is effective in a wider scope than merely the thought of Derrida.

To do this, some key facets of the promise and of phenomenological futurity must be outlined and their correlations shown. This will help to clarify both what is meant by the promise and also its role in a phenomenological conception of the future.

A. Essential Aspects of the Promise

Derrida's conception of the promise can be summarized by the following: The "radical structure of the promise" is that "the promise prohibits the (metaphysical) gathering of Being in presence"; it "is the remainder of the necessary undecidability of thinking and action upon which any *act* of thought" or language is premised, and this remainder "is an absolute past (it cannot be recalled in any act) which *gives the chance* of the future" (NM, 16). As such, it is listed as one of the essential "predicates" of messianicity, along with the affirmation of the future, the relation to the other, affirmation, and justice (33). The promise, then, is in its essence both essentially past-oriented and essentially futural.[1]

It is this double directionality that makes the promise an excellent *metaphor* for futurity, but is it more than that? It seems that it is, for not only is the promise doubly directional from a temporal perspective (i.e., related both to the past and the future), but it is also doubly directional from an intersubjective standpoint. It goes, so to speak, not only from one person (the promiser) to another person (the receiver of the promise) but also from that dyad out toward all other people via the linguistic culture in which the promise is made. This linguistic aspect of the promise introduces justice (in the Levinasian sense)[2] into the promise, in addition to its ethical aspect relating one to the Other. The linguistic aspect of the promise also opens the promise onto iterability and hence ideality, in Husserl's sense: The promise is not only a temporal act, but it is also an ethical, cultural, and linguistic act. The promise therefore is essentially subjective, intersubjective, empirical, *and* ideal.

B. Essential Aspects of Phenomenological Futurity

Ultimately, though, the only way to fully prove that the promise is more than merely a metaphor for futurity is to show its central place in futurity, that is, to demonstrate that without this concept of the promise, futurity would not be what it is. This can be done only by outlining the essential aspects of phenomenological futurity and then examining whether such aspects can be achieved without the promise.

Futurity, conceived phenomenologically, is defined primarily by a certain lack of fulfillment: Because the object of the futural act is, by necessity, not present (i.e., is precisely in the future, not the present), the futural act, *qua* futural act, cannot be fulfilled. In the moment of fulfillment, it ceases to be the futural act and becomes some other act; protention, for example, is "fulfilled" only by being retained, and expectation is "fulfilled" only in confirmation (or disappointment, negation, etc.).[3] There is, then, a certain striving character to futurity: It pushes forward (i.e., toward the future).

But futurity also simultaneously carries within itself a passive moment: Not only does it strive toward the future, but it awaits the arrival of the future. To a certain extent, this reverses the direction of futurity:[4] Rather than striving from the present to the future, as does the active moment of futurity, the passive moment of futurity awaits in the present the coming of the future. This passive moment also cannot be characterized by a fulfillment; the object here remains again, by necessity, not present.

The nonpresence of the object of futurity is matched by the presence of the ground of the futural act. This entails two things: first, that the futural act seeks *in the present* a nonpresent object. This does not mean that the object sought is thought to be discoverable in the present; rather it means that the seeking of the object occurs in the present: Every futural act occurs now, that is, in the present. Its object might be deferred, but the act itself is not, at least to the extent that it occurs in the living present (though, as Derrida has shown, the living present itself bears the marks of deferral, to some degree).

The presence of the ground of the futural act entails, second, that the futural act opens necessarily onto an intersubjective world beyond the egoic consciousness of the subject. Because the futural act occurs in the present though its object is in the future, there is always something (the ground) that justifies the egoic movement from past to future. This ground, however, bears a similar duality to that of the object of the futural act: Where the futural act moved toward its object and waited for the arrival of its object, the ground of the futural act lies both in the evidence for the object and in the validity or trustworthiness of the subject. Not only must there be adequate evidence and the proper functioning of the subject[5] to justify the move to the futural object, but there must also be some opening of the present to the possibility of the arrival of something outside itself. The proper functioning of the subject must be intersubjectively verified,[6] and therefore the ground of the futural act opens onto the intersubjective world, an opening that is itself premised on the necessary relation between the subject and the Other.

The necessity of holding together this pair of essential dualities (object as striving toward the future and awaiting the arrival of the future; ground as present to the subject but opening to that which is beyond the subject) was recognized by Derrida, first in his notion of *différance* (which trades on the deferral of the object and the differing of the ground), and later in the messianic (which emphasizes the waiting for the future and the necessity of the intersubjective Other). This double necessity was Derrida's unique contribution to a notion of futurity in phenomenology.

C. Correlating the Promise and Phenomenological Futurity

But the messianic is able to operate only because of the structure of the promise (SM, 59). It is only by conceiving the future as the fulfillment of a promise that I primarily *am*, not a promise that I primarily *make*, that the holding together of the two competing visions of futurity can make sense: If we can understand the past as a past that occurs before I am on the scene, a past that precedes my past but thereby makes it possible (what Levinas would call a diachronous, an-archic past, the past of the trace), then we can make sense of the necessity of the future being something that must arrive also from elsewhere, that is, a future I do not wholly constitute. Yet because this anarchic past is not abandoned but is *taken up* by me, the future that is to come will also show some continuity with my past, though the shape and nature of this continuity cannot be precisely forecast. In other words, because the promise that I am is also the promise that I take up, my horizons of experience are not purely solipsistic or egoic but are, by their nature, already infused with the alterity of the Other who promises me; my horizons are not purely teleological but are already opened to the possibility of eschatology.[7]

Conversely, because the promise that I take up is *my* promise only by virtue of its being a promise I am committed to by someone else (beyond my experience), like Hamlet's quest for vengeance which commits him before he commits himself and which therefore gives him such great pause for existential and ontological concern ("To be or not to be"),[8] because I can promise only because I am already promised, my waiting for the irruptive arrival of the other takes the form of working with my horizons: Eschatological waiting is teleologically active. This means both that it takes place within horizons[9] and that its taking place, as a waiting, is an activity (in addition to its passivity).[10] To speak of the coming of the event of the Other as "absolutely unprecedented" is, as Derrida admits, "just a form of emphasis" (NM, 44), a hyperbole. Even the absolutely unprecedented must come within my horizons and, in some way, come *from* within my horizons: "[T]he unprecedented is never possible without repetition, there is never something absolutely unprecedented, totally original or new. . . . The new cannot be invented without memory or repetition" (44–45). This is the twofold necessity of inheritance, or of the work of mourning, discussed at the end of chapter 8, and it defines phenomenological futurity.

II. Futurity and Phenomenology

This duality-in-unity therefore constitutes the heart of phenomenological futurity. Its double necessity is not solely futural but is also phenomenological; it is not only phenomenological *futurity* that is so doubly oriented, but so is phenomenology itself. The double necessity of horizons and opening, construction and reception, self and other—what is this but the holding together of constituting and constituted, structure and intuition, consciousness and world? What is this, in other words, but an elaboration of the phenomenological doctrine of intentionality and therefore an elaboration of phenomenology itself?

The phenomenological doctrine of intentionality is that of transcendental world-constitution:[11] The world and consciousness can be held as always already in contact only if we can understand that the world is "immanent to the absolute" that constitutes it (PCC, 99). This occurs, of course, in transcendental constitution. But this constitution, that is, the unity of (without collapsing the distinction between) consciousness and the world, can be *primordial* only if transcendental constitution is concerned with what is itself most primary. Hence, in Fink's famous phrase, "phenomenology sees its decisive problem in the question concerning the origin of the world" (96). By investigating the "origin of the world," phenomenology is able to get beneath "dogmatic metaphysics" and its ontological and "naïve" conception of the world and critical (neo-Kantian) philosophy's concern with "the *meaning* of beings" (96). Phenomenology, in its essence, seeks to unite elements of both critical philosophy (i.e., its transcendental charac-ter) and metaphysics (i.e., its concern for the origin of the world) without falling into the traps and pitfalls of either (i.e., the sharp divorce between the world and the nonworld, or between world and another world).

It is the reduction that enables the passage to the transcendental realm of phenomenology (cf. PCC, 98–99). As such, the reduction constitutes a "movement" of knowledge that enables both the transcending of the world and "at the same time the *retention of the world*" within the absolute that is revealed by the reduction, that is, the absolute of transcendental subjec-tivity (99). By this movement, phenomenology "questions the bond . . . between the 'founded' and the 'foundational' sphere" (97) by showing that the world is not "founded" on a distinct "foundational" sphere (i.e., the God or Being of speculative metaphysics or the 'world-form' of critical philoso-phy); rather there is a necessary correlation between founded and founda-tional, or between constituted and constituting (to return again to our earlier terminology). The world, then, is both transcended and yet still pres-ent; that is, the world is simultaneously constituted and constituting, by reference to its inclusion in the absolute (subject) that constitutes it, an in-clusion that is prephenomenological, that is, before the reduction (100).

The reduction therefore reveals the proper theme of phenomenological philosophy: the transcendental constitution of the origin of the world within transcendent *life* (PCC, 99). Via the "habitualities and potentialities of transcendental life" we see that transcendental life is "communalized in the process of constitution" and therefore that transcendental subjectivity is essentially intersubjective.[12]

In its essence, therefore, phenomenology seeks to challenge the sharp divide between the world and the nonworld, in part by showing that the world is both transcendental and immanent to the absolute that consti-tutes it, and therefore that the world is both constituted and constituting. This is the essence of intentionality, itself the great breakthrough of Hus-serlian phenomenology. By way of the reduction, which is the method and way of knowing that is "the most essential feature of phenomenology's unique character" (PCC, 99), phenomenology exposes itself as a move-ment that both transcends the world and simultaneously acknowledges the givenness of the world and hence waits for the sensuousness of that given-ness. By so doing, the reduction reveals a transcendental subjectivity that is simultaneously monadic and intersubjective or communal. And all of these apparent contradictions take place within the sphere of "life."

But "life," in its phenomenological sense as a "strange unity" of "two parallels" (i.e., the transcendental and the empirical Egos) that are simul-taneously different but yet united, and which is therefore united while being "its own division and its own opposition to its other" (SP, 14–15), is nothing but another name for *différance* (cf. 82). In other words, the very double necessities that characterized futurity—the simultaneous necessity of immanence to experience and transcendence of experience, of striving forward in activity while also awaiting in passivity, the necessary intersubjectivity of the subject—also characterize phenomenology itself.

At the least, this would suggest that a study of futurity provides an excellent way into an understanding of phenomenology. But is there anything more than that? Can we also say that futurity provides a way into understanding phenomenology because futurity is integral to phenomenology, that is, that futurity not only *helps* us understand phenomenology but is *necessary* to our understanding of it? I think we can. First, there is the oft-stated importance of temporality to phenomenology (temporality as absolute consciousness, as our characteristic mode of being, etc.), and the necessity of a distinctly futural analysis for any understanding of phenomenological temporality, and of the constituting subject more generally (as I hope was demonstrated in part 1). Second, there is the necessary connection between not just temporality but specifically futurity and the subject's openness onto the world and the Other (as discussed in part 2).

Both of these points are premised upon the centrality of futurity to phenomenological temporality: What is distinctive about the phenomenological analysis of time is precisely its emphasis, often noted but rarely studied indepth, on the futural aspect of time. But there is another avenue that seems to tie futurity essentially to phenomenology. It is premised not on the correlation between futurity and temporality but on a certain openness that seems to characterize both futurity (nonfulfillment, striving, etc.) and phenomenology (intentionality, transcendence of immanence, etc.). This openness goes by a somewhat peculiar (at first glance) name in Levinas's phenomenology: ethics.

III. Ethics and Phenomenology

I have tried to show that the promise is central to the phenomenological conception of futurity and that that conception of futurity, in turn, is central to phenomenology as a discipline. It would seem to follow, then, that the promise is central in some way to phenomenology as a discipline. In evaluating the possible significance of this, one must look at the somewhat contentious issue of the possibility of an essentially ethical phenomenology (as phenomenology is essentially promissory, and the promise is an ethical act). But what would an essentially ethical phenomenology look like, and what could it tell us about ethics and about phenomenology?

I have already suggested what would form the beginning of an answer to this question: An essentially ethical phenomenology would be one that is essentially open—to the Other, to the world, to the other-than-subjectivity—in two directions: the subject can access that to which it is open, and that to which it is open has always already accessed (or is "within") the subject. That such a conception is phenomenological has, I hope, been shown through the arguments and analyses above. But why should such a notion be conceived of as *ethical*? This is a question that bears further examination.

A. Disambiguating "Ethics"

We must admit from the outset a certain equivocation in the term "ethical." On the one hand, "ethical" refers to a theory that seeks to provide a framework for what will constitute "good" or moral actions in the world. As such, it is often particularized to different situations; we speak, for example, of business ethics, environmental ethics, medical ethics, and so on. The framework provided by these theories can also be narrowed based on differing conceptions of the good that will guide that theory; in this manner, we speak of care ethics, utilitarian ethics, virtue ethics, and so on. This is a rather standard view of ethics and is what most people have in mind when they speak of a desire to act ethically; such a desire seeks to act in accordance with some conception of what is good or right.

So conceived, however, ethics clearly seems to be a particular branch of the sciences, and as such could never have an essential function in phenomenology, which seeks to ground all worldly sciences (cf. PCC, 98).[13] Premised as it is upon some conception of what is good or right, ethics seems to remain always subordinate in its deployment, always fit within a context that it can only be applied to, not one that it helps to constitute.

But the conception of ethics at work in phenomenology—especially the phenomenologies of Levinas and Derrida—is different from the standard definition of ethics. For Levinas and Derrida, ethics refers to a relation that respects the alterity of the Other (person).[14] Such a conception of ethics is most definitely not an ethics in the standard sense of the term,[15] but this does not mean it is pure equivocation either. There is a relation between ethics, traditionally conceived, and the ethical relation of Levinas. If phenomenological ethics are not traditional ethics, then what have they to teach us about traditional ethics? To return to a question from earlier in this work but now further clarified: Given the difference between phenomenological and traditional conceptions of ethics, what does it mean to suggest that there is something essentially ethical about my waiting for my wife to arrive home from work?

B. Meta- and Arche-ethics

Let me begin by attempting to explain the relationship between phenomenological ethics, as conceived especially by Levinas and Derrida, and ethics, more traditionally understood. Derrida is quick to note that "Levinas does not seek to propose laws or moral rules, does not seek to determine *a* morality, but rather the essence of the ethical relation in general" (VM, 111). Instead Derrida speaks of "a step back behind the ethical in order to explain it," a move he calls "arche-ethical" (NM, 27). Levinas supports such a reading when he states, "My task does not consist in constructing ethics; I only try to find its sense. . . . One can without a doubt construct an ethics in function of what I have just said, but this is not my own theme" (EI, 90). Both thinkers seem to be suggesting that what they refer to as ethics is actually an attempt to understand the (nontological)[16] ground of ethics itself: What is it in the subject, in the Other, and in the world that enables ethics, traditionally conceived, to be possible? What kind of subject can be ethical?

Phenomenological ethics, then, seems to be metaethical, and as such bears a somewhat conventional relationship to the standard conception of ethics. Ethics—especially sympathy, empathy, pity, and other forms of "solidarity with another"—are possible only because of the conception of the self put forward by Levinas and Derrida (cf. OB, 102). The self they suggest, it will be recalled, is one in which the continuity of the self as subject is found not in its relation to the "I can" of the ego but to the ipseity and uniqueness of the I, founded on the "Here I am" of responsibility to and for another. For Levinas, this took the form of the subject's persecution by, being held hostage of, and ultimately substitution for the Other. In Derrida, this took the form of the subject as promising only because it was first promised by another. In both cases, the key move is that the subject is not only constituting but is primarily constituted. Hence phenomenology is based primarily on something other than the constituting ego of ontology; it is based on the constituting relation to the Other that goes by the name of "ethics."[17] But what is this but a redescription of the idea of intentionality? To say that phenomenology is primarily ethical, therefore, is to say nothing other than that the phenomenological subject is constituted and constituting, intuitive and structuring, hyletic and morphic, and is so essentially. Such a claim is not meant to upend phenomenology but to return it to its original foundations, its unique insights, and to use those insights

to criticize some analyses that have occurred under the name of phenomenology but that have failed to take seriously the precise meaning of that
name. To say that phenomenology is fundamentally ethical, in this sense,
is not to mystify or sacralize phenomenology but to de-metaphysicize it, to
re-phenomenologize it.[18]

C. The "Ethicality" of Phenomenological Futurity?

To claim the fundamental ethicality of phenomenology is to make a claim
that is within the bounds of the most rigorously orthodox phenomenology—
but as such, it is also a claim that perhaps loses some of its apparent significance. As a critical tool, the rediscovered ethicality of phenomenology has
proven invaluable in discovering phenomenological analyses that seem to
have drifted away from the fundamentally intentional nature of phenomenology but in fact constitute precisely its recovery. But as a positive tool,
what does ethicality contribute to our understanding of phenomenology?
Given the focus of our analyses, and the attempt to prove the centrality of
futurity to phenomenology contained therein, let it suffice to answer this
question by looking at what ethicality adds to the phenomenological notion of futurity. What precisely is *ethical* about my waiting for my wife to
arrive home from work?

The openness of the subject is of course central to the notion of futurity,
and vice versa, but beyond that, ethicality so conceived gives us a way of
understanding our (present) experience as a whole. Recall Lacoste's claim
that "[t]he logic of anticipation is calmly inscribed in the logic of experience" (PA 31). For both anticipation and experience, the present experience
is experienced and is a harbinger of a future experience that will add something more to the present experience; we came to define this twofold nature of experience as (pre-)experience. That this is true of anticipation is
obvious: We experience in the present an act that seeks a future object. In
experience in general, however, we see the same basic principle at stake.
Our experience of an object is never complete but can always be supplemented by further, optimalizing experiences:[19] I currently experience the
chair by sitting on it, but I could know more about it by, at some later
moment, examining it more closely or in different ways—by moving to
other sides of it, by speaking with a chairmaker to appreciate its construction, by speaking with a designer to appreciate its design or with a store
clerk to appreciate its economic value, and so on. Hence in my current
experience of sitting on a chair, I not only experience the chair, but I also
pre-experience the other aspects of the chair that could ultimately become
the focus of some later experience of the chair. I also pre-experience all the

later experiences that my current experience of the chair will, in part, help me make sense of: later experiences with chairs, for example, but perhaps also with social customs more generally, with the balance of rest and work, with aesthetic appreciation, with economic exchange, and so on.

We can now understand why anticipation can so accord with (pre-) experience: Both are premised on the openness of the subject. Anticipation strives for (and waits for) a future, while (pre-)experience waits for another immediate contact with the world via sensibility, intentionality, and so on. The openness of the subject, however, is not only the reason for what is *not* (presently) experienced in the (pre-)experience; it is also the condition for what *is* experienced there: Without the futural relation to the Other (conceived as deferral, promise, or awaiting), and without being open to an entire cultural and environing world,[20] the subject would not experience the world at all. Openness therefore is not only the condition of absence in (pre-)experience but also the possibility of presence—it is the very condition of constituting subjectivity. In this regard, to say that my waiting for my wife is an ethical act is merely to say that it is something I experience and that it opens up the question of presence and absence.

Futurity is fundamentally ethical, then, but only in a particularly phenomenological understanding of that term. This ethicality of futurity does not seem to lend any new ethical weight to the action of waiting for my wife to arrive home from work (for example), save to show that every act that we consciously take up has an anticipatory aspect to it, that is, that every egoically directed act is anticipatory in some way. Combined with the fundamentality of protention (to temporality and absolute consciousness) and expectation (to our constitution of objects and the world), we see that futurity is a key theme of phenomenology.

Conclusion

The Promissory Discipline

The significance of futurity for phenomenology should be apparent by now: By connecting the phenomenological method essentially with the notion of promise, futurity shows phenomenology to be an essentially promissory discipline. In doing so, it opens phenomenology to a set of problems and questions that otherwise might seem to fall outside its scope. It is only in examining these problems and questions that the full scope of the promissory nature of phenomenology comes to the fore. Thus we can see that what has been at stake in our discussion—and what remains at stake—is our understanding of phenomenology itself: its purpose, function, relation to other disciplines, and to life in general.

I. The Tension in the Principle of Principles

We have seen throughout that focusing on the role of futurity in phenomenology has brought the necessary interplay of presence and absence back to the forefront of phenomenological research. Though this idea can be found already in Husserl,[1] its importance is not always fully recognized there. Fully recognizing the essential nature of absence, for example, would seem to problematize the phenomenological principle of principles: that *"every originary presentive intuition is a legitimizing source of cognition, that everything originarily* (so to speak, in its 'personal' authority) *offered to us in 'intuition' is to be accepted simply as what it is presented as being, but also only within the limits in which it is presented there"* (Hua III, 43–44).

If we were to understand consciousness as a container, like a box or a bag that holds within it images or representations of what is otherwise essentially outside of it, then this principle seems fairly straightforward: We can take as true our representations of things, provided we realize that they are true only as representations. The purpose of phenomenology would then be to understand what goes into our construction of these representations: the various types of intentional strands, the differing modes of givenness of the objects being represented, and so on (where both intentionality and givenness would be essentially related to objectification and objects).[2]

Our analysis of futurity has shown us, however, that intentionality cannot be equated solely with objectification (chapter 4), and consciousness is not a box or a bag.[3] But if this relatively straightforward understanding of the principle is inadequate, this is because there is nothing straightforward about this principle. Rather, as may not surprise us after our investigation into the relationship between constitution and openness in part 3, there is a certain tension at work in this formulation of the principle, which offers two distinct movements that seem to be contradictory. On the one hand, things must give themselves to us originarily, with their own 'personal authority,' an authority that clearly undercuts the authority of the constituting subject; on the other hand, the constituting subject provides the 'limits' of appearance and therefore takes pride of place.[4] Without the former, there is no possibility for the phenomenon to appear *legitimately* and thereby establish phenomenology as a rigorous science, as it is the self-giving nature of the phenomenon alone that provides the "legitimizing source of cognition." Without the latter movement, however, there is no possibility for the phenomenon to *appear*, as it is the subject alone to which things can appear, can become phenomena.[5] Since both aspects are necessary to the possibility of phenomenality itself, the question for phenomenology becomes how to balance these two distinct movements—how to hold them in tension—so as to preserve the possibility of phenomena and of phenomenology.

Historically speaking, phenomenology has at times been understood as overemphasizing the first aspect, resulting in a naïve, empirical intuitionism that privileges perception as the only way of knowing (cf. PCC, 76–82); at other times, the second aspect has been overemphasized, resulting in a speculative, transcendent idealism that privileges individual power and freedom. Though both naïve realism and speculative idealism are undoubtedly poor understandings of phenomenology, one can understand the reason for them, especially when Husserl puts off—at least in *Ideas I*—any transcendental examination of the mediation between these two movements.

But a transcendental examination of this mediation is not entirely missing from Husserlian phenomenology. This fact was brought to the fore most notably in Derrida's *Introduction* to Husserl's "Origin of Geometry." In this work, we see Derrida discover a thorough going reexamination not just of the principle of principles but of the entire phenomenological epistemology that it entails. Already in *différance*, Derrida has shown the necessity of supplementation in the very heart of the lived present and tied this supplementation to the in-the-place-of (*für etwas*) structure of the sign in general (SP, 88). As in *Speech and Phenomena*, in the *Introduction* Derrida is adamant to show that this necessary supplementation is constitutive of transcendental phenomenology itself. Though he marks this necessary supplementation at times with the term "writing," this constitutes a philosophy of language only in a very modified sense. Indeed it is precisely this modification of sense that is at stake in phenomenology.[6]

Using the "Origin of Geometry," Derrida is able to show that a certain kind of history—even tradition[7]—is necessarily a part of phenomenological investigation. This is only possible, however, given the principle of principles, if we are able to speak not merely of historical facts but of a "historical *intuition* in which the intentional reactivation of sense should—*de jure*—precede and condition the empirical determination of fact" (OoG, 26, emphasis added). Derrida will then go on to show that this "reactivation of sense" is the guiding thread not only of the "Origin" but of the phenomenological project as a whole.

The pursuit of knowledge characterized by this "reactivation of sense" requires a move beyond classical epistemology (OoG, 34) and hence lays out not only our examination of the principle of principles but also the nonepistemological nature of phenomenology revealed by our analysis of futurity. The search for an 'origin' at work in a reactivation of sense (e.g., the "origin of geometry") is a search not for the foundational axioms on which a science or discipline can be built but for the "primordial evidence" that is presupposed in any axiom (55). These presuppositions cannot, then, be a series of rules, concepts, or any other ideas or ideals that would themselves function axiomatically. Rather they must be essentially pre-axiomatic, pre-ideal, and this occurs only in the "historical interconnections" that function as "interconnections of sense and value" (56). These historical interconnections are called sedimentations (56).[8]

Now the notion of sedimentation was first broached in our discussion of the second level of constituting consciousness (i.e., passive synthesis), where it functioned as expectative horizons that enabled us to constitute a world by providing us with clarificational intuitions. That is, our horizons enable us to clarify what is coming, so that when it comes (in a confirming intuition) we can experience it not only as the object it is but also as the fulfillment of what we were expecting. Via the distinction between clarifying and confirming intuition (first introduced by the positive account of protention provided in chapter 1), we are able to experience not only objects but also, precisely, our *experience* of objects as *our* (or, better, *my*) experience. In this double intentionality (of transverse and horizontal intentionality, in Husserl's language) the two seemingly contradictory movements of the principle of principles are confirmed.

II. Making Sense of Making-Sense (*Sinnbildung*)

If we have seemed to confirm the principle of principles, we have done so only by critiquing how it is often understood.[9] For the reactivation of sense that we are here discussing is not merely a 'received' sense, nor a 'constituted' sense, but is a sense that is received and constituted—that is made or formed, but not by me. This "primordial evidence" or sense is therefore called, by Derrida and by Husserl, not only primordial but preprimordial, "a radical ground which is [always] already past" (OoG, 55), a "transcendental prehistory" (40), a "protohistory" (42). We have encountered such a prehistory before: in the "pre-history of the I" of Levinasian diachrony. This prehistory, as we noted then, is essentially marked by a futural element: the "surprise" that comes not just when the self encounters something from beyond itself but when the self encounters the Other as always already within itself, encounters itself as constituted by the Other. We call this "surprise" because it is characterized by a lack of "decidability" (52–56), implying that everything follows from and is contained in the axioms in an axiomatic system, and hence everything in that system is decided— even if not yet fully understood—in advance in those axioms. Our horizons, while providing us the ability to "expect" a world (see chapter 2) are not, for all that, wholly decidable axioms. As we shall see shortly, there remains within horizons a certain "undecidability," a lack of knowledge, first in that here are things that I "know" but that I do not understand, that I do not know that I know (as they are the products of passive synthesis for me and not of explicit judgment), and second, that these horizons always remain open to impression (my clarifying intuitions must always be matched—confirmed, disappointed, etc.—by a confirming intuition).

This lack of knowledge moves us beyond thinking of all knowledge along the lines of objectivity and hence spurs us to wonder.[10] Wonder, in turn, is nothing but another name for the phenomenological reduction, which does not lose the world but precisely reveals to us again the world "as strange and paradoxical" in its very familiarity.[11] Indeed, as Husserl himself writes, the "phenomenologist lives in the paradox of having to look upon the obvious as questionable."[12] It is precisely this making questionable of the obvious that is the task of the phenomenological enterprise: The phenomenologist must recover what was once a novel and interesting thought but has now become a truism, an empty formula, just "the way things are." It is this recovery that is at the heart of the project of the "re-activation of sense," but it can occur only by way of a historical reduction that would bracket factual history "in order to respect and show the normative independence of the ideal object in its own right" (OoG, 44). However, this "independent" ideal object is not then revealed as atemporal but as inhabiting its own "unique historicity" (44), a genuinely transcendental, phenomenological historicity.

This historicity goes back again to the notion of sedimentation. Our sedimented horizons are given to us from beyond ourselves.[13] We then employ these horizons in our constitution of objects via clarification,[14] so as to permit the possibility of receiving a (confirming) intuition that can come only from the self-givenness (*Selbstgegebenheit*) of the things themselves.[15] The very "infinite" nature of ideal objects (as omnitemporal, etc.) is then tied inextricably with "a certain finitude" (OoG, 37) that phenomenology cannot ignore if it is to provide ideal and transcendental knowledge.

But accounting for empirical and historical conditions in this way is not a simple task. It must avoid the twin scourges of "the philosophical nonsense of a purely empirical history" (i.e., historicism; cf. OoG, 103), on the one hand, and "the impotence of an ahistorical rationalism" on the other (51). To return to economic metaphors employed in earlier chapters, we can say that we "can never keep [our] sedimentary deposits out of circulation" (56) but that those deposits are not the sum total of our epistemological assets. We are neither restricted only to what we receive from the world, nor are we the purely constituting masters of our domain; we are neither wholly determined nor wholly free.[16] Rather the phenomenological task is to make sense precisely of what we receive from others and our responsibility for it.

III. Tradition, Phenomenology, Responsibility

In the "Origin of Geometry" (and in, at least, the *Crisis* and *Formal and Transcendental Logic*), "a doctrine of *tradition* as the historical ether of perception" emerges (OoG, 49). Here we must take account of the way our perception requires horizons, and these horizons are not merely our own, but are given to us via sedimentation. The world we constitute in passive synthesis is a lifeworld, a cultural world, a "spiritual"[17] world that "exists entirely 'through tradition' (168)" (56).[18] We must start with this tradition if we are to make any transcendental breakthroughs;[19] we cannot reactivate the sense of geometry, for example, without beginning from geometry as it is currently constituted (Hua VI, §9). In order to make sense of this, we must think of the tradition as analogous to internal time-consciousness.[20] Just as the living present is nothing other than the "*dialectic* of protention and retention," so too is our tradition nothing other than "a cultural structure which is animated by a project" (OoG, 58) that it both lives out of and strives to enact.

But while tradition clearly plays an epistemological role, Husserl is adamant that our knowledge—especially scientific knowledge, including phenomenology—is not the product of a mere 'worldview' (*Weltanschauung*). While our knowledge is historically situated, and in an essential and not merely an accidental way, science remains by its very nature "supratemporal," "limited by no relatedness to the spirit of one time . . . (135–146)" (OoG, 58–59).[21] Husserl attributes this to science's grasping of truth, but the analogy with time-consciousness now helps us make sense of this in a new way. As we saw with Levinas, time-consciousness is not merely the "dialectic of protention and retention" but is also marked by the preprimordial engagement with alterity that constitutes the subject as a subject that constitutes. Now this contact with alterity is twofold: We are in contact with the world (via materiality, sensibility, the concrete, etc.) and with the Other (via the trace, substitution, etc.).[22] It is precisely this contact with alterity that marks science—specifically phenomenology, as that science whose job it is to reduce the natural attitude so as to recover the self-givenness of the things themselves[23]—as not merely the product of a time and place but also as transcendent. This distinction can be marked between the realms of validity, on the one hand, and the realm of truth, on the other (59). Phenomenology enables us to move beyond mere validity to truth, because phenomenology enables us to directly engage alterity.[24]

But this engagement with alterity is not simple, as we saw in part 3. For while we may wish to think of alterity in terms of supratemporal (i.e., acultural, etc.) individuals, and then posit that these individuals (i.e., the 'things themselves' [as *Ding an Sich*], the Other[s], etc.) are the ground not only of objectivity but of phenomenological validity, we must realize that even the very "infinitization" of these individuals (at work in the infinite alterity of Levinas's Other, but also in the Idea in the Kantian sense of Husserlian epistemology) is necessarily inscribed within a certain finitude, "the infinite limit of a finite and qualitative intuition" (OoG, 106). We are confronted here again with the distinction between the domain of nonintuitive differentiation (which is, in principle, infinite) and the domain of intuition (which is finite) that we discussed in chapter 1. The mode of nonintuitive differentiation is marked by ideation, most notably by the Idea in the Kantian sense, which is to say, by an infinite theoretical Telos (Hua III, §83; Hua VI, appendix IV; Hua I, §41). This infinite Telos is contained in the very structure of absolute consciousness itself—the infinite series of protentions protending protentions and retentions and retentions retaining protentions and retentions discussed in chapter 1. If this is true, Derrida points out, "the unity of infinity, the condition for . . . temporalization, must then be *thought*, since it is announced without appearing and without being contained in a Present. This thought unity, which makes the phenomenalization of time as such possible, is therefore always the Idea in the Kantian sense which never phenomenalizes itself" (OoG, 137). The Idea in the Kantian sense, as infinite, plays an essential role in phenomenology, but it can never itself be given as such in an intuition. However, it structures and conditions the entirety of the realm of intuition and hence unites the two domains in the essential dual core of phenomenology. For although the transcendent thing of nature cannot be given "with complete determinacy and with similarly complete intuitability in any limited finite consciousness," "*as Idea* (in the Kantian sense), [*its*] *complete givenness is . . . prescribed*" (Hua III, §143; see also OoG, 139). While finite consciousness can never intuit the entirety of the transcendent thing as such, it remains in a project of ever-increasing givenness, of gaining more and more knowledge of the thing that gives itself.[25] This infinite telos is built into the heart of the phenomenological project, from its characterization of absolute (time-constituting) consciousness to the duality of the principle of principles, and was revealed to us clearly in our analysis of anticipation in chapter 3.

Derrida will relate this infinite telos to "intentionality itself" (OoG, 139). In doing so, he not only highlights the essentially futural nature of this infinity further (because of the essential relationship between intentionality and protention discussed in chapter 1 and in part 2), but he also opens up the entire problematic discussion of intentionality itself. At the least, we can begin to see that the infinite telos of constituting consciousness is, in part, necessarily characterized by the infinite alterity of that onto which it is opened. That is, the realm of nonintuitive differentiation is not the only infinity at work in intentionality; there is also the counterintentionality coming from the (infinite) Other that both constitutes the subject as able to constitute and also provides that constituted constituting subject with an (infinite) responsibility to constitute the world well.[26] In so doing, it reveals a certain infinity at work in the domain of intuition itself, even as that domain must be marked by an essential finitude.

Intentionality, then, cannot be separated either from the movement of temporalization nor from the passive horizons of sedimented sense by which we constitute the world—both of which are essentially marked by futurity, as we saw in chapters 1 and 2. Rather intentionality is the coming together of these two aspects, each opened, in its own way, to the infinite:[27] "[I]ntentionality is traditionality. At its greatest depth—i.e., in the pure movement of phenomenological temporalization . . . intentionality is the root of historicity,"[28] and historicity itself "is *sense*" (OoG, 150).[29] This opens the phenomenological project onto its essential problem: The ideality of ideal objects and the corresponding unity of sense is "always relative, because it is always inscribed within a mobile system of relations and takes its source in an infinitely open project of acquisition" (104), whether we think of this project as the project of science, the project of truth, or the project of transcendental consciousness. This project, then—the very project of phenomenology—must now be understood as the paradoxical and problematic relation between the "objective-exact" truths of theoretical science and the "subjective-relative" truths of the passively received lifeworld (cf. Hua VI, §§33–39; OoG, 119–20). While this duality is not symmetrical—there is a clear preference for the ideal, the univocal, the infinite, and the exact at work in phenomenology[30]—this does not eliminate the essential necessity of the duality; indeed phenomenology's task is precisely to "keep alive the *question: How can the a priori of scientific Objectivity be constituted starting from those of the life-world?*" (OoG, 120).[31]

Despite the very pretentions to univocity that characterize science, including the science of phenomenology, its "inscription" within particular historico-lingual situations will necessarily give rise to multiple singular perspectives, "multiple interconnections of sense, and therefore some mediate and potential aims" (OoG, 120). It is never possible, therefore, for the phenomenologist to fully know or fully control how her work is inserted into her horizons (disciplinary or otherwise).[32] The pursuit of truth can never happen apart from particular normative pursuits (of validity, etc.), but those very normative pursuits operate on more levels than just those of the pursuit of truth. In pursuing truth, the phenomenologist—or the scientist or philosopher in general—is necessarily opened onto more than just her own pursuits or the normative pursuits of her discipline (though she also never fully leaves them behind); she is opened also onto the lifeworld itself. One moves beyond validity and toward truth, then, only by moving within validity in a certain way.[33]

These entwined movements of validity and truth echo our earlier discussion of the relationship between inference and trustworthiness, between epistemology and ethics. In this regard, it should not surprise us that this futural phenomenological epistemology (if we can still rightly call this an epistemology) concerns nothing less than responsibility. The project of phenomenology is a project of taking responsibility for our horizons, our presuppositions, that which is most "obvious" (cf. Hua XVII, especially pp. 2–10 of the English translation): "[R]esponsibility here means shouldering a word one hears spoken, as well as taking on oneself the transfer of sense, in order to look after its advance" (OoG, 149). But this responsibility therefore has a twofold nature that is essentially futural: It involves both a clarification and a confirmation (or denial), and this responsibility is always a "co-responsibility" involving "the one who receives, but also . . . the one who creates" (100).[34]

The clarification of responsibility can occur only via a clarification of our own tradition and the possibilities inherent within it.[35] Our tradition provides "the associational consciousness of the historical community,"[36] which I earlier called our sedimented horizons. But these horizons are made up not only of facts (or previous acts) but also of norms (or "validity-systems"), and these latter are not reduced with the former (cf. Hua III, §56; OoG, 43n.34). Even the norms of logic are themselves rooted—in a particular way—in the lived experience of individuals.[37] Because of this distinction (between facts and norms), we are able to see that our tradition provides us not only with the "content" of our experience but with the very structures that shape our experience.[38] Hence it is our tradition, via these norms, that provides us with the horizon that enables us to expect what is coming and therefore gives us a world.[39]

These expectations, then, provide the majority of what is "most obvious" to us in our horizons (e.g., that objects subsist through time). If it is, as I have said, the task of phenomenology to "look upon the obvious as questionable," then a major task of the phenomenological project must be to clarify—to ourselves and to others—what precisely are the expectational horizons that guide our constitution of the world and to enter them into scientific discourse.[40] If objectivity is the watchword of modern science, then perhaps attestation (e.g., TI, 176), confession,[41] or testimony[42] are the watchwords of phenomenological science: No longer seeking the view from nowhere, phenomenology is able to clarify and discuss *where*[43] it is viewing (from) as a way of discussing what it is viewing.

This point bears further elucidation, for it signals something significant about our project of clarifying phenomenology understood as a promissory discipline. In beginning with a reevaluation of the principle of principles, we seemed to have begun in the realm of epistemology. But this realm cannot stay separated from other realms, other philosophical problems, now that we are attempting to understand the phenomenological project.

Husserl himself says that"the ruling dogma of the separation . . . between epistemological and genetic origin is fundamentally mistaken."[44] In this regard, Derrida's claim that "[h]istory itself establishes the possibility of its own appearing" (OoG, 66) is telling. Not only does it bear directly on the very sense of tradition that is currently under discussion, but it does so in a way that problematizes the duality inherent in the principle of principles as discussed above, in which the subject is the condition of the appearance of any phenomenon; in doing so, it perhaps suggests that (transcendental) History is not a phenomenon, properly speaking, and so invokes the infinite telos of phenomenology discussed under the rubric of the Idea in the Kantian sense.[45] In "establishing the possibility of its own appearing," then, (transcendental) History not only gives itself (in the self-givenness characteristic of phenomena), but it also gives the very possibility of the subject to receive its very self-givenness. Transcendental History[46] (also called Tradition, transcendental intersubjectivity,[47] transcendental language, etc.) thereby coheres structurally with the Levinasian Other, even as it cannot be equated with it precisely because of its structural (i.e., institutional rather than personal and individual) character; while transcendental History does not have a Face, it can still be seen in the Face of the singular Other (which perhaps might explain Levinas's claims that, in the very face-to-face encounter I already invoke the third).[48] The relationship between reception and constitution that has been a major theme of this work is here crystallized: I receive the tradition, but only after the tradition has given me the very "tools" I need to receive it (e.g., language, concepts, clothing, arts, music).[49] As such, in clarifying the horizons we have received from our tradition, we are not (only) clearing the ground to make room for the self-givenness of the things themselves[50]—things that, like History, need not be restricted to objects—but we are (also) furthering the reception of that givenness itself. Clarifying our horizons not only helps us see the 'things themselves' better; it also gives us another 'thing itself,' another *Sache* though not a *Ding*: transcendental History (or Historicity), the very focus of the phenomenological project itself, and co-given with the self-givenness of any object.[51]

In seeking to clarify its own horizons, then, phenomenology not only acknowledges the limits of its own discourse but, more importantly, enters those very limits into discussion, that is, makes those limits also the object of its inquiry. This not only enables us to determine in what ways our project does (and does not) operate within and according to those limits, but, perhaps more importantly, it clearly reveals the connection between scope and method: Without clarifying our methodological presuppositions, we can never be sure that our work coheres properly with our method, and conversely, in clarifying our method we open the door to renewed discussion of what we can and cannot do within and according to that method.[52]

IV. The Promissory Discipline

So coherence—and indeed classical epistemology—is not the sum total of the phenomenological project. Once we have made ourselves aware of our expectational horizons, we must still evaluate whether or not those horizons are "good" horizons.[53] As opposed to measuring whether or not our results accord with our method, here we discuss whether or not our method itself is a good one. But according to what standards can we measure our horizons, if our horizons shape and constitute the world for us? Here we run into a problem of circularity, found in Husserl, Heidegger, Gadamer, Levinas, and Derrida (to name a few): If our tradition provides us with our norms (or validity systems), then we seem able to analyze our tradition only from within that very tradition itself (i.e., according to the norms it itself provides).[54] The only way to avoid this circularity for phenomenology is by giving in to it; one goes beyond it only by passing through it in a certain way:[55]

> [A] subjectivity 'normed' in its Present by a constituted objective sense (which is therefore its 'absolute logic') 'fastens' its 'norms' to a 'higher subjectivity,' i.e., to *itself*, in the creative movement by which it goes beyond itself and produces a new sense, and so on. This new sense will also be the moment of a *higher* sense-investigation in which the past sense, sedimented and retained first in a sort of objectivist attitude, will be reawakened in its dependent relation to living subjectivity. . . . Of course, all this remains paradoxical and contradictory as long as we continue to consider—implicitly or not—the Idea as *some thing* and Reason as an *ability*. (OoG, 143–44)

In order to avoid these misconceptions, and thereby to make sense of the essential functioning of absolute subjectivity within (and as) history, we must remind ourselves of the essentially promissory nature of phenomenology. We have already said that, in phenomenology, we are both the recipient and the content of the promise—we *are* the promise, given to us by our tradition. These norms help constitute the promise that we are called to live up to, even as they already make us who we are. If our tradition (or messianism, in Derrida's language) promises us validity, for example, then we work within that tradition to ensure that it achieves that promise; when it does not, in order to live up to the promise we try to change it accordingly. Such "promises" are at work in all the "regional" sciences and guide the work of those sciences. The crisis in the sciences that Husserl points out is that many of these sciences have lost the sense of their promise, and hence they no longer know what they are doing. This does not decrease their effectiveness as a particular science, but it does limit their value in the constitution of the (life) world. The task of phenomenological science, then, is to clarify and evaluate these promises that lie at the core of the sciences. To do this, we must reactivate the sense of the promise that guides each science, cultural institution, or political institution (which would also each be a promise that it is trying to live up to), by determining its own (transcendental or proto-)historicity, a historicity that is "parallel" to but distinct from the mere facts of empirical history (OoG, 132). This empirical-transcendental parallel is held together, as we discussed in chapter 7, only in and as "*life*" (SP, 14).[56] Because of this being-held-together, in reactivation we can not only distinguish between the different promises and different sciences, but we can also begin to clarify the connections between them to see how they influence and shape each other and life itself. In this manner, phenomenology finds "in reactivation [of sense] the medium of its *fidelity*" (OoG, 99n.106, emphasis modified).

Hence, in addition to evaluating the coherence of method and results within each discipline, institution, or 'promise,' we must also be able to evaluate these promises vis-à-vis each other. Here it is not primarily the coherence between the promises that must guide us, as these come together in the identity-in-difference that characterizes life, but the affirmation as well of the difference(s). In this regard, we cannot be content to merely study the acts of (epistemological) constitution but must also seek the self-givenness of the things themselves (*die Sachen selbst* and not *Ding an sich*): The very duality of the principle of principles provides us not only with an epistemological but now also with an ethical promise or project. With this in mind, we can begin to evaluate not only whether or not we are coherent but whether or not we are sufficiently Just, Democratic, Truthful, and so on, where the capital letters in these words indicate the (quasi-)transcendental[57] nature of certain promises we receive from our tradition, not just as mere 'facts' within that tradition but as constitutive of that tradition—as the characteristic mark of that tradition's constitution of its adherents.[58] If we can examine the coherence of our tradition, or of our own work within that tradition, via the epistemological aspect of phenomenology, we can examine the confirmation (or denial) of that tradition itself via the nonepistemological aspect of phenomenology (which can now, finally, perhaps be understood as 'ethical' in something like the traditional use of that word). This confirmation (or denial) will consist primarily not of statements and judgments but of the kinds of 'things' (subjects, objects, institutions, ideas, etc.) that tradition constitutes, the 'things' it enables to appear, and the ability it gives to others to allow itself to appear.

We are now in a position to see how a book on phenomenological method in fact opens onto issues that are of central importance across a variety of disciplines, philosophical and otherwise. By showing the essentially promissory nature of phenomenology, we can see that issues of 'empirical concerns' are of central importance to any epistemological claim (though not in a straightforwardly deterministic fashion). But we see too that epistemological claims, by taking up a position within a tradition of promise and inheritance (as discussed, via different terminology, in both the *Crisis of the European Sciences* and *Specters of Marx*), are themselves making claims that have ethical and political value; not only do our judgments provide the sedimented deposits of other people's horizons of expectations, but the claims of the various sciences are united together in the lives of individual people, who live in and as the promise of their respective traditions.[59] As such, not only are we held hostage to our tradition (that we never seem able to escape), but we also find ourselves responsible for this being-hostage, as we live out and pass on the tradition not merely as something we do or know but as something we are (cf. *Otherwise than Being*). For not only do we receive an intuition of alterity in the self-givenness of objects, but the very capacity that we have to receive (and constitute) is itself the ongoing revelation of the Other: My life is the trace of the Other in me, and therefore my life is not only the response to a preprimordial revelation, but it is also the continuing unfolding of that revelation.[60]

This would be true not only for me as an individual but also communally and institutionally: Communities and institutions, and not just individuals, are called to live in, as, and up to the promise.[61] Hence the phenomenological project is not only communal and intersubjective in its method (i.e., in the constitution and discovery of its object of inquiry) but also in its application and scope; phenomenology bears on issues that are communal and institutional and therefore political, ethical, ecological, juridical, religious, and so on.[62] Phenomenology is not confined to speaking strictly of the individual and its acts, and therefore its insights and breakthroughs are similarly not confined strictly to the individual.[63] Hence employing a (quasi-)transcendental move does not prevent us from acting or thinking positively, contra Rorty and Wood.[64] Rather in undertaking a genuinely transcendental analysis, we can come to understand the sense that our actions, communities, and institutions have received via traditionality and therefore, in turn, the sense that they pass on, via that same traditionality, to others. Such a transcendental analysis is, in and of itself, not merely a negation but a positive, ethical action.[65] By opening ourselves to the essential role of futurity in phenomenology, we have opened ourselves also to new possibilities, new pursuits, for the present and future of phenomenology.

Notes

Introduction

1. As we will see, this is at least in part because, pursuing phenomenology, we will be pushed toward a transcendental (or quasi- or ultra-transcendental) understanding of time rather than being content to discuss "real" or empirical time. This is a point that McInerney seems to miss in his discussion of phenomenology ("About the Future").

2. This might be essentially the case and not merely a methodological choice. Derrida claims in *Edmund Husserl's* Origin of Geometry: *An Introduction* that "phenomenology cannot be reflected on in a phenomenology of phenomenology. The *Endstiftung* of phenomenology (phenomenology's ultimate critical legitimation: i.e., what its sense, value and right tell us about it), then, never directly measures up to a phenomenology. At least this *Endstiftung* can give access to itself in a philosophy, insofar as it is announced in a concrete phenomenological evidence, in a concrete *consciousness* which is made *responsible* for it despite the finitude of that consciousness, and insofar as it grounds transcendental historicity and transcendental intersubjectivity" (OoG, 141). This quote not only justifies or shapes the method of this book, but it also announces the essentially responsible (and therefore) ethical nature of phenomenology and therefore announces also a major part of the content of this book.

3. For example, the notion of "awaiting" in Romano, "Awaiting."

4. Heidegger, *Sein und Zeit*, 406; *Being and Time*, especially §79.

5. Merleau-Ponty, *Phenomenology of Perception*, especially pt.3, chap.2, "Temporality."

6. Sartre, *L'Être et le néant*; *Being and Nothingness*, especially pt. 2, chap. 2.

7. Cf. Janicaud et al., *Phenomenology*.

8. For methodological reasons, therefore, I begin from the standpoint that the 'theological turn' is in need of justification before it can be considered 'phenomenological.' This is not to say that I will never discuss those thinkers deemed 'theological' phenomenologists, but rather that I shall engage with them primarily as phenomenologists rather than as theologians or philosophers of religion. This will show itself in my selection of texts. For example, I spend significant time in chapter 3 on a relatively little-known article by Lacoste, "The Phenomenality of Anticipation," while failing to spend significant time on his much better-known book *Experience and the Absolute*. The article is, I think, more amenable to a wider phenomenological audience, whereas some of the terminology employed in the book makes it more comfortable for theological audiences than for certain phenomenological ones. While I do not wish to separate their phenomenology from their philosophy of religion too strictly (since, in the minds of theological phenomenologists anyway, they are obviously closely connected), I hope that my focus will prove helpful both to philosophy of religion and to phenomenology.

9. The building of this bridge will largely be confined to footnotes and marginal comments and will not be rendered in any sort of systematic fashion. While I hope that such a systematic bridge will be constructed someday and that this book will prove to be a helpful stone for that bridge, pursuing this project directly would take us away from our overall theme and focus.

10. To anticipate those who would object that these have *always* been phenomenological concerns, I say only that I do not disagree with that statement. As the patient reader will see, eventually the concerns and problems brought up by Levinas and Derrida will be related back to the work of Husserl, where most of those concerns find an initial voice, if not always a satisfactory hearing.

11. While the recourse to the past could perhaps accomplish the same purpose, there is a difference with futurity that, we will see, becomes significant. The "lack" or "absence" of the object of memorative acts (including retention, "primary memory") is of a different nature, it seems, than that of futural acts: In memorative acts, the object is no longer present, though at one time it was; in futural acts, however, the object has never been present (though implicitly it will be, or at least could be, someday).

12. Cf. *Being and Time*, §9: "The Being of any such entity is *in each case mine*."

13. This reveals itself in the ultimately reflexive nature of Dasein, which is never opened onto anything other than itself, since alterity is never anything other than a 'nowhere and a nothing.' To cite a few of many examples illustrating this theme: in "Being-towards-death, Dasein comports itself towards itself" (*Being and Time*, §51); the "*constancy of the self* . . . is the *authentic* counter-possibility to the non-Self-constancy which is characteristic of irresolute falling" (§64); "What does the conscience call to him to whom it appeals? Taken strictly, nothing. The call asserts nothing, gives no information about world events, has nothing to tell" (§56); "In that in the face of which one has anxiety, the 'nothing and nowhere' becomes manifest" (§40).

14. Marion discusses Heidegger's critique of the subject at length in §25 of *Being Given*. He acknowledges there much of what we have been saying here: "Dasein is still exposed to solipsism," but now "a new solipsism, no longer ontic (being-in-the-world preserves it), but ontological (the transcendence of Dasein secures it)" (259–60). See also Henry, "The Critique of the Subject."

15. As chronicled most famously in Richardson, *Heidegger*.

16. This marks a significant difference between this work and David Wood's, *The Deconstruction of Time*, a difference that follows from methodological choices that orient the respective texts. While Wood employs a method that is "historical as well as analytical" (5), focusing primarily on the understanding of time, I employ an analysis that is methodological, focusing primarily on the understanding of phenomenology. This difference causes Wood to order his text around the question of "what reading of the history of philosophy leads Derrida to make" his claims (5), whereas my book is not a historical reading that culminates somehow in Derrida; rather it is a methodological analysis of a problem, an analysis that is also necessarily in a certain way historical, since "[m]ethod is not the neutral preface or *perambulatory* exercise of thought. Rather, it is thought itself in the consciousness of its complete historicity" (OoG, 149). This is not merely a play on language on my part; this difference on the status of method, on the historicity of method and method as historicity, goes a long way in explaining our different positions toward the (quasi-transcendent) nature of Derrida's texts. In short, where Wood seems to find the sense of Derrida's work to be necessarily at odds with transcendental thinking (cf. *Deconstruction of Time*, pt. 4; see especially the postscript to chapter 3), I will argue that Derrida's work is in some essential way marked by a transcendental nature. It seems to me that this is merely a disagreement about the word "transcendental," in which case I hope my explanation of that term in part 3 and especially the conclusion will help alleviate this apparent tension.

The present work can, then, perhaps be best understood vis-à-vis Wood's book as an attempt to (a) develop the theory that, in 1989, Wood was only beginning to "grow aware" of, that is, that "the concept of time . . . only ever appears with some such tacit or explicit theoretical implication" (*Deconstruction of Time*, 3–4), within (b) the more narrowly defined phenomenological tradition. These two points mark significant differences from Wood's attempt to "free" time "from the shackles of its traditional moral and metaphysical understanding" (xi) via an exploration of a tradition that "includes Kant, Hegel, Nietzsche, Husserl, Heidegger, and recent structuralist thought" (4). Still, my project is not entirely divorced from Wood's attempt; I do make an attempt to explain the "two distinct levels of articulation: that of primitive event [equated with 'Time as absolute openness to the Other'] and that of structure," in a way that attempts not a synthesis but at the least "an account of their inner unity," a unity (in difference) whose very possibility "remains a matter of speculation" for Wood (xii).

17. I have also undertaken this endeavor elsewhere: DeRoo, "The Future Matters"; DeRoo, "A Positive Account of Protention."

18. That is, as will become clear, both in the constitutive powers of transcendental subjectivity and in the (self-)constitution of that subjectivity itself.

19. In deeming Derrida's work "quasi-transcendental," I echo Wood's claim, though I contest that this makes Derrida in some way incoherent; rather than reading Derrida as "open[ing] another concept of time" (*Deconstruction of Time*, 6), I see in Derrida a way of holding two other accounts of time together in tension. But rather than viewing this way as "new" or as "another," I will argue that it is the outworking of a certain tradition and methodology, Derrida's attempt to live up to a certain "promise" he sees inherent in phenomenology. This language of quasi-transcendentality comes to replace the earlier talk of "ultratranscendental" (cf. OG) in *Glas* and for the most part thereafter. See Bennington, "Derridabase."

20. To say "transcending" at this moment would not be inappropriate but could lead to unnecessary confusion; hence I will stay with the somewhat ambiguous "going-beyond." One could argue that the difference between Husserl and Levinas is captured most succinctly in their respective understandings of the word "transcendent."

21. See Hua XII and Husserl, *Philosophie der Arithmetik*.

22. For one of the many places that Derrida discusses the theme of the other "in" me, see Derrida, *A Taste for the Secret*, 84. Compare this to Husserl's discussion of intersubjectivity "in" me (e.g., in Hua VI, §54) and Levinas's discussion of "the idea of Infinity in us" (TI, 79).

23. For example, both the noesis and the noema are "products" of consciousness, so to speak, even though it is through the noema that we know the world itself rather than merely knowing our own consciousness. For more, see Drummond, *Husserlian Intentionality*.

1. Protention as More than Inverse Retention

1. For Husserl's discussions of Meinong and Stern, consult Hua X, "Supplementary Texts" nos. 29, 30, 33, 31. Husserl's understanding of Stern's position is based largely on Stern, "Psychische Präsenzzeit."

2. The debate concerning the relationship between intentional acts and the absolute flow of consciousness is discussed at length in Zahavi's *Self-Awareness and Alterity* chap. 5. There Zahavi pits his conception of this relationship against the standard view supported by J.B. Brough and Robert Sokolowski. For an explanation of the Brough and Sokolowski position, see Brough's introduction to *On the Phenomenology of the Consciousness of Internal Time* (Hua X), especially xlviii–lv. At the heart of the debate is Brough's characterization of the relationship between intentional acts and the absolute flow of consciousness in the following manner: "[Primary impression, retention and protention] are no longer taken to be names for moments belonging to a *perceptual* act; they are rather moments of the ultimate level of consciousness through which one is aware of the perceptual act—and of any other act or content—as an immanent temporal object" (Brough, "Translator's Introduction" xlix). Zahavi, on the other hand, does not want to distinguish so sharply between acts of the second level and the absolute flow of

consciousness, instead mapping the second and third levels on to Husserl's distinction between thematized and functioning subjectivity, respectively (Zahavi, *Self-Awareness and Alterity*, 71). It is not immediately clear to me that Brough and Sokolowski do not also make the same move, although Zahavi clearly thinks that they do not.

3. William James, who seems to have a similar model of the time of consciousness and the consciousness of time, uses the metaphor of a rainbow before a waterfall to illustrate the flow: Although the rainbow remains constant, the material that makes up the rainbow, the individual particles of water that reflect sunlight and hence give off the appearance of the rainbow, are constantly changing, constantly moving, as the water continues to flow (*The Principles of Psychology*, 593). For a more thorough explanation of the relation between Husserl's and James's theories of time-consciousness, see Cobb-Stevens, "James and Husserl."

4. The importance of this flow for the overall phenomenological project cannot be overestimated. Husserl explicitly equates this flow with absolute subjectivity (Hua X, 75). As such, it would seem to be central to the project of a phenomenological study of "transcendental subjectivity," as put forward, e.g., in Hua I.

5. It is not until the time of Texts no. 50 and 51 (dated by R. Bernet between October 1908 and Summer 1909) that Husserl replaces his initial talk of "primary memory" with language of "retention." For simplicity's sake, I have stayed with retention throughout. For more on the development of Husserl's account of time-consciousness in Hua X, see Brough, "The Emergence of an Absolute Consciousness"; for the change in terminology, see 314–15.

6. The instant is what Husserl calls the "now-point": It exists only as the phase of a continuum and "is conceivable only as the limit of a continuum of retentions, just as every retentional phase is itself conceivable only as a point belonging to such a continuum; and this is true of every now of time-consciousness" (Hua X, 33). Even as a limit, the now is only an "ideal limit" (Hua X, 40). We will see that as the analysis of protention deepens in the later works, this concept of the "now-point" is de-emphasized.

7. Husserl makes similar claims in Hua III, §§77, 81.

8. Though this must be kept distinct from actively anticipating a future event, which would be the intentional act of anticipation rather than the protentional modification of the intentional act of perception. The same goes for retention, which must be kept distinct from the intentional act of reproducing or recollecting (cf. Hua X, §§14–19, especially 19).

9. That is, a retention (Ec) of the retention (Dc) of C.

10. The inspiration for the preceding comes from Hua X, 28. The actual terminology, however, is based on a diagram by Dan Zahavi in *Self-Awareness and Alterity*, 66.

11. Meinong was the major proponent of the view that temporally distributed objects can be presented only by temporally undistributed presentations; see A. Meinong, "Über Gegenstände höherer Ordnung und deren Verhältnis zur inneren Wahrnehmung," *Zeitschrift für Psychologie und Physiologie der Sinnesorgane*

21 (1899): 182–72, translated as "On Objects of Higher Order and Their Relationship to Internal Perception." See also Kortooms, *Phenomenology of Time*, 39–43.

12. The translation is from Kortooms, "Phenomenology of Time," 95.

The invocation of fantasy at this point calls to mind the essential role of imagination in Husserlian phenomenology. While this theme is explored in many places—most notably in Sartre's *Imagination* but also in Kuspit, "Fiction and Phenomenology"; Kaufmann, "On Imagination"; and Saraiva, *L'Imagination selon Husserl*—the most comprehensive account of imagination's role in the phenomenological method occurs in Richard Kearney's *Poetics of Imagining*. However, even Kearney acknowledges that the account of imagination is severely underdeveloped by Husserl, so that the very advantages that Husserl claims from imagination (e.g., its nature as an intentional, "bi-polar" act, its role in the reduction, etc.) are never established on a firm footing. As Kearney states, "[O]ne remains especially perplexed as to how, for example, the Husserlian account can succeed in relating the *essential* to the *existential*, the *transcendental* to the *historical*, the *subjective* to the *intersubjective*" (35). We will see that futurity provides us with precisely the necessary resources to relate these seeming opposites, by revealing the essential connection between futurity and intentionality, the very intentionality that is central to Husserl's account of imagination. In this regard, futurity becomes necessary to better understand the phenomenological account of the imagination, not the least because of the ways it will challenge the equation between imagination and freedom that threatens to mistake phenomenological insights for mere Kantian idealism (a mistake that Sartre seems to make at several key junctures). This challenge will occur not only in the Levinasian inversion of *Sinngebung* discussed in part 2 and the Derridean phenomenology of tension discussed in part 3 but already by the expectative horizons of futurity at work in the second level of constituting consciousness (see chapter 2). This last point accords with Kearney's claim that imagination, for Husserl, is primarily the work of that second level of constituting consciousness (*Poetics*, 36n.20).

13. As we will see, there is a problem with labeling this doubly intentional act "retention" and simultaneously claiming that retention is operational only on the level of absolute consciousness.

14. This difference does not affect the tonal quality of the note but rather its givenness: I hear the next note as following the former, in some kind of unity; i.e., I hear it precisely as a *second* note.

15. We will see in later chapters that expectation and anticipation must also be distinguished. For now, however, it is enough to mark them as distinct from protention; whatever expectation and anticipation might turn out to be, they are not protention. It will turn out that the described scenario is an example of expectation, but this is to "anticipate" the second chapter. Peter K. McInerney seems to conflate protention and expectation in his account of "immediate anticipation" and therefore misses what is essential about protention, as we will see momentarily. This might be at least partially explainable given the different con-

text within which he is operating (i.e., a combination of "real" time and neuroscience rather than the methodological concerns that are primary for us here); see McInerney, "About the Future."

16. Indeed this could indicate why Husserl says little about protention in his early analyses of time-consciousness: because he does not know what to say about it, given the framework he was then using. As we will see, when he begins to develop a positive account of protention, he abandons the earlier model of protention as inverse retention.

17. In doing so, we will see that the notion of retention itself is reevaluated when one accounts for protention.

18. Hua X, §24, from which the above quotes were taken, was composed at a later date than most of the rest of the first portion of Hua X. Written specifically for the compiled edition edited by Edith Stein, §24 was written in 1917; see Boehm's note on Hua X, 52 in Brough's translation, 54 n.36.

19. All translations from this volume are by Toine Kortooms, unless otherwise noted.

20. The truth of this claim is difficult to evaluate at this early stage of the analysis. On the one hand, it is easy to understand that the *content* of a protention (though it is not clear that one can speak this way and still be talking about protention) grows out of a past horizon: "The style of the past becomes projected into the future" (Ms. L I 15, p. 32b, translated by James R. Mensch in "Husserl's Concept of the Future," 43, 57n.7). However, such a situation seems better attributed to *expectation*, as chapter 2 will show. On the other hand, Husserl ties protention itself to the *instincts*; hence it would seem to have some basis in past experience (see Ms. A VI 34, p.34b and Ms. E III 9, p. 4a; for a more coherent account of the instincts, one that draws from throughout Husserl's manuscripts, see Mensch, *Husserl's Account of our Consciousness of Time*).

The L manuscripts, from which the first quote from Husserl was taken, form the textual basis of Hua XXXIII. Some of the research on Husserl's concept of protention precedes the publication of Hua XXXIII (2001). For accuracy's sake, I have maintained the reference to the L manuscript when using translations of this material that predate Hua XXXIII. Some later scholars (e.g., Rodemeyer; see note 46 below) have persisted in using the L manuscripts rather than Hua XXXIII. Though the reason for their decision is not explained, I have chosen to again maintain reference to the L manuscripts rather than Hua XXXIII when using translations from those scholars in keeping with their own preference.

21. To go back to our earlier example: If a moment E contains an impression of E, a retention of D, Ed, a secondary retention of C, Ec, and a protention of F, 'F, then we must understand each of these moments, and not just 'F, as protentional: just as 'F protends its givenness in the next instant as F, so too E protends its givenness in the next instant as Fe, Ed protends its givenness as Fd, and Ec as Fc (see Hua XXXIII, 21–22; Kortooms, *Phenomenology of Time*,160; Zahavi, *Self-Awareness and Alterity*, 66). Husserl revises his earlier diagram on internal time-consciousness (Hua X, 28) with more complex diagrams of retention, drawn

out by Kortooms (167, 168), based on Husserl's descriptions in Hua XXXIII, 34–35.

22. As was the case in the early accounts of internal time consciousness (e.g., when Husserl was still employing the content-apprehension schema, as described in section 1 above) and as would be the case if he maintained the notion of fulfillment introduced in the sixth of the *Logical Investigations*. This suggests that the *Logical Investigations* still operate largely on the content-apprehension schema that Husserl later abandons.

23. That it is able to do away with such talk does not mean that Husserl always consistently does so. The talk of primal impression will remain intermittently throughout the middle and later writings. Lanei Rodemeyer would prefer to replace talk of primal impression with that of "moment of actualization," which she claims is less likely to reify the idea of a "now-point," which has always been an idealized abstraction for Husserl (see. Hua X, 40; n.29 above). See Rodemeyer, "Developments in the Theory of Time-Consciousness," 131 ff., 150n.11. Levinas, however, will demonstrate the supreme importance of maintaining talk of impression for a phenomenological account of futurity and for phenomenology itself as a whole; see part 2 below.

24. This constitutes an advance of sorts on Husserl's earlier claims that retentions retain retentions (Hua X, 81).

25. Ms. L I 15, 24a–b, as translated by Rodemeyer in "Developments in the Theory of Time-Consciousness," 131.

26. Ms. L I 16, 9a, as translated by Rodemeyer in "Developments in the Theory of Time-Consciousness," 138.

27. The retention of previous retentions and protentions would also border on infinite. However, the openness of protention marks an essential difference from the necessarily "bound" nature of retention (cf. note on Hua X, 297). This will be discussed in greater detail below.

28. With protention we can describe only the "form" of particular fulfillment; it will not be given fuller content until our discussion of expectation in chapter 2.

29. This distinction is called for by the double meaning of retention and protention implied by the striving character that marks fulfillment. This double meaning implies that the same retentional instant can be simultaneously seen as a fulfillment (of the protentional directedness of the previous instant) and as a de-filling (*Entfüllung*; Hua XXXIII, 30) with regard to the fullness of the object's givenness.

30. Kortooms gives a much more in-depth discussion of this new problem of infinite regress and its potential solutions than is needed for our argument here (*Phenomenology of Time*, 169–74).

31. Cf. Ms. L I 15, 24a–b and note 48 above.

32. This seems to be in line with some of the later texts from Hua X, e.g., Text no. 54 (which is dated no earlier than the end of 1911): "We rather call it the *retention of the earlier primal sensation*, when it is a question of a consciousness in the original flow of the modifications of sensation; otherwise we call it a *repro-*

duction of the earlier sensation. We must adhere to this distinction consistently" (Hua X, 377).

33. On the distinction between protention and expectation, see Hua XI, 125–29 and chapter 2 below. Briefly protention is a "synthetically constituted form in which all other possible syntheses must participate" (Hua XI, 125). Association is one of these "other possible syntheses." What protention is to internal time-consciousness, expectation is to association and passive constitution: the subject's mode of relating to the future within that specific type of constituting consciousness. The positive account of protention gives us the resources to differentiate protention from other modes of relating to the future (e.g., expectation or anticipation) in a way that the account of protention as inverse retention was not able to do, as our discussion of the symphony example indicated.

34. Hence these two modes of bringing to intuition help us see even more clearly how the type of fulfillment necessary for the self-constitution of the absolute stream of consciousness is possible.

35. As Eugen Fink, Husserl's longtime assistant, wrote, "Directedness, tending-to, is the fundamental character of consciousness-of in its most original essential composition" (Eugen-Fink-Archiv B-II 307). This is Fink's (slight) modification of Husserl-Archiv L I 15, 35a, as translated by Ronald Bruzina, "The Revision of the Bernau Time-Consciousness Manuscripts," 369, 382n.51.

36. Though, as discussed earlier, this "does not rule out that in certain circumstances and in their own way they can assume this intentional character later" (Hua XI, 77).

37. My thanks to Osborne Wiggins for pointing out this inconsistency and to the participants of the thirty-eighth annual conference of the International Husserl Circle, whose comments on an earlier draft of this chapter were very helpful in developing the conclusions that I am now putting forth.

38. This "passive" level of constitution can itself be divided into two distinct realms of constitution: the "lawful regularity of immanent genesis that constantly belongs to consciousness in general" (Hua XI, 117), of which association is the prime example, and the "universal, formal framework . . . in which all other possible syntheses must participate" (125) that is internal time-consciousness. This will be discussed in much greater detail in chapter 2.

39. J.N. Mohanty describes intentionality as "a directedness towards a fulfillment" (*The Concept of Intentionality*, 124). Given the discussion of protention and its relationship to fulfillment in section 2 above, this helps us see the inherent connection between protention and intentionality. This definition of intentionality also helps open the question of intentionality itself: Is intentionality the act of consciousness constituting an object, or is it some more fundamental openness onto the world? The broad definition of intentionality provided by Mohanty does not decide this question one way or the other. We will see later that the issue of intentionality is key to our understanding of the transcendental nature of subjectivity and to phenomenology as a discipline.

40. For more on the implications of Husserl's account of absolute consciousness for discussion of identity and self-consciousness, see Zahavi, *Self-Awareness and Alterity*; Zahavi, "Self and Consciousness"; Zahavi, "Phenomenology of Self."

41. Such an analysis of the relation between protention—or at least futurity operating on a fundamental level of consciousness—and intentionality is a major theme of this work. Here in part 1 I focus especially on one aspect of that relation, namely, constitution. In parts 2 and 3 this relation will be expanded to include talk of openness onto the world. Here I can say only that the necessary connection between futurity, intentionality, and openness that will be discussed at length in part 2 is prefigured here in an analysis of Husserl's phenomenology.

2. Expecting the World

1. The "shift" to genetic phenomenology within Husserl is chronicled most famously in Steinbock, *Home and Beyond*.

2. Such issues are raised from outside of genetic phenomenology as well. For example, it is easy to question the phenomenological basis of Husserl's analysis of internal time-consciousness, especially after one sees that retention and protention are not acts of consciousness: If they aren't acts that we do, properly speaking, how do we have phenomenological access to them? How are they given to us? Though this question is slightly different from the question at hand, both seek an account of the relationship between the most basic level of internal time-consciousness and the intuitive givenness of presentational consciousness.

3. These remain passively operative; they do not require the active interest of an ego to be accomplished, but rather their accomplishment is presupposed in every activity of the active ego (Hua XXXI, 3–4). Hua XXXI, 3–83 are included as the third part of Anthony Steinbock's translation of Hua XI in *Analyses concerning Passive and Active Synthesis*. Quotations from these pages of Hua XXXI will use Steinbock's translation.

4. See the debate between Dan Zahavi and John B. Brough and Robert Sokolowski. Zahavi contends that Brough and Sokolowski's attempt to make sense of the trinitary structure of consciousness leads to grave problems for a Husserlian theory of awareness. Hence the twofold structure (for Zahavi, the distinction is between self- and hetero-manifestation) is a more accurate description of Husserl's theory of consciousness. See Zahavi, *Self-Awareness and Alterity*, especially 69–75. I have argued that something like the analysis of the relationship between the twofold and the threefold structures of consciousness could go a long way in mediating the debate between Zahavi and Brough and Sokolowski; see Neal DeRoo, "Re-visiting the Zahavi-Brough/Sokolowski Debate," *Husserl Studies* 27.1 (2011): 1–12.

5. Also called at times by Husserl "prepredicative experience" or functioning subjectivity. These refer to the same basic functions, if from different perspectives.

6. One must be careful to note that affecting (*Affektion*) is a living quality belonging to the formal structure of association and constitution; it is not part of

the content of what is being intended (cf. Hua XI, 167–68;Ryan, "Passive and Active Elements," 43).

7. Cf. EU §§16–18. For more on these elements, see Ryan, "Passive and Active Elements." For a helpful summary of association, see John J. Drummond, "Time History and Tradition," 130–33.

8. *Reiz* is often translated as "stimulus," which, though perhaps misleading in some contexts, is helpful to us here to indicate the manner or the level on which this "pull" occurs: Just as the heat of the fire is a stimulus that prompts us to remove our hand without the active involvement of the ego but automatically, reflexively, so the allure (*Reiz*) of the thing stimulates the ego to constitute it (i.e., the thing), but to do so automatically, like a reflex, before the active involvement of the ego.

9. For this reason it is not entirely proper to speak here of objects, as only the categorical object is an object according to Husserl (EU, 81 n.1). One can say, though, as Husserl does, that without affecting "there would be no objects at all and no present organized with objects" (Hua XI, 164).

10. For those primarily familiar with the *Logical Investigations*, the use of "association" as a key term in Husserl may be surprising. In LI, Husserl is painstakingly detailed in his critique of empiricist and psychologistic uses of association. In this secondary sense, association belongs properly in the realm of "indication" and hence is accidental rather than necessary to the ego (unlike, e.g., the eidetic functioning of the ego at work in expression; cf. LI I,§§1–10). Derrida's reading of Husserl in *La Voix et la Phénomène* seems to point in the same direction as the later Husserl: Association is essential to the ego's functioning. The point that remains to be clarified, however, is whether association, as it works in these later texts, still belongs in the realm of indication as it does when understood along the lines of the empiricists and psychologists. Husserl seems to suggest that it does (EU, 78). The question of how this fits into Derrida's argument in *La Voix et la Phénomène* must be suspended for now.

11. This recalling is purely phenomenological, happening within the epoche and hence distinct from the recollection of empirical and psychological notions of association; cf. Hua XI, 117–18.

12. Cf. Alemany, "In Continuity."

13. Cf. Drummond, "Time History and Tradition," 133 ff. The full significance of this claim will become explicit in the conclusion.

14. Rudolf Bernet makes this point, though in somewhat different language, in "My Time and the Time of the Other." He suggests that, already with the recourse to history, the subject is opened up to the "time of the other." We cannot yet evaluate this proposal and must suspend an answer until at least part 2 of this book. For now let it mark a potential opening onto Levinas's analyses from within Husserl's phenomenology.

15. Cf., for example, Hua XI, 120 where Husserl speaks of passivity as "the founding level of all the active-logical processes."

16. This seems to be in line, to a certain extent, with Zahavi's understanding of Husserl's theory of consciousness in *Self-Awareness and Alterity*, where he states

that two of the levels differentiated by Husserl are but two different ways of looking at one and the same thing, and hence there are only two distinct things at issue (80).

17. Cf. EU §§80–83 and Hua XI, 3. For more, see also Ryan, "Active and Passive Elements," 49. The issue of empirical types and their relation to general types and to different levels of *eidos* would need to be examined further in any attempt to distill a distinctly phenomenological epistemology. Such an attempt must be bracketed here, though I hope to show that futurity would play an important role in any such attempt.

18. I do not wish to either condone or condemn the suggestion that there is a qualitative difference between humans and animals and that this difference is based on humans possessing reason and animals not possessing it. There are arguments for both sides, and that discussion is not crucial to the argument of this chapter. For now, let us merely adopt it as a hypothetical.

19. Much later Husserl will begin to use the language of instincts also for the levels of passive constitution in humans. James Mensch ties together several references spread over the C manuscripts into a coherent theory of the instincts in his *Husserl's Account of our Consciousness of Time.*

20. This raises the question of whether or not the animals in our scenario "perceive" the world, properly speaking. The answer comes down to one's definition of perception. Our argument so far would seem to suggest that perception, as a conscious act (in the pregnant sense of that term), lies on the third level of constitution and hence cannot be experienced by those animals we posited as not possessing that level. However, since the technical Husserlian definition of perception is an original giving to consciousness (a presentifying), Husserl can use perception for even the second level of constitution. On this level one has to distinguish perception as a type of intuition (i.e., a presentifying one) from perception as a possible conscious act. For Husserl, perception would not be, strictly speaking, an act but rather an intuition.

21. The distinction between *bedeutung* and *sinn* in phenomenological theories of knowledge is significant and cannot be fully elaborated here. The most significant point for our current context is perhaps that sense is not equivalent to an attitude of the active ego (see. Hua III, 191). For more on this distinction, especially as it relates to Levinas's reception of Husserl, see Drabinski, *Sensibility and Singularity*, 25–28.

22. See Ryan, "Passive and Active Elements," 46.

23. We must bracket the epistemological discussion of the move from the empirical type of passive constitution to the general type of active constitution, and the subsequent move (within active constitution) from the general type to the *eidos*, as such epistemological questions will distract us from the question of futurity, which remains our goal.

24. One could, I suppose, characterize this activation of interest as an activation or change of intentionality. To do so, however, one must be careful to adequately distinguish between different levels or concepts of intentionality in Husserlian

phenomenology. See Mohanty, *Concept of Intentionality*. We will revisit the question of intentionality throughout the remainder of this work.

25. Husserl's account of interest is greatly expanded by Scheler, who distinguishes it from "attention," "perception," and "experienced efficacy." See Scheler, *Gesammelte Werke II*, especially 164 ff; see also Steinbock, *Home and Beyond*, 151–57.

26. For a more thorough treatment of the reciprocal influence of passive and active syntheses, see DeRoo, "Phenomenological Insights into Oppression."

27. Hence Husserl can also refer to expectative association as "inductive association" (Hua XI, 120). One could be tempted to think that induction lies in the sphere of active synthesis, given its use in scientific judgments; however, induction remains wholly in the sphere of passive synthesis. Husserl will contend that the scientific and philosophico-logical use of induction is in fact founded on an earlier, experiential, and passive level of induction (Hua VI, 29), which is ubiquitous in all human practices and experience (Hua VI, 51; see also Mohanty, *Edmund Husserl's Theory of Meaning*, 142–43).

28. Nor would I be surprised: Surprise also presupposes a system of expectations that are then unfulfilled. This is why I do not find someone's loud yell to be startling during a sporting event at which I am a spectator, though I would find the same yell quite startling in the study carrels of a library. In the first case, I expect such noises, so the yell is a fulfillment of what is expected. In the second case, I expect the maintenance of a certain level of silence, and the yell disappoints (and disrupts) this expectation.

29. For more on the distinction between the mode of intuition and the mode of nonintuitive differentiation, see chapter, 1 section 2; Hua XXXIII, 227 ff.

3. Experience and the Essential Possibility of Anticipation

1. Though, strictly speaking, protention and expectation also bear some essential relation to intentionality, they do so in a particular sense of intentionality that does not bear on the consciousness of objects. The shift in intentionality at work here, that is, the shift to intentionality as consciousness of objects properly speaking, bears a specific relation to constituting consciousness, a relation that Levinas will accuse Husserl of equating with intentionality itself. We will return to this issue in part 2.

2. Some might question the wisdom of trying to determine anticipation by focusing only on hope. There are two potential objections here: (1) It is not wise to seek characteristics of the genus by reflecting on only one of the species; (2) hope has some unique characteristics that make it a particularly bad model of anticipation. The first of these objections might be warranted if I talked *only* about hope, but, as we will see, hope will be the starting point that will enable us to speak, if only in passing, also of other distinct kinds of anticipation. The second objection has some merit, but I do not feel that Smith's account of hope in DH is sufficiently idiosyncratic to warrant its exclusion as a potential type of anticipation. Whether this reflects poorly on my account of anticipation or Smith's account of

hope—or neither—is an issue that we must suspend for now. I thank Jeffrey Bloechl for bringing this objection to my attention.

3. This holds true even if that subject is constituted by alterity, as the phenomenologies of both Levinas and Marion suggest.

4. Here we see a distinct difference between futurity in a Husserlian phenomenology of constituting consciousness and futurity after its reconception by Levinas. For Levinas, the future must occur as an "absolute surprise"; indeed this is the very mark of futurity itself (see TO, 76). This might suggest, in light of our later analyses, that Smith's analysis of hope bears some necessary connection to eschatology, but we are not yet in a position to evaluate this claim.

5. Equating intentionality with an act would mark a particularly Husserlian understanding of intentionality. We will see in the analysis of anticipation below and especially in part 2, that a phenomenological account of futurity will begin to problematize this account of intentionality, opening it up to a deeper (and arguably more phenomenological) meaning by problematizing the distinction between subject and object.

6. We will return to this theme in the next section.

7. This does not rule out the possibility of radical hope, of the hope for something radically different from our current conditions. Even the most utopian of thinkers, in Moltmann's sense of that term as indicating a radical break between present and future, still understands the present as in some way providing evidence for his hope in the radically different future. The utopian Christian believes in the power of God, not just in the eschaton but also here and now; the utopian Marxist believes in the working of dialectical materialism, not just in the future but here and now; and so on. See Moltmann, *Theology of Hope* and *The Coming of God*. However, there does seem to be a certain difficulty in getting from one's horizons of expectation to the "radically new" in a futurity that is based on a strong sense of constituting subjectivity, as is Husserl's. The "radically new" becomes a main theme in the phenomenological account of futurity when the privilege of the constituting subject is called into question via a revaluation of intentionality (see chapters 4 and 5 below).

8. I reiterate that this is not as nonradical as it may at first seem. The point is not that nothing surprising can occur; the point is that we must understand the present in such a way as to admit of surprises—we must acknowledge that we can be surprised. We will return to this in part 3.

9. I use the term in its standard theological usage. It will not gain its specifically phenomenological meaning until our analysis of Levinas in part 2.

10. This is why Husserl says that there is no essential distinction between clarifying and confirming modes of intuition during remembering (Hua XI, 80–81).

11. We will return to this theme of enjoyment, especially its phenomenological or ontological weight, when we examine Levinas's conception of time in *Totality and Infinity* in chapter 5.

12. This, of course, is different from experiences that I like or that make me happy; enjoyment here bears only its phenomenological sense of an experience in

which the subject is totally absorbed, totally engrossed, totally satisfied. See translator's note on PA, 20.

13. This is reminiscent of Husserl's analysis of indication in *Logical Investigations*. To this extent, I suppose, there are affinities between anticipation and language, though I am not sure this would satisfy Romano ("Awaiting").

14. See, e.g., Hua XI, 3: "[I]t is inconceivable that a perceptual object could be given in the entirety of its sensibly intuitive features, literally, from all sides at once in a self-contained perception."

15. But also, perhaps, of nonpresence; see Lawlor, "Temporality and Spatiality."

16. There we read Husserl himself talking of a "phenomenologically clarifiable infinite anticipation" that "*as* an anticipation, has an evidence of its own." Derrida makes a similar claim: "The phenomenological attitude is first an availability of attention for the future of a truth which is always already announced" (OoG, 148).

17. This is at least true when I promise to do something (e.g., the promise to honor and cherish your spouse given in the wedding vows), if not always true when I promise-that something (e.g., I promise that I have been faithful). The latter is more accurately a case of swearing (I swear that it is true) than of promising, as the object of promising-that is always verifiable in the present, whereas no promise-to can be presently verified.

18. Though not necessarily a passive waiting. For a phenomenological analysis of waiting, see Romano, "Awaiting."

19. Which is also the issue of the nonepistemological nature of phenomenology itself. We will see that Levinas will combine the nonepistemological nature of phenomenology with an essential openness (given inchoately in the mode of a hint or promise above) to challenge the privilege accorded to transcendental subjectivity within phenomenology (at least as he understood its being employed by Husserl and Heidegger). In doing so, Levinas will focus on the openness to alterity as the root of his nonepistemological challenge to transcendental subjectivity. This challenge is at work in the evocation of "ethics" here, especially in "ethics as first philosophy." See chapter 4, especially section 3.

20. See chapter 2, based on Hua XI, 125–26.

4. Phenomenology, Openness, and Ethics as First Philosophy

1. This begins already in Levinas's dissertation; see TIHP.

2. See Bernet, "Levinas's Critique of Husserl," 89.

3. Ibid.

4. See chapter 3 above, especially notes 5 and 8.

5. See also Bernet, "Levinas's Critique of Husserl," 89.

6. I will henceforth follow the standard practice of translating *l'autrui* (other person) as Other. This is to distinguish it from *l'autre* (other). Cf. Translator's introduction to TO.

7. Contra certain readers of Levinas who suggest that the "ruptures and interruptions of moral consciousness are too much for phenomenology to contend

with. . . . To fully engage the ethical relation, one has to leave phenomenology for an ethical (metaphysical?) language" (Drabinski, *Sensibility and Singularity*, 5). Drabinski himself does not read Levinas this way. His comment is made to summarize the views of Jan de Greef, Stephan Strasser, Jacques Colette, and others. See de Greef, "Levinas et la phénoménologie"; Strasser, "Antiphénoménologie et phénoménologie dans la philosophie d'Emmanuel Levinas"; Colette, "Lévinas et la phénoménologie husserlienne"; Large, "On the Meaning of the Word Other in Levinas."

8. This seems to run counter to the proposals of some other readers of Levinas, who believe that his critique is motivated by concerns brought from someone outside the phenomenological tradition (usually Rosenzweig). As evidence of this, mention is made of the preface to *Totality and Infinity*, where Rosenzweig's *Star of Redemption* is described by Levinas as "too often present in this book to be cited" (TI, 28). My own proposal here, however, tends to focus on the statement immediately following this: "[T]he presentation and development of the notions employed [in *Totality and Infinity*] owe everything to the phenomenological method" (TI, 28). For an analysis of this passage, see Cohen, "Levinas, Rosenzweig and the Phenomenologies of Husserl and Heidegger." Other statements of this "supplementary" (cf. Drabinski, *Sensibility and Singularity*, 4–6) reading of Levinas's critique of phenomenology can be found in Cohen, *Elevations*; Gibbs, *Correlations in Rosenzweig and Levinas*; and, in a distinctly Heideggerian register, Manning, *Interpreting Otherwise than Heidegger*.

9. Let me state here explicitly that I am not intending to show that Levinas's readings of Husserl ground his other philosophical and religious claims or vice versa; rather I am merely trying to show that Levinas's philosophical claims echo—and greatly expand upon—certain statements of Husserl's already and, further, that Levinas himself saw and understood this.

10. Several readers of Levinas interpret him distinctly in this way: Drabinski, *Sensibility and Singularity*; Wyschogrod, *Emmanuel Levinas*, especially xxii, where she states, "Levinas's thought is nevertheless a phenomenology"; Peperzak, *Beyond*, especially 84–85, where he claims that "Levinas's oeuvre itself is the illustration of an expanded phenomenology and ontology."

11. See, e.g., Mohanty's discussion in *The Concept of Intentionality* of (at least) two distinct accounts of intentionality in Husserl, as well as still different accounts of it offered by Brentano, Heidegger, Sartre, Merleau-Ponty, and Ricoeur.

12. Such a thesis is too large to be fully argued for here. Fortunately Drabinski has argued for it at length, and compellingly in my opinion, in *Sensibility and Singularity*, so it is not necessary for me to repeat the entirety of the argument in the present context. Instead I will attempt to highlight key moments of this argument to prove the legitimacy of the claim and so to set the stage for our analysis of Levinas's account of the future in the next chapter.

13. "World" here must be understood in the distinctly phenomenological sense discussed in chapter 2 and not in a physical-materialist sense, or any other sense constitutive of the "natural attitude." Indeed these other senses of "world"

must be suspended in the *epoche* that makes possible the phenomenological reduction(s). See "World as Phenomenological Problem," in Landgrebe, *The Phenomenology of Edmund Husserl*, 122–48.

14. Cohen and Smith translate *sens* as "meaning" throughout DEH. I, however, follow Drabinski in translating it as "sense," for reasons that I hope will become clear in the following discussion of *Sinngebung* and sensibility. For more on the difference between *sinn, bedeutung,* and *meinung,* and the difficulties of translating these into French and English, see Drabinski, *Sensibility and Singularity*, 25–28.

15. Though the world that bestows sense must be differentiated from the brute existence of the *il y a*, which has no meaning, no sense. The world can bestow sense because sense is first bestowed on the world by the Other. Hence the reversed *Sinngebung* is ultimately an intention from the Other (through the world) to me.

16. Though I have begun here with the 1940 essay, Levinas's impetus to reevaluate Husserlian intentionality as putting us in relation with the reality of concrete life is found already in his dissertation of 1930. See TIHP, 158.

17. In addition to passive synthesis, Husserl will call this action "axiological" or "practical" attitudes and intentions (Hua IV, 7; Hua III, 244).

18. Though one cannot rule out the possibility that Levinas was brought to this realization, and even perhaps to this understanding of Husserl, by some other considerations, be they investigations of particular phenomena (e.g., insomnia, desire, ethics) or the work of other thinkers (e.g., Rosenzweig). That is, Levinas's reading of Husserl in TIHP is different from his reading of Husserl in some of the later texts under discussion here; whatever the reason for this difference, however, my point is to illustrate that the difference was still one of *reading Husserl* and that Levinas at least saw a continuity between his philosophical project and Husserl's.

19. See also Mirvish, "The Presuppositions of Husserl's Presuppositionless Philosophy."

20. Derrida also makes this point about phenomenology in *Speech and Phenomena*, as we will see later.

21. This seems to be true of Derrida's critique of Husserl as well. See ' "Genesis and Structure' and Phenomenology" in *Writing and Difference*, 154–231, especially 163.

22. See chapter 1, p. 20.

23. This calls to mind Lacoste's characterization of anticipation as "(pre-) experience and (pre-)givenness." See PA, 31, and chapter 3 above. We will return to the significance of this in later chapters.

24. See also our earlier discussion of the role of *Gefuhl* (feeling) in passive synthesis (p. 32).

25. Levinas's notion of the trace makes this point especially clearly in terms of temporality and the non-re-presentability of the subject's past. I will discuss this in greater detail in the next chapter.

26. See Levinas, "Lévy-Bruhl and Contemporary Philosophy," especially 41.

27. Critchley, *The Ethics of Deconstruction*, 3–13.

28. I recognize that "derivative of" and "the condition of" are not synonymous; hence the disjunction here is a true disjunction, not the joining of like with like. The question of the precise status of the relationship between 'material' sensibility and the exteriority of the face cannot yet be settled. In time the answer will emerge more clearly.

29. See OB, passim; GDT, 115; Levinas, "Language and Proximity," 114. I do have time to go into the specifics of the differences between the face-to-face encounter of *Totality and Infinity* and the situation of substitution or hostage described in *Otherwise than Being*. For now, I hope it will suffice to suggest that the two, despite differences, maintain a similar trajectory and that substitution provides a clarification of the face-to-face rather than a radical departure. See Levinas, "Preface to the German edition of *Totality and Infinity*," 197. I attempt to argue for this continuity in more detail in DeRoo, "Re-constituting Phenomenology."

30. This could also read "The face of the other, which remains a modality of sensation, expresses the 'eminence' of the Other . . .". The exact nature of the relationship between the Other and others, between *l'autrui* and *l'autre*, is up for debate. Derrida, for example, contends, in *Gift of Death*, that "every other is wholly Other" and that "every Other is wholly other," an ambiguity encapsulated in the French *tout autre est tout autre*.

31. That is, affective immersion in the elements. See my discussion of enjoyment and *jouissance* in chapter 3 above.

32. Or, from *Otherwise than Being*: ' "Me" is not an inimitable nuance of *Jemeinigkeit* that would be added onto a being belonging to the genus 'soul' or 'man' or 'individual,' and would thus be common to several souls, men and individuals, making reciprocity possible among them from the first. The uniqueness of the ego . . . is the other in the same, the psyche" (OB, 126).

33. See Marion, *Being Given* and *Reduction and Givenness*. Marion's notion of an interlocuted or called subject is very reminiscent of Levinas's account of the subject as I have described it here.

34. Levinas, "Entretien," 10.Cf. Drabinski, *Sensibility and Singularity*, 8.

35. Levinas more explicitly discusses the impossibility of nonhuman animals constituting the Other in The Name of a Dog" and in "The Paradox of Morality." See also Llewelyn, "Am I Obsessed by Bobby?"and *The Middle Voice of Ecological Conscience*, especially chap. 3.

36. The issue of the status of the subject in the primordial relation is far from settled in Levinas scholarship, in large part because it is far from settled (and stable) in Levinas himself. While his language seems to equivocate at times, I put this down to the difficulty inherent in discussing matters that take place "otherwise than being or beyond essence." In fact I think that *Otherwise than Being* is more consistent on this point. I thank John Drabinski for providing a coherent account, via the notion of sense, of a presubjective encounter within the logic

of *Totality and Infinity* (*Sensibility and Singularity*, 230n.29). See also DeRoo, "Re-constituting Phenomenology."

5. From Eschatology to Awaiting: Futurity in Levinas

1. Indeed relating "ethics" in this sense to (the reversal of) *Sinngebung* threatens to recast it precisely as an epistemological exercise. As we go forward, I hope it will become clear why this is not primarily an epistemological *Sinngebung*—or, if it is, we must significantly reconceive of what we mean by epistemology.

2. This emerging is detailed in *Existence and Existents*. The title is a poor translation of Levinas's *De l'existence à l'existant* (1947), which could also be translated as *From Existence to the Existent*, a translation that better captures the movement characteristic of the text. Much of the content of *Existence and Existents* is similar to that in *Time and the Other*. I will focus mainly on the latter.

3. In this regard, it seems to have certain affinities with Derrida's notions of *différance* and *khora*. These latter terms will be discussed in greater detail in part 3.

4. Westphal, "The Welcome Wound," 216.

5. Cf. *Being and Time*, especially §§14, 15.

6. Here we see in a nutshell the major aspect of Levinas's critique of Heidegger, namely that Heidegger ultimately reduces everything to the self (everything becomes something *for me*, for *my* projects, etc.), whereas Levinas wants to more radically place the self in relation with that which is other than it; that is, he wants to place the self in a world (and in relations with people) that is there on its own. This does not make it *for-itself* in the Sartrean sense; rather the world is neither for-itself nor for-me; it is for nothing, anonymous, just there (*il y a*). The world can become endowed with sense and thereby a gift that can be given by or to the Other (cf. TI, 76–77), but this is subsequent to its being the *il y a*.

7. Compare this account of enjoyment to Lacoste's phenomenological use of enjoyment in "The Phenomenality of Anticipation" and my discussion of it in chapter 3.

8. Here we see already the basis of much of Levinas's critique of phenomenology as discussed in chapter 4.

9. There are obvious Hegelian overtones to this description of work, overtones that are not, I think, accidental: If nothing is more totalizing than the Ego, no philosophy is more totalizing than Hegel's; on this score, cf. Derrida's "Violence and Metaphysics," a more thorough elaboration of which will occur in part 3, when we turn to Derrida's contributions to a phenomenology of futurity, contributions that develop in large part out of Derrida's reading of Levinas.

10. Cf. Heidegger, *Being and Time*, §§46–53.

11. Cf. ibid.,especially §26; TO, 41; VM, 90.

12. One can see here the beginnings of Levinas's notion of "eschatology," which will be examined in more detail later.

13. Here we have already a foreshadowing of the development of diachronic time in Levinas's later works.

14. For more on the difference between need and desire, and their relation to ontology and metaphysics, respectively, see Westphal, "The Welcome Wound," 213.

15. We will return to the relationship between the promise and that which is "always to come" in part 3, when we examine Derrida's notion of the messianic.

16. This is reminiscent of the distinction between the striving of protention and concrete expectations.

17. Hence the analysis of futurity causes us to pause before Adriaan Peperzak's assessment that "[t]he second chapter of *Totality and Infinity* describes the manner in which nature is made to submit by the ego through consumption, dwelling, manipulation, work, and technology, as well as through aesthetic contemplation," a project that Peperzak admits is never fully completed (*To the Other*, 42). Futurity helps us see that the second chapter of *Totality and Infinity* announces both the submission of nature to the ego and the openness that entails that this submission will never be completed; in this section of TI, then, are announced both Husserl's constituting intentionality and its inversion in Levinas's ethical or metaphysical intentionality.

18. Though, as mentioned earlier, there is a certain amount of confusion or ambiguity in Levinas on this point. Later on in *Totality and Infinity*, for example, he will say that time recognizes the distance from self to self (TI, 210), a point that both coincides with *Time and the Other*'s analysis of the distance between the self (as Ego) and the self (as Me) and conflicts with *Time and the Other*'s analysis of time as the relation to the Other.

19. The date of this essay is important, in that it shows that the "move" from the ethics of the face-to-face in *Totality and Infinity* to the ethics of substitution in *Otherwise than Being* was begun *before* the publication of Derrida's "Violence and Metaphysics," and hence the motivation for that "move" was internal to Levinas's project, and is not the result of Derrida's criticisms.

20. Levinas will take up the criticism of Heidegger's being-toward-death, begun implicitly in *Time and the Other*, more explicitly in *God, Death and Time*. We must suspend an investigation into these criticisms for the time being.

21. There are interesting resonances here with Derrida's account of metaphor in "White Mythology." This and other similarities between the philosophies of Levinas and Derrida marked throughout this work begin implicitly to justify the move we will make from Levinasian futurity to Derrida's *différance* and the messianic. These themes will be revisited more explicitly—and several key distinctions also noted—in part 3.

22. The latter is the name of an article first published by Levinas in 1968. It was "the germ" of *Otherwise than Being* (see OB, 193n.1).

23. Derrida's suggestion in "Violence and Metaphysics" that Levinas does not adequately account for the role of phenomenology in his ethics applies much more forcefully to the writings before "The Trace of the Other" than it does to the writings after that essay (including *Otherwise than Being*). If Levinas's later works are able to avoid some of the problems highlighted by Derrida, they still do not sufficiently account for the role of genesis in phenomenology and hence

for the role of phenomenology in Levinasian ethics. Phrased alternately, and in a manner that will necessarily prove unclear at the present moment but will be clarified in part 3, Levinas's philosophy can perhaps accommodate *différance* but not the messianic. Interestingly, supplementing Levinas's philosophy with his theology might begin to remedy this situation, before any move to Derrida is necessary (though whether one could supplement Levinas's philosophy with his theology without doing so by some move through Derrida, even if an implicit one, remains to be seen).

24. Again, we will return to this strange notion of unity in difference with Derrida's account of futurity that builds on both Levinas's and Husserl's accounts of futurity.

25. One can distinguish in Levinas at least four distinct "moments" of the self: the ego (self as constituting power), the subject (self as continuous), the oneself or ipseity (self as infinite depth/uniqueness), the (empirical) person encountered in experience. Levinas's project, especially in *Otherwise than Being*, is to show that the subjectivity of the self is based on its ipseity, not its egoity; that is, the self is continuous (and hence can be ethical in the traditional sense: can make promises, etc.) not because of its constituting power, but because it is constituted in responsibility.

26. For more on the distinction between history and the time of ethics, cf. Bernet, "My Time and the Time of the Other."

27. Cf. Romano, "Awaiting."

28. Levinas's notion—though not very well developed—of "synopsia" attempts to explain how the subject experiences this disquieting interruption nevertheless as a unity. Synopsia is "the unifying force of consciousness that continually integrates the interruption that [Levinas] calls 'diachrony'" (GDT, 259n.5; see also 116; *Of God Who Comes to Mind*, 60, 64, 139).

29. Therefore fulfilling the goal of *Totality and Infinity*, namely to find an account of subjectivity that is able to contain within itself the infinite as that which is more than it can contain. See TI, 48, 79.

30. Westphal speaks of Desire as "for the contact that converts, that inverts, that overwhelms, that decenters, that so radically changes one's mode of being that one could be said to exist otherwise than being"("The Welcome Wound," 213).

6. Levinas's Unique Contribution to Futurity in Phenomenology

1. In this way, Levinas perhaps opens himself up again to the infinite regress problem that caused Husserl to posit absolute consciousness as self-constituting. For if I am most basically constituted by the Other, who constitutes the Other? We would need an infinite regress of constituting Others, or a self-constituting Self that would ground all others. However, Levinas avoids this objection, as it were, by embracing and then redefining it. By reinscribing the meaning of infinity, he can posit the Other as infinite, thereby removing the sting of the *regressus ad infinitum*. This reinterpretation of infinity will take on added significance in Derrida's interactions with Levinas and Husserl, discussed in part 3.

2. We see in this parenthetical remark the two main strands of the early French appropriation of Husserl: first, Levinas, and second, Merleau-Ponty. I am clearly suggesting a deep continuity between the two projects, though the specific role of other people would be the fundamental distinction that remains between them: Where Merleau-Ponty seems to focus more on people as indicative of a wider phenomenon (broadly speaking, as institutions), Levinas seems to prefer to focus on the individual person I see before me. The significance of this distinction would have to be brought out further before one could fully clarify the relationship between these two projects.

3. This can be mapped on to the four senses of the Self in Levinas described earlier (see chapter 5, note 62): Here we have ipseity; the self as subject is shown in the continuity exhibited by the flow of absolute consciousness; the self as Ego takes place in world-constituting abilities of passive synthesis; and the empirical self corresponds to the active engagement with the world of the third level of Husserl's constituting consciousness.

4. Cf. Husserl's "Origin of Geometry" in Hua VI, and Derrida's introduction to it in *Edmund Husserl's* Origin of Geometry.

5. We will pursue this point further in part 3, when we turn to Derrida's account of futurity, especially *différance*.

6. Though the notion of self involved in Husserl marks it as also essentially different from Levinas's conception of the *il y* a; as such, the similarity is strictly formal. This formal similarity appears in Husserl's development of a theory of the instincts in the C manuscripts, a theory that occasionally explicitly relates to protention and time-consciousness (see especially Ms. C 16). James Mensch ties together several references to the instincts spread over the C manuscripts into a coherent theory of the instincts in a paper titled "Instincts." Material from this unpublished paper is included in Mensch, *Husserl's Account of our Consciousness of Time*.

7. It is on this point that one could begin to undertake a project of comparing Levinas and Henry as phenomenologists.

8. Further, these similarities help us make sense of the otherwise ambiguous transition in Levinas from the impersonal striving of existence to the sensibility of the world of the subject. What the distinct modes of intuition make possible in world-constitution, the *il y a* makes possible (if this is the right way of talking about this in Levinas) in sensibility. Levinas's radical reinterpretation of protention, discussed below, would be the starting point of such a "possibility."

9. This awaiting is based on the trace, then, and must be related to the to-come of Derrida's messianic, as will be discussed in part 3.

10. Merleau-Ponty's notion of "style" would seem to describe this passivity; See "Indirect Language and the Voices of Silence." See also Singer, "Merleau-Ponty on the Concept of Style"; Santilli, "The Notion of Style in Merleau-Ponty."

11. Cf. Levinas's account of the idea of the infinite in Descartes as being "lodged within a thought that cannot contain it" (OB, 146–47).

12. Though he does not evoke absolute consciousness here, Levinas does associate synopsia explicitly with the "immanence" of time in Husserl (GDT, 116).

13. This is also the key theme of "Substitution," the fourth chapter of *Otherwise than Being.*

14. For more on this notion of optimalization, see Gyllenhammer, "The Passivity of Optimalizing Practices"; Steinbock, *Home and Beyond*, especially 138–47.

15. It is this redefinition of protention that would underlie a theory of testimony and the necessity of discourse: If there is a ceaseless striving of the sense of the other in me, then I must acknowledge this alterity within me, and silence would truly be the worst violence, that is, the worst way of failing to recognize the alterity of the other (because I would take it only as myself; cf. "Substitution"). One can see this in Levinas's invocation of discourse in *Totality and Infinity* and in Derrida's statement that the worst violence is "the violence of the night which precedes or represses discourse" (VM, 117; note too the use of the night metaphor, here and in Levinas's invocation of the futurity of the *il y a* in TI, 142). For more on discourse in Levinas, see Dudiak, *The Intrigue of Ethics.*

16. Indeed the object of anticipation can even be something negative, as was discussed in chapter 3. As such, the object of anticipation can also be negatively ethical, that is, unethical in a traditional sense of the word "ethics"; we can anticipate the knock of the Gestapo on our door, for example. Such an anticipation would still be premised on a certain openness and hence would remain "ethical" in the Levinasian sense of that word as developed so far. This clearly points to a major problem, that of the relationship between Levinasian ethics and ethics as traditionally conceived; we will return to this problem in chapter 9, where it will emerge also in Derrida's discussion of the promise and the *arrivant(e)* as being potentially helpful or harmful—we have no way, right now, of knowing for sure.

17. In phenomenology more generally, the idea of intentionality begins to describe this essential openness, as we will see in chapter 9.

18. This would seem to help Levinas avoid some of Derrida's arguments in "Violence and Metaphysics" regarding the impossibility of the appearance of the Wholly Other.

19. We will see that, for Derrida, the subject is, in a certain sense, both the recipient and the content of the promise. See NM and chapters 8 and 9 below.

20. In terms of intentionality, this would suggest that the self is not the agent of intentionality (i.e., the one "doing" intentionality, performing intentional acts) but is the content, so to speak, of intentionality: The self *is* intentionality. Indeed this must be the case if intentionality is to be a "transcendental foundation of objectivity" rather than merely the "psychological 'character' of thought" (PG, 1) that would not avoid the charge of psychologism leveled against Husserl by the neo-Kantians (cf. PCC, especially 73–78) and that Husserl takes great pains to dissociate himself from (e.g., in the "Prolegomena" to LI).

7. Genesis, Beginnings, and Futurity

1. A hypothesis supported by Leonard Lawlor; see *Derrida and Husserl*, especially chap.1, "Genesis as the Basic Problem of Phenomenology." In this chapter, Lawlor claims that "only an examination of Fink's 1933 essay shows that Derrida's

philosophy—his deconstruction—is continuous with Husserl's phenomenology" (11). It is my hope that the present work demonstrates another avenue that can reveal the continuity between Husserl and Derrida, namely, futurity, though I will return to an analysis of Fink's 1933 essay (PCC) in chapter 9.

2. In describing genesis as bringing together the "contradictory" meanings of absolute origin and temporal immanence, we begin to see what further analysis will only make more explicit: At work in genesis, and therefore in phenomenology more generally, is a tension between Levinasian (absolute surprise) and Husserlian (temporal horizons) accounts of futurity.

3. Anthony Steinbock discusses in more detail the genetic movements of Husserl's phenomenology in *Home and Beyond*.

4. Cf. the overtones of the analysis of anticipation as (pre-)experience in chapter 3.

5. As Derrida will make clear in *Speech and Phenomena* but also in "'Genesis and Structure' and Phenomenology," "Ousia and Grammē," and even, as I will argue momentarily, "Violence and Metaphysics."

6. For example, in §81 of *Ideas I*, when Husserl acknowledges that the analyses of *Ideas I*, the absolute that is discovered there, "is, in truth, not what is ultimate" and highlights the need for a later examination of internal time-consciousness to access "what is ultimately and truly absolute." (In a footnote [n.26 in Kersten's English translation], he claims that this is achieved and set out in lectures delivered in Göttingen in 1905, lectures that are part of the basis for Hua X.) Unfortunately for Husserl, Derrida will demonstrate in *The Problem of Genesis* that the sentence that follows these quotes does not hold true. In that sentence Husserl claims, "Fortunately, we can leave out of account the enigma of consciousness of time in our preliminary analyses without endangering their rigor" (Hua III, 163).

7. The phrase "already constituted" (*déjà constitué*) or "already there" (*déjà là*) occurs no fewer than fifty times in *The Problem of Genesis*. Lawlor lists these uses in *Derrida and Husserl*, 252n.71.

8. On this, see PCC, passim.

9. See chapter 1, n.2; chapter 2, n.4 and DeRoo, "Revisiting the Zahavi-Brough/Sokolowski Debate."

10. Similarly, though the search for essences is confined to the sphere of the already constituted, and hence cannot accurately take account of genesis, Derrida still claims that the "absolute beginning of all philosophy must be essentialist" (PG, 138).

11. We will examine Derrida's (somewhat surprising) use of this term in section 3 of this chapter.

12. Or, perhaps more accurately, to avoid that dichotomy altogether.

13. By this phrase Derrida seems to mean transcendental constitution; to describe this as "intentionality" is to decide already the nature of intentionality along the theoretical lines of Husserl. The struggle between fact and essence, between being and sense, takes place within the sense or definition of intentionality itself.

14. In *The Problem of Genesis*, Derrida shows this to be the case with Husserl's entire discourse on the "infinite task" of philosophy, beginning already in *Ideas I* and continuing through the *Cartesian Meditations* up to the Vienna Lecture, the *Crisis*, and the "Origin of Geometry." In the introduction to his French translation of the "Origin of Geometry," Derrida discusses this in more detail.

15. This phrasing of the problem of genesis, and the claim that such passage occurs originarily, that is, that the originary situation of the phenomenological subject is one that already links (without uniting) primitive existence and originary sense, helps explain the otherwise enigmatic statement from Derrida's *Introduction* to Husserl's 'Origin of Geometry': "The Absolute is passage" (OoG, 149). See also John D. Caputo, "The Return of Anti-Religion," §6: "If there were something like a law in 'deconstruction' this 'ultra-transcendentality' is the law, meaning 'the necessity of the pathway (*parcours*),' the *passage through the transcendental* to a displaced quasi-, post-, or ultra-transcendental, which always leaves its tracks in the text it passes through." There is contained in this quote a reference to OG, 60–62.

16. Here, as I will continue to do throughout, I change Hobson's translation of *antéprédicative* from "antepredicative" to "prepredicative" in order to maintain continuity with our earlier discussions of Husserl and prepredicative experience. I will no longer mark this modification, which occurs every time one reads "prepredicative" in a direct quotation from *The Problem of Genesis*.

17. Though Derrida made significant additions to "Violence and Metaphysics" for its 1967 publication, the section titled "Difference and Eschatology" constituted the entire second half of the 1964 version of the essay. This is not to say that additions were not made to this section also, but merely to note that already in 1964, the reference to eschatology was prominent. This is significant given that "La Trace de l'Autre" was published in 1963, after most of the essay was already written. Hence Derrida "can make but brief allusions" to that text in this essay (VM, 311n.1). Therefore the Levinasian account of futurity with which Derrida was working at the time was largely confined to the "first" period of Levinas's thought on time, as discussed in chapter 5 above. For more on the evolution of "Violence and Metaphysics" over time, and the differences between the 1963 and 1967 versions, see Bernasconi, "The Trace of Levinas in Derrida"; Bernasconi, "Levinas and Derrida"; Bernasconi, "Skepticism in the Face of Philosophy."

18. See chapters 5 and 6.

19. Part of the difficulty here seems to stem from what Derrida holds to be Levinas's too simple opposition of constitution with encounter: "Constitution is not opposed to encounter. It goes without saying that constitution creates, constructs, engenders, nothing" (WD, 315–316n.44).

20. Here we see the difficulty in the "parallelism" between the empirical and the transcendental egos, a parallelism that must be rigorously maintained (to prevent empiricism and psychologism), but one in which the difference that holds between the two parallels is a difference of nothing. Derrida treats this theme at length in *Speech and Phenomena*.

21. Puzzlingly, the English translation leaves out precisely the phrase that I quote: "without relation to the same." Here is the French version of the first sentence following the quotation from Nicholas of Cusa: "En faisant du rapport à l'infiniment autre l'origine du langage, du sense et de la différence, sans rapport au même, Levinas se résout donc à trahir son intention dans son discourse philosophique" (*L'écriture et La différence*, 224).

22. See also chapter 4, section 2.

23. Derrida discusses this theme at length in the last two sections of *The Problem of Genesis*, as well as in *Edmund Husserl's* Origin of Geometry.

24. For a summary and a critique of the notion of "presuppositionlessness" in phenomenology, see Mirvish, "The Presuppositions of Husserl's Presuppositionless Philosophy."

25. Placing this in the context of a discussion of adequation now enables one to see insights into Marion's project of the "saturated phenomenon"; see Marion, *Being Given*, §§21–22; Marion, "The Saturated Phenomenon"; and John Panteleimon Manoussakis' very helpful discussion of this idea in *God after Metaphysics*, especially chap. 1.

26. Cf. Lawlor, *Derrida and Husserl*, 160.

27. See Derrida, *A Taste for the Secret*, 84: "The other is in me before me: . . . there is no 'I' that ethically makes room for the other, but rather an 'I' that is structured by the alterity within it."

28. Derrida discusses some of the potential danger of such logic of purity in "Faith and Knowledge" and its connection to problems of "auto-immunity" in "Auto-immunity."

29. Cf. Smith, *The Fall of Interpretation*, especially 127–29.

30. See Derrida, "The Principle of Reason," 132.

31. Perhaps is even a sign of sin; see Smith, *The Fall of Interpretation*.

32. See Baudrillard, "The Precession of Simulacra."

33. Cf. Husserl, "Origin of Geometry."

34. See, in just one of many possible examples, VM, 151, where Derrida uses the economics language of "circulation" to describe the relationship between Levinasian ethics, philosophical discourse, and the sameness of Being.

35. A discussion of the relationship between the thought of Derrida and that of Henry must, I think, begin here, with this complex account of life provided by Derrida.

36. For more on the distinction between *ipse* and *idem*, see Ricoeur, *Oneself as Another*.

37. Cf. Lawlor, *Husserl and Derrida*, 161–62.

8. From Deferring to Waiting (for the Messiah): Derrida's Account of Futurity

1. Recall Derrida's earlier quote that intelligibility and significance depend essentially on an anticipation that precedes past and present(PG, xxvi; see also chapter 7, pp. 101.

2. The following analysis will focus almost exclusively on the temporal aspect of *différance*, in keeping with the theme of this work. However, no discussion of *différance* can help but focus on both temporality and spatiality, given the temporalization of space and the spatialization of time at work in the play between differing and deferring in *différance*: "[D]ifferance . . . (is) (both) spacing (and) temporalizing" (SP, 143). In this regard, spatiality will always remain in our discussion, emerging again later under the guise of intersubjectivity, the to-another that opens space as much as time. Understood in this manner (i.e., as differing), spatiality will be a constant part of our discussion, even if it is rarely mentioned explicitly. For more on Derrida's notion of spatiality or spacing (*espacement*), see Derrida, "Khora"; Derrida, FK; Caputo, *Deconstruction in a Nutshell*, especially the section "Khora: Being Serious with Plato"; Sallis, *Chorology*; Lawlor, "Temporality and Spatiality"; Lawlor, *This Is Not Sufficient*, 41–45.

3. Cf. OG, especially 141–64.

4. The deferral that is characteristic of *différance* also characterizes the sign, and it raises a series of questions and problems for any epistemology premised on ideality, an ideality that must itself be infinitely deferred, not just in being signified, but already in Husserl, by the invocation of the Idea in the Kantian sense. This leads Derrida to state the enigmatic (but, for our current discussion, very interesting) phrase, "[Sense] does not await truth as expecting it; it only precedes truth as its anticipation" (SP, 98). Whether such a statement can withstand an analysis premised on our earlier arguments concerning Husserl's threefold sense of futurity remains—and must remain, at least for the time being—unclear.

5. Cf. Husserl, "Origin of Geometry."

6. Discussed in greater detail in Derrida, *Limited Inc.*

7. In this regard, recall also Levinas's discussion of death and its relation to futurity and alterity in *Time and the Other*, discussed in chapter 5.

8. Here we see the essentially 'ethical' (or at least Levinasian) theme at work in Derrida's account of spatiality.

9. Cf. VM; chapter 7, section 2B above.

10. Cf. Janicaud, "The Theological Turn of French Phenomenology."

11. For more on the relationship between future and past conceived as *telos* and *arche*, see Derrida, "The Ends of Man."

12. See also Lawlor, *Derrida and Husserl*, 211–12.

13. This "always-already called to us" is why the ghost is a *revenant* (one who comes back; see translator's note, SM, 177n.1) who "begins by coming back," as cited above. The connection between this and the diachronic and an-archic time of Levinas will be explored more fully in the final section of this chapter.

14. I follow Kamuf's translation of *l'à-venir* as future-to-come; see translator's note, SM 177n.5.

15. Cf. Derrida, *Adieu to Emmanuel Levinas*. This not only opens the future onto intersubjective elements, but it also, via both its intersubjective and prepositional aspects, shows the spatialization of time and the temporalization of space that is characteristic of *différance*. Hence we begin to challenge what seemed to

be our overemphasis on time at the expense of space by showing how the two are held together not just in *différance* but in Derrida's account of the future more generally.

16. For the Levinasian definition of eschatology, see TA, 349 and chapter 5 above. Briefly, the use of eschatology to denote the being-for-beyond-my-death is my justification for its use of this second sense of futurity in Derrida, that which must "carry beyond *present* life, beyond life as *my* life or *our* life. *In general*" (SM, xx). Though Derrida himself will seem at times to equate eschatology with teleology, I would suggest that this equation stems from a lack of proper understanding of the relationship between eschatology and phenomenological futurity. Whether this lack is Derrida's or theology's is a question that must be temporarily suspended.

17. It must be noted that, in *Specters of Marx*, Derrida does not always rigorously distinguish between the messianic and messianicity. It seems that, as time goes on (SM is the first book in which Derrida employs the term "messianic" in any kind of systematic way), Derrida begins more coherently to distinguish between messianicity and the messianic (cf. for example, "Faith and Knowledge: The Two Sources of 'Religion' within the Bounds of Reason Alone"), however, one can also not ignore certain exigencies of language: messianicity does not lend itself easily to an adjectival form other than messianic (e.g., "a messianic structure of experience" could be equivalent to "the structure of experience known as messianicity"). Hence, one must try to distinguish between the messianic (as umbrella term) and messianic (as the adjectival form of messianicity).

18. Elsewhere Derrida refers to a "bond between singularities," a bond that "cannot be contained within traditional concepts of community, obligation or responsibility". (NM, 47–48).

19. This heritage is also named in the title of the fifth chapter of *Specters of Marx*: "Apparition of the Inapparent: The Phenomenological 'Conjuring Trick.'"

20. Cf. Derrida, *Adieu to Emmanuel Levinas*; Derrida and Dufourmantelle, *Of Hospitality*.

21. Cf. Levinas's description of futurity as "an awaiting without something being awaited" (GDT, 115). See also chapter 5 above.

22. I am disagreeing here with James K.A. Smith, who would want to read the tension between the structure and history of experience in Derrida as a tension between Heideggerian and Levinasian influences, respectively. I read the tension as one between Levinasian and Husserlian influences, respectively, for reasons that will be explored further below. For Smith's argument, see his *Jacques Derrida*. Another name to introduce here would be Kierkegaard, or rather Climacus, and the *Philosophical Fragments*.

23. Cf. Derrida, *Adieu to Emmanuel Levinas*.

24. Prominent members of this group include James K.A. Smith (see "The Logic of Incarnation") and perhaps Kevin Hart (see, e.g., "Without").

25. For example, Smith, "Re-Kanting Postmodernism?"

26. I am purposive in calling this new "spin" non-Kantian rather than non-Husserlian. As I have been at pains to show throughout this book, the "Levinasian" reading that I am opposing here to the "Husserlian" reading is itself an outgrowth of the phenomenological project laid out by Husserl. In trying to balance these two moments (Levinasian and Husserlian) within one account of the messianic, then, Derrida is abandoning an exclusive universality that dismisses empiricism (e.g., that of Kant) while holding another universality (e.g., that of Husserl) in tension with a quasi-empirical nonuniversality (inspired by Levinas). This strange blend is captured in Derrida's enigmatic pursuit of a "universalizable culture of singularities" (FK, 56).

27. For example, in Kant's *Religion within the Limits of Reason Alone* and Eliade's *The Sacred and the Profane*. Another prominent proponent of a project similar to Eliade's is Cantwell Smith, *The Meaning and End of Religion*.

28. I am not trying to argue that Derrida's messianicity is a form of abstracted religion or politics. This, I believe, is to conflate messianicity with a messianism. On the other hand, I am also not arguing for or against the claim that Derrida is perhaps guilty of this conflation at times. Rather my purpose here is to argue that, *if* Derrida is guilty of this conflation, such a conflation is not necessary to the concept of the messianic; in other words, one can employ the messianic and talk of messianicity without immediately falling into an abstracted form of religion or politics.

29. Derrida, "Foi et savoir," 28.

30. On the "mystical foundation of authority," see also Derrida, "Force of Law," as well as Montaigne and Pascal.

31. Such a reading would have consequences for the entire understanding of Derrida's view of religion, and perhaps for his view of politics as well. Both religion and politics come together, for Derrida, in his notion of testimony. For one account of how this might work, see DeRoo, "The Testimonial Function of Reason and Religion in the Public Sphere."

32. It must be noted that 'trustworthiness' is no guarantee that the promise will be kept; it does not even, in a sense, deal with 'likeliness' or 'probability,' as these remain in the realm of inference and justification. Someone's being trustworthy does not entail that he will always keep his word. Nor is trustworthiness itself always a good thing; for example, one can trust that the Buffalo Bills or Chicago Cubs will find a way to lose the big game. They are trustworthy in this regard, but this is not a 'good' thing to be trustworthy about. Alternatively, someone can keep his word—live up to his promise in a 'trustworthy' fashion—but do so in a fashion that we do not appreciate (the character of Rumpelstiltskin in the *Shrek* movies is an excellent example of this). To speak of the promise in terms of trustworthiness, then, is not to say that all promises are good or yield good results. I bring this up here because, for Derrida especially, there is no guarantee that what fulfills the promise will be good, or will be better than what we have right now. In this sense, the promise can be menacing as much as it is comforting or beneficial.

33. And, as such, is distinctly epistemological in nature, as Alvin Plantinga and others have demonstrated.

34. In this regard, I disagree with Lawlor's conception of the injunction of the promise, in which we promise something (justice) to the other (*Derrida and Husserl*, 219–20). Though this is true, it is only secondary to our being the promise.

35. "[L]ike all promises, it must be assumed" (NM, 30).

36. "[T]he one who is promising is *already* the promise, or is *almost* already the promise, [the] promise is imminent" (NM, 30).

37. For this reason, Derrida has spoken of the appearance of the other as a *revenant*, that is, one who "*begins by coming back*" (SM, 11). The first appearance of the Other of which I am aware is already the Other's return to a scene at which it was present before I was. The Other of the promise is a *revenant*; it appears, but its appearance is always a return that ensures that I will have arrived too late. There are obvious resonances here with diachronic time in Levinas and the "prehistory of the I."

38. For more on the possibility of a prediscursive, preverbal 'yes', see Derrida, "Ulysses Gramophone."

39. Cf. Derrida, *Adieu to Emmanuel Levinas* and *The Work of Mourning*.

40. Mark Dooley and Liam Kavanagh provide an excellent account of the work of mourning and its centrality to Derrida's work in *The Philosophy of Derrida*.

9. The Promise of the Future

1. This notion is not as idiosyncratic as it may originally seem. Recall that the promise has a future object but a present ground, a ground that is based on our horizons of experience.

2. Cf. Levinas, "Philosophy, Justice, and Love" and "Dialogue on Thinking the Other."

3. Though expectation does introduce a distinct act, clarification, that could be understood as a type of fulfillment, it is not, I would argue, fulfillment properly speaking, in that it does not bring about an intuitive fullness; that is, it is not an "adequation," to use Husserl's language.

4. As it also, importantly, reverses the movements of intentionality and *Sinngebung*; see chapter 4.

5. For more on the necessity of "proper functioning" for the knowledge of objects, see Plantinga, *Warrant and Proper Function*.

6. Cf. *Logical Investigations*.

7. This point seems to have great consequences for a (phenomenological) theory of eschatology. Some of these consequences are discussed in DeRoo and Manoussakis, *Phenomenology and Eschatology*.

8. It is interesting to note that Hamlet is not the only one struggling to live up to a promise that he made and to which he was committed by another: Ophelia too, as the betrothed, must live up to her status as the promised. When Hamlet's apparent madness strikes at the very possibility of living up to this promise (not just whether she can marry a madman but also whether this madman is anymore

Hamlet, the Hamlet to whom she is promised), Ophelia is struck with a similar dilemma: to be (i.e., to live, up to and as, her promise, to be [the betrothed, the promised]) or not to be (to fail to live, up to and as, her promise, to fail to be [the betrothed, the promised]). Her choice, then, is "not to be" (because she cannot bear not being able to live up to the promise), while Hamlet ultimately chooses "to be." Both choices end in death, and this perhaps is the ultimate tragedy of *Hamlet*: To be or not to be, to keep or not to keep the promise (that one made and that one is)—the end of both is death. This is why Levinas, and Derrida after him, will try to get beyond the duality of being/not-being by establishing being on the basis of the beyond being. If this does not escape death, it at least makes possible life (which is another name for ultratranscendental *différance*; SP, 14–15, 82).

9. See, e.g., NM, 51: "But let me be clear—the experience of an absence of horizon is not one that has no horizon at all; it's where the horizon is, in a sense, 'punctured' by the other."

10. See, e.g., NM, 40: "[T]o allow the future to arrive as the future . . . is not to be understood in a [wholly] passive sense. This relation to the future is active, it is affirmative; and yet, however active it is, the relation is also a passive one. Otherwise the future will not be future."

11. Cf. Lawlor, *Derrida and Husserl*, 16.

12. Cf. Fink and Husserl, *Sixth Cartesian Meditation*, 10.

13. Cf. Husserl, "Philosophy as a Rigorous Science."

14. One must put "person" within brackets when speaking of Levinas and Derrida together, because they disagree on the question of whether or not there can be nonhuman others. For Levinas, there cannot be a nonhuman other (see chapter 4, note 36 above), while Derrida holds out the possibility of animals being Other (see Derrida, *The Animal That Therefore I Am*; Lawlor, *This Is Not Sufficient*; Calarco, *Zoographies*).

15. "The ethical language we have resorted to does not arise out of a special moral experience, independent of the description hitherto elaborated. The ethical situation of responsibility is not comprehensible on the basis of ethics" (OB, 120).

16. I designate this ground "nontological" to acknowledge Levinas's critique of Heideggerian ontology, while also showing its proximity to Heidegger's fundamental ontology. For more on this (though not the phrase "nontological" itself), see Bernasconi, "Deconstruction and the Possibility of Ethics."

17. Cf. Levinas, "Is Ontology Fundamental?"

18. One could ask whether this does not understate the case of ethical phenomenology: Does not Levinas's ethics of the substitution and the face-to-face suggest more than just that the subject is constituted by the same world that it constitutes? Does it not suggest, at the least, the importance of the other person in this constitution? It does—but so does Husserl's analysis of the necessary intersubjectivity of transcendental subjectivity, and his entire analysis of the lifeworld. One must not forget that, unlike, perhaps, for Buber, for Levinas the I-Other relationship never occurs without simultaneously invoking the Third, and hence institutions, laws, morals, politics, etc. (see, e.g., "Philosophy, Justice

and Love," 106), an invocation that would seem to put it back in line with the lifeworld.

19. Put simply, the optimal is that which enables me to understand something better. For more on the optimal, see Gyllenhammer, "The Passivity of Optimalizing Practices," especially 99; Steinbock, *Home and Beyond*, 138–69.

20. Cf. Steinbock, *Home and Beyond*, 146.

Conclusion: The Promissory Discipline

1. As many commentators have noted. For one example, see Sokolowski, *Introduction to Phenomenology*.

2. Not only does Deleuze try to divorce sense from this necessary relation to an object (e.g., in *the Logic of Sense*), but so too do Levinas and Derrida, as I have shown.

3. See Hua II, 52, 55, 68. See also Brough, "Consciousness Is Not a Bag."

4. These two movements clearly map onto the openness of intentionality, on the one hand, and the constituting subject, on the other, and therefore relate essentially to our analysis of futurity so far.

5. For more on this duality, see Manoussakis, *God after Metaphysics*, 14–19.

6. Derrida will be at pains to show that the invocation of language here is not merely incidental but indicates an essential connection between the stakes of phenomenology under discussion here and language itself. He is not alone, as several notable phenomenologists speak of the importance of language for phenomenology. Fink, for example, says that the phenomenological reduction "cannot be presented by means of simple sentences of the natural attitude. It can be spoken of only by transforming the natural function of language" (letter of May 11, 1936, cited in Berger, *The* Cogito *in Husserl's Philosophy*, 49). Suzanne Bachelard echoes a similar thought in her excellent *Study of Husserl's Formal and Transcendental Logic*. After bemoaning the fact that "language does not know the phenomenological reduction and so holds us in the natural attitude," she then asks of phenomenological philosophy, "[C]an it not imbue language with a new thought?" (xxxi). Derrida discusses this in a key footnote (OoG, 69n.66).

7. This word will have to hold at least two distinct meanings: "a set of generationally transmitted beliefs, practices, customs and rules," and "a philosophical meaning: tradition is a complex form of associational, intersubjective—better, communal—intentionality"(Drummond, "Time History and Tradition," 128). We will see that these two meanings cannot be held entirely separate from each other.

8. We will see that we can view these sedimentations more fundamentally as promises. This is perhaps to say that we should view them as injunctions rather than as concepts or ideas. This perhaps begins to get at Husserl's understanding of "calling," for example in Hua XVII, 28; it also is reminiscent of Levinas's discussion of the saying and of the call coming from the voice of the Other, Derrida's multiple discussions of the injunction/call, Heidegger's notion of the Call (see *Being and Time*, §56), as well as several key notions at work in Chrétien, Henry, and Marion.

9. On *Sinnbildung*, see Husserl's "Origin of Geometry" and Derrida's discussion of it in OoG, 55. I have modified the translation as "making-sense."

10. Cf. Marion, *Being Given*, 269.

11. Cf. Merleau-Ponty's reference to Fink in the preface to the *Phenomenology of Perception*, xii.

12. Husserl, *Crisis*, 180.

13. This beyond is both temporal and spatial. Temporally some of my sedimentations are given to me now by a past person (perhaps—even essentially, ideally—myself; cf. OoG, 85–86) that transcends the present me. Spatially—or, better, intersubjectively, though I suggested above that these two terms come together in Derrida's discussion of futurity—the act of "primordial *depositing* [that constitutes our sedimented horizons] is not the recording of a private thing, but the production of a *common* object, i.e., of an *object* whose original owner is dispossessed" (78).

14. This reception of our horizons can help explain how the clarifying process can be considered an 'intuition' rather than an act, properly speaking. In this regard, it is perhaps on par with the categorical intuition of the *Logical Investigations*.

15. Though this 'self-givenness' is itself a complicated process, as Marion points out in *Being Given*.

16. Within phenomenology, Marion seems at times to fall victim to this first temptation, and Sartre to the second.

17. Husserl makes use of the notion of "spiritual" acts and a "spiritual" world throughout the *Crisis* and the "Origin" and studies it in more detail in Hua IV. One would have to be careful in relating this to the "theological turn" in phenomenology.

18. The parenthetical reference in the quotation is to Husserl's "Origin of Geometry," published as an appendix in OoG, 157–80.

19. For example: "Only within a facto-historical language is the noun '*Löwe*' free, and therefore ideal" (OoG, 70); and "Historical incarnation sets free the transcendental, instead of binding it. This last notion, the transcendental, must then be re-thought" (77). These kind of statements give a new sense to Derrida's discussion of the messianic, allowing us to make sense of statements there such as that the Abrahamic messianisms are "the only events on the basis of which we approach and first of all name the messianic in general" (SM, 168). As such, the relationship between messianisms and messianicity requires all the resources of phenomenology to decipher, and any attempt to make sense of Derrida's messianic must "pass through the transcendental" movement of phenomenology, as Derrida himself makes clear (SP, 82; VM, 129).

20. See also Drummond, "Time History and Tradition," 137–38.

21. Parenthetical references again to the version of Husserl's "Origin of Geometry" appended to OoG.

22. Though these two are intimately related: "The horizon of fellow mankind supposes the horizon of the world: it stands out and articulates its unity against

the unity of the world. Of course, the world and fellow mankind here designate the all-inclusive, but infinitely open, unity of possible experiences and not this world right here, these fellow men right here, whose factuality for Husserl is never anything but a variable example" (OoG, 79).

23. See not only Marion, *Being Given*, but also *Being and Time*, where Heidegger essentially relates the letting-appear of phenomenology with the project of the *Destruktion* of metaphysics and ontology.

24. Here we can play on the connections, etymological and otherwise, between truth, trust, and troth (as in the betrothed).

25. Though, of course, there is no guarantee that we will in fact gain more and more knowledge of the thing. The project, and its telos, are in this sense theoretical rather than intuitive.

26. To justify the (implicit) invocation of Levinas here, we must note that Derrida himself describes the Idea as "beyond being" (OoG, 144), a phrase whose Levinasian overtones cannot be denied, even if the explicit reference is to Plato. This is not to conflate Levinas's Other with the Idea; I merely wish to signal an Infinite common to both (even if the precise nature of that infinity is not equivalent; cf. the two senses of infinity discussed in chapter 8).

27. This can help us begin to make sense of Ricoeur's claim that the distinction "between intention and intuition," "fundamental in Kant, [is] totally unknown in Husserl"(*Husserl: An Analysis*, 189). Such a claim might be surprising to certain readers of Husserl, especially of the *Logical Investigations*.

28. John J. Drummond also notes the tight relationship, if not the equation, between intention and the transcendental intersubjectivity that I am calling tradition: "Husserl characterizes all experiences . . . as intersubjective . . . [not] in fact but intersubjective in intention"("Time History and Tradition," 134).

29. Here is but one place where one could begin to bridge the gap between Husserlian and Heideggerian phenomenology (cf. OoG, 150–53).

30. Recall Derrida's claim, cited in chapter 7, that the "absolute beginning of all philosophy must be essentialist" (PG, 138). However, such a preference cannot be simply acceded to, as our discussion of Levinas and Derrida has, I hope, made clear.

31. John J. Drummond seems to agree, at least in principle, when he says, "We must instead recognize the full force of this problem [of traditionality] as a theoretical problem" ("Time History and Tradition," 128). Pushing this further, one can say that the task of phenomenology is to explore how we can make universal and objective claims beginning from particular (perhaps even individual) standpoints.

32. Which is not to say that she has *no* control, nor that she should not take every available precaution in order to determine, as strongly as possible, how her work will be received. Surely the rigor of Husserl's analyses prove this as well as anything.

33. See note 19.

34. It should be clear that these two invoke the two distinct—but essentially related—accounts of futurity at work in phenomenology.

35. This could perhaps pass itself off as a suitable definition of deconstruction which, we can now see, is nothing more—and nothing less—than one aspect of the phenomenological project. See Michael Naas's claim that "taking on the tradition" is "another way of glossing 'deconstruction' " (*Taking on the Tradition*, xix).

36. Drummond, "Time History, Tradition," 138.

37. Though obviously not in a psychologistic way; cf. *Logical Investigations, Formal and Transcendental Logic*, and *Experience and Judgment*.

38. As noted at the end of chapter 2, what moves Husserl beyond Kant is that for Husserl, unlike for Kant, the very structures of subjectivity themselves are constituted and not merely given a priori.

39. "Tradition . . . as the associational consciousness of the historical community, shapes the individual's openness to the future in the light of the community's past" (Drummond, "Time History, Tradition," 138). See also Steinbock, *Home and Beyond*, passim.

40. However, we must be careful not to view these horizons as mere objects, or to objectify the transcendental history or sense. See Derrida's lengthy explorations of horizons, historicity, and objectivity in the *Introduction*, but also in *The Problem of Genesis, Speech and Phenomena*, and *Of Grammatology*.

41. Or, perhaps better, profession. See Derrida, "The University without Condition," 202–37.

42. For example, in Derrida, *Demeure*.

43. Here we must remember the spatialization of time and the temporalization of space at work in our discussion of futurity, most notably in *différance*. Thus we are able to see that the 'where' of our viewing is not distinct from the 'when' of our viewing, and vice versa. The notion of tradition perhaps makes this most clear, as one's tradition is both temporally and spatially located: It is not just that I grew up *here* or that I grew up *now*, but that I grew up here and now, as any cursory examination of traditionality will reveal (e.g., by comparing the tradition[s] of one place in two distinct times, or by comparing the tradition[s] of one time in two distinct places).

44. "Origin of Geometry," 172 (in the version appended to OoG).

45. It should be clear by this point that the invocation of an "Idea in the Kantian sense" is not done to tie the notion of sense to an object but precisely to problematize this relation via the notion of historicity, that is, of essential traditionality. In this regard, it invokes not merely the infinity of asymptotic approach, but also the infinity of self-givenness, revelation, and alterity.

46. While this phrase occurs throughout Derrida's *Introduction* to the "Origin of Geometry," it seems to appear only once in Husserl's work itself; see manuscript C VIII 2, p. 3, referenced in OoG, 121n.134.

47. Dan Zahavi discusses the constitutive role that intersubjectivity plays in the various levels of constituting experience in "Husserl's Intersubjective Transformation of Transcendental Philosophy."

48. It also gives new insight into Derrida's famous phrase "tout autre est tout autre," discussed at length in *The Gift of Death*.

49. A notion that invokes the Teacher who provides the condition for the reception of the teaching in the listener in Kierkegaard's *Philosophical Fragments*.

50. Cf. Marion, *Being Given*, 10.

51. We are now drawing near the work of Henry, Marion, and Chrétien (to name a few), work that, we can now see, is continuing to explore the problem of infinity opened first—and in numerous places, from *Ideas I* through the *Crisis*—by Husserl himself. If Henry et al. work within a (religious) tradition that is perhaps not one's own, this does not disqualify, phenomenologically, the necessity of working within a tradition that is their own. In this sense, the invocation of a religious tradition does nothing in and of itself to defeat the phenomenological nature of the work. That one could draw the reduction otherwise than do these figures no more denies their work phenomenological status than do Husserl's several different reductions disqualify his own work as phenomenological. Rather it calls for further phenomenological work to be done, including perhaps the phenomenological work of deconstruction. On this, see Husserl's own later discussions of God (e.g., Ms. K III, 106; Ms. F I 24, 68) and "transcendental divinity," as well as Derrida's remarks on them (OoG, 147–48). By indicating the validity of a certain "metaphorical and indicative" invocation of God within phenomenology, Derrida allows for "theological" claims that "would be only the indefinite *openness* to truth and to phenomenality for a subjectivity that is always finite in its factual being" (148). Whether such claims could still be considered "theological" in a meaningful sense, and whether Henry et al. would consider their work to be examples of such claims, still needs to be investigated.

52. We can then think of the debate concerning the 'theological turn' as a debate about the nature of phenomenology itself—not unlike the project of this work itself.

53. These two moments of the phenomenological project are not easily separable. One does not neutrally describe and then evaluate, but rather every description is an evaluation: One describes as a way of evaluating, and one evaluates as a way of describing: "constantly to maintain a questioning of the origin, ground and limits of our conceptual, theoretical or normative apparatus . . . this is, from the point of view of a rigorous deconstruction, anything but a neutralization" (Derrida, *Acts of Religion*, 248). In this way, the project of making ourselves aware of our horizons is, in and of itself, a question also of evaluating those horizons, and hence a question of responsibility. See also Derrida, "Remarks on Deconstruction and Pragmatism," 83–85.

54. This difficulty is the main theme of Derrida's "Ends of Man."

55. See OG, 60–62. See also Caputo's discussion of the passage through the transcendental in "The Return of Anti-Religion," §§ 6–9, and Wood's discussion of the way out of metaphysics involving a displacement within metaphysics (*Deconstruction of Time*, 370).

56. It is here, I think, that the distinctly *phenomenological* significance of Henry can begin to be discerned. This also opens a dialogue with Deleuze and Guattari on their notion of immanence in *What Is Philosophy?* See also Lawlor,

This Is Not Sufficient, 3–5. It also begins to come close to some of Deleuze's formulations of the notion of event in *The Logic of Sense*.

57. Derrida will sometimes refer to these as "unconditionals." See, e.g., *Paper Machine*, 79; *Rogues*, 90, 135, 142, 151; *The Beast and the Sovereign*, passim.

58. But again, there is no guarantee either that we will live up to this promise (i.e., that we will remain coherent with our professed intentions) nor that the promise itself is "good" (i.e., that what fulfills the promise will be in keeping with the other, quasi-transcendental promises that have been given to us), and therefore to discuss this under the rubric of the promise does not glaze over the fact that what is to-come might in fact be the worst. Rather the promise is an infinite task that can never, even in principle, be finished and therefore fully fulfilled. See Drummond, "Time History and Tradition," 140. This suggests that the authenticity discussed by Drummond in his text (taken from Husserl) might be understood by us here as fidelity to the promise, precisely as trustworthiness in a transcendental and nonepistemological (i.e., not merely valid) sense.

59. I do not discuss the implications of this for nonhuman animals, though I think the pieces are in place here to begin such a discussion, one that would probably look quite similar to that in Lawlor, *This Is Not Sufficient*.

60. This seems to me to be one of the most significant ways that focusing on his phenomenological aspects can help us rethink Levinas's philosophy of religion (such as it is).

61. Cf. Drummond's discussion of communal authenticity in "Time History Tradition," 141–43. Derrida makes this most clear in "Force of Law," with his distinction between the law (as an institution) and Justice (as the promise animating and driving that institution).

62. To cite a few examples of work already being done to think phenomenologically in these areas: Several of these issues are explored in Atterton and Calarco, *Radicalizing Levinas*. J. Aaron Simmons explores the political and ethical implications of phenomenology, especially Levinas, in *God and the Other*. Drucilla Cornell explores the impact of Derrida's thought on legal theory throughout her work; the most obvious examples are perhaps *Beyond Accommodation* and the edited volume *Deconstruction and the Possibility of Justice*. Chantal Mouffe, among others, explores how this impacts political theory; see *The Democratic Paradox* and the edited volume *Deconstruction and Pragmatism*. Some of the ecological aspects—at least in relation to the treatment of nonhuman animals—are explored in Lawlor, *This Is Not sufficient*. While all of these works cite phenomenological figures, it is not clear that they all adequately account for the phenomenological nature of their work. So although such thinking has begun, it is a project that is far from complete and may not yet even be fully recognized as a project in its own right (a phenomenological [take on] politics, or on ethics, for example).

63. Though a community is composed of and founded on individuals. Cf. Hua XXVII, 22, 48; Drummond, "Time History Tradition," 141–42; Drummond, "The 'Spiritual' World."

64. Cf. Rorty, *Philosophy and the Mirror of Nature*; Rorty, "From Ironist Theory to Private Allusions"; Wood, *Deconstruction of Time*, 311.

65. Cf. Eaglestone, "Postmodernism and Ethics against the Metaphysics of Comprehension." For more on the connection between the figures studied in this work, especially Levinas, and the theoretical presumptions of postmodernism, see my "Re-constituting Phenomenology," especially §4.

Bibliography

Alemany, Francisco Salto. "In Continuity: A Reflection on the Passive Synthesis of Sameness." In *Analecta Husserliana,* vol. 34, ed. A. T. Tymieniecka. Boston: Kluwer Academic, 1991. 195–202.

Aristotle. *The Basic Works of Aristotle.* Ed. Richard McKeon. New York: Modern Library, 2001.

———. *Physics.* Trans. R.P. Hardie and R.K. Gaye. In *The Basic Works of Aristotle*, ed. Richard McKeon.New York: Modern Library, 2001. 218–394.

Atterton, Peter,and Matthew Calarco,eds. *Radicalizing Levinas.* New York: State University of New York Press, 2010.

Augustine. *Confessions.* Trans. Henry Chadwick. Oxford World's Classics. Oxford: Oxford University Press, 1998.

Bachelard, Suzanne. *A Study of Husserl's Formal and Transcendental Logic.* Trans. Lester E. Embree. Evanston, Ill.: Northwestern University Press, 1968.

Baudrillard, Jean. "The Precession of Simulacra." In *Simulacra and Simulations*. Trans. Sheila Faria Glaser. Ann Arbor: University of Michigan Press, 1994. 1–42.

———. *Simulacra and Simulations.* Trans. Sheila Faria Glaser. Ann Arbor: University of Michigan Press, 1994.

Bennington, Geoffrey. "Derridabase."In *Jacques Derrida*, by Geoffrey Bennington and Jacques Derrida. Chicago: University of Chicago Press, 1993; 1–316.

Bennington, Geoffrey, and Jacques Derrida. *Jacques Derrida.* Chicago: University of Chicago Press, 1993.

Berger, Gaston. *The Cogito in Husserl's Philosophy.* Trans. Kathleen McLaughlin. Evanston, Ill.: Northwestern University Press, 1972.

Bernasconi, Robert. "Deconstruction and the Possibility of Ethics." In *Deconstruction and Philosophy: The Texts of Jacques Derrida*, ed. John Sallis. Chicago: University of Chicago Press, 1987. 122–39.

———. "Levinas and Derrida: The Question of the Closure of Metaphysics." In *Face to Face with Levinas*, ed. Richard A. Cohen. Albany: State University of New York Press, 2007.181–303.

———. "Skepticism in the Face of Philosophy."In *Re-Reading Levinas*, ed. Robert Bernasconi and Simon Critchley. Bloomington: Indiana University Press, 1991. 149–61.

———. "The Trace of Levinas in Derrida."In *Derrida and Différance*, ed. David Wood and Robert Bernasconi. Evanston, Ill.: Northwestern University Press, 1988; 13–30.

Bernasconi, Robert, and Simon Critchley, eds.Re-*Reading Levinas*. Bloomington: Indiana University Press, 1991.

Bernasconi, Robert, and David Wood, eds. *The Provocation of Levinas: Rethinking the Other*. New York: Routledge, 1988.

Bernet, Rudolf. "Levinas's Critique of Husserl." In *The Cambridge Companion to Levinas*, ed. Simon Critchley and Robert Bernasconi. Cambridge: Cambridge University Press, 2002. 82–99.

———. "My Time and the Time of the Other." In *Self-Awareness, Temporality and Alterity: Central Topics in Phenomenology*, ed. Dan Zahavi. Dordrecht: Kluwer Academic, 1998. 137–49.

Bloechl, Jeffrey. *The Liturgy of the Neighbor: Emmanuel Levinas and the Religion of Responsibility*. Pittsburgh: Duquesne University Press, 2000.

Borradori, Giovanna, ed. Philosophy *in a Time of Terror: Dialogues with Jürgen Habermas and Jacques Derrida*. Chicago: University of Chicago Press, 2003.

Bouwsma, O.K. *Philosophical Essays*. Lincoln: University of Nebraska Press, 1965.

Bowman, Curtis. "*Speech and Phenomena* on Expression and Indication: Derrida's Dual Critique of Husserl's Demand for Apodictic Evidence and the Phenomenological Reduction." *International Studies in Philosophy* 31.4 [1999] 1–21.

Brough, John Barnett. "Consciousness Is Not a Bag: Immanence, Transcendence and Constitution in *The Idea of Phenomenology*." Lecture delivered at Boston College, April 2008.

———. "The Emergence of an Absolute Consciousness in Husserl's Early Writings on Time-Consciousness."*Man and World* 5 (1972): 298–326.

———. "Translator's Introduction." In Edmund Husserl, *On the Phenomenology of the Consciousness of Internal Time (1893–1917)*. Trans. John Barnett Brough. Dordrecht: Kluwer Academic, 1991. Xi–lvii.

Brough, John Barnett, and Lester Embree, eds. *The Many Faces of Time*. Vol. 41 of *Contributions to Phenomenology*. Dordrecht: Kluwer Academic, 2000.

Bruzina, Ronald. "The Revision of the Bernau Time-Consciousness Manuscripts: Status Questionis—Freiburg, 1928–30." *Alter* 1 (1993): 357–83.

Cadava, Eduardo, Peter Connor, and Jean-Luc Nancy, eds. *Who Comes after the Subject?* New York: Routledge, 1991.

Calarco, Matthew. *Zoographies: The Question of the Animal from Heidegger to Derrida*. New York: Columbia University Press, 2008.

Cantwell Smith, Wilfred. *The Meaning and End of Religion: A New Approach to the Religious Traditions of Mankind*. New York: Mentor Books, 1963.

Caputo, John D. *Deconstruction in a Nutshell*. New York: Fordham University Press, 1999.

———. "The Possibility of the Impossible: A Response to Kearney." In *Cross and Khora: Deconstruction and Christianity in the Work of John D. Caputo*, ed.Neal DeRoo and Marko Zlomisliç. Eugene, Ore.: Pickwick, 2010, 140–50.

———. *The Prayers and Tears of Jacques Derrida: Religion with/out Religion*. Bloomington: Indiana University Press, 1997.

———. "The Return of Anti-Religion: From Radical Atheism to Radical Theology." *Journal for Cultural and Religious Theory*, Spring 2011. Online.

———. "Temporal Transcendence: The Very Idea of *à-venir* in Derrida." In *Transcendence and Beyond: A Postmodern Inquiry*, ed. John D. Caputo and Michael Scanlon. Bloomington: Indiana University Press, 2007. 188–203.

———. *The Weakness of God: A Theology of the Event*. Bloomington: Indiana University Press, 2006.

Caputo, John D., and Michael Scanlon, eds. *Transcendence and Beyond: A Postmodern Inquiry*.Bloomington: Indiana University Press, 2007.

Caputo, John D., Michael Scanlon, and Mark Dooley, eds. *Questioning God*. Bloomington: Indiana University Press, 2001.

Cobb-Stevens, Richard. "James and Husserl: Time-consciousness and the Intentionality of Presence and Absence." In *Self-Awareness, Temporality and Alterity: Central Topics in Phenomenology*, ed. Dan Zahavi. Dordrecht: Kluwer Academic, 1998. 41–57.

Cohen, Richard A. *Elevations*. Chicago: University of Chicago Press, 1995.

Cohen, Richard A., ed. *Face to Face with Levinas*. Albany: State University of New York Press, 2007.

———. "Levinas, Rosenzweig and the Phenomenologies of Husserl and Heidegger."*Philosophy Today* 32.2 (1998): 165–78.

Colette, Jacques. "Lévinas et la phénoménologie husserlienne." In *Emmanuel Levinas: Les Cahiers de La nuit surveillée*, no. 3, ed. J. Rolland. Lagrasse, France: Verdier, 1984. 19–36.

Cornell, Drucilla. *Beyond Accommodation: Ethical Feminism, Deconstruction and the Law*. New ed. Lanham, Md.: Rowman and Littlefield, 1999.

Cornell, Drucilla, Michael Rosenfeld, and David Gray Carlson, eds. *Deconstruction and the Possibility of Justice*. New York: Routledge, 1992.

Critchley, Simon. *The Ethics of Deconstruction*. Oxford: Blackwell, 1992.

de Greef, Jan. "Levinas et la phénoménologie." *Revue de Métaphysique et de Morale* 76.4 (1971): 448–65.

Deleuze, Gilles. *The Logic of Sense*. Trans. Mark Lester. New York: Columbia University Press, 1990.

Deleuze, Gilles, and Félix Guattari. *What Is Philosophy?* Trans. Hugh Tomlinson and Graham Burchell. New York: Columbia University Press, 1994.

DeRoo, Neal. "Determined to Reveal: Determination and Revelation in Derrida." In *The Logic of Incarnation: A Critique of Postmodern Religion*, ed. Neal DeRoo and Brian Lightbody. Eugene, Ore.: Pickwick, 2008. 41–56.

———. "The Future Matters: Protention as More than Inverse Retention." *Bulletin d'Analyse Phénoménologique* 4.7 (2008), 1–18.

———. "Phenomenological Insights into Oppression: Passive Synthesis and Personal Responsibility," *Janus Head* (forthcoming).

———. "A Positive Account of Protention and Its Implications for Internal Time-Consciousness." In *Phenomenology, Archaeology, Ethics: Current Investigations of Husserl's Corpus*, ed. Sebastian Luft and Pol Vandevelde. London: Continuum, 2010. 102–19.

———. "Re-constituting Phenomenology: Continuity in Levinas' Account of Time and Ethics." *Dialogue: Canadian Philosophical Review* 49.2 (2010): 223–43.

———. "Re-visiting the Zahavi-Brough/Sokolowski Debate," *Husserl Studies* 27.1 (2011): 1–12.

———. "The Testimonial Function of Reason and Religion in the Public Sphere." *Symposia* 1.1 (2009): 35–47.

DeRoo, Neal, and Brian Lightbody, eds. *The Logic of Incarnation: A Critique of Postmodern Religion*. Eugene, Ore.: Pickwick, 2008.

DeRoo, Neal, and John Panteleimon Manoussakins, eds. *Phenomenology and Eschatology: Not Yet in the Now*. Aldershot, England: Ashgate, 2009.

DeRoo, Neal, and Kascha Snavely, eds. *Merleau-Ponty at the Limits of Art, Religion and Perception*. London: Continuum, 2010.

DeRoo, Neal, and Marko Zlomisliç, eds. *Cross and Khora: Deconstruction and Christianity in the Work of John D. Caputo*. Eugene, Ore.: Pickwick, 2010.

Derrida, Jacques. *Acts of Literature*. Ed. Derek Attridge. London: Routledge, 1992.

———. *Acts of Religion*. Ed. Gil Anidjar. New York: Routledge, 2002.

———. *Adieu to Emmanuel Levinas*. Trans. Pascale-Anne Brault and Michael Naas. Stanford: Stanford University Press, 1999.

———. *The Animal That Therefore I Am*. Ed. Marie-Louise Mallet, Trans. David Wills. New York: Fordham University Press, 2008.

———. "At This Very Moment in This Work Here I Am." Trans. Ruben Berezdivin. In *Re-Reading Levinas*, ed. Robert Bernasconi and Simon Critchley. London: Routledge, 1990; 11–48.

———. "Auto-immunity: Real and Symbolic Suicides—A Dialogue with Jacques Derrida." In *Philosophy in a Time of Terror: Dialogues with Jürgen Habermas and Jacques Derrida*, ed. Giovanna Borradori. Chicago: University of Chicago Press, 2003. 85–136.

———. *The Beast and the Sovereign*. Vol. 1. Trans. Geoffrey Bennington. Chicago: University of Chicago Press, 2009.

————. "Demeure: Fiction and Testimony." In *The Instant of My Death and Demeure: Fiction and Testimony*, by Jacques Derrida and Maurice Blanchot. Stanford: Stanford University Press, 2000. 13–103.

————. "Des Tours de Babel." In *Psyché: L'inventions de l'Autre*. Paris: Galilée, 1987. 203–35.

————. "The Ends of Man." In *Margins of Philosophy*. Trans. Alan Bass. Chicago: University of Chicago Press, 1982. 109–36.

————. *L'écriture et La différence*. Paris: Seuil, 1967.

————. *Eyes of the University: Right to Philosophy 2*. Trans. Jan Plug and others. Stanford: Stanford University Press, 2004.

————. "Foi et savoir: Les deux sources de la 'religion' aux limites de la simple raison." In *La Religion*, ed. Jacques Derrida and Gianni Vattimo. Paris: Editions du Seuil, 1996. 9–86.

————. "Force of Law: The Mystical Foundation of Authority." In *Acts of Religion*, ed. Gil Anidjar. New York: Routledge, 2002. 228–98.

————. *The Gift of Death*. Trans. David Wills. Chicago: University of Chicago Press, 1995.

————. *Glas*. Trans. John P. Leavey Jr. and Richard Rand. Lincoln: University of Nebraska Press, 1986.

————. "Khora." in *On the Name*. Trans. Thomas Dutoit. Stanford: Stanford University Press, 1995. 89–127.

————. *Limited Inc*. Ed. Gerald Graff.Trans. Jeffrey Mehlman and Samuel Weber. Evanston, Ill.: Northwestern University Press, 1988.

————. *Margins of Philosophy*. Trans. Alan Bass. Chicago: University of Chicago Press, 1984.

————. *Negotiations: Interventions and Interviews*. Ed. and trans. Elizabeth Rottenberg. Stanford: Stanford University Press, 2002.

————. *Paper Machine*. Trans. Rachel Bowlby. Stanford: Stanford University Press, 2005.

————. "Politics and Friendship." In *Negotiations: Interventions and Interviews*, ed. and trans. Elizabeth Rottenberg. Stanford: Stanford University Press, 2002. 147–98.

————. *The Post Card: From Socrates to Freud and Beyond*. Trans. Alan Bass. Chicago: University of Chicago Press, 1987.

————. "The Principle of Reason: The University in the Eyes of Its Pupils." Trans. Catherine Porter and Edward P. Morris. In *Eyes of the University: Right to Philosophy 2*. Stanford: Stanford University Press, 2004. 129–55.

————. *Psyché: L'inventions de l'Autre*. Paris: Galilée, 1987.

————. "Remarks on Deconstruction and Pragmatism."Trans. Simon Critchley. In *Deconstruction andPragmatism*, ed. Chantal Mouffe. New York: Routledge, 1996. 77–88.

————. *Rogues: Two Essays on Reason*. Trans. Pascale-Anne Brault and Michael Naas. Stanford: Stanford University Press, 2005.

———. *A Taste for the Secret*. Ed. Giocomo Donis and David Webb. Trans. Giocomo Donis. Cambridge, England: Polity, 2001.

———. "Ulysses Gramophone: Hear Say Yes in Joyce." Trans. Tina Kendall and Shari Benstock. In *Acts of Literature*, ed. Derek Attridge. New York: Routledge, 1991. 253–309.

———. "The University without Condition." In *Without Alibi*. Trans. and ed. Peggy Kamuf. Stanford: Stanford University Press, 2002. 202–37.

———. *La Voix et la Phénomène*. Paris: Presses Universitaires de France, 1967.

———. "White Mythology: Metaphor in the Text of Philosophy." In *Margins of Philosophy*. Trans. Alan Bass. Chicago: University of Chicago Press, 1982. 207–71.

———. *The Work of Mourning*. Trans. Pascale-Anne Brault and Michael Naas. Chicago: University of Chicago Press, 2003.

Derrida, Jacques, and Maurice Blanchot. *The Instant of My Death and Demeure: Fiction and Testimony*. Trans. Elizabeth Rottenberg. Stanford: Stanford University Press, 2000.

Derrida, Jacques, and Anne Dufourmantelle. *Of Hospitality: Anne Dufourmantelle Invites Jacques Derrida to Respond*. Trans. Rachel Bowlby. Stanford: Stanford University Press, 2000.

Derrida, Jacques, and Gianni Vattimo, eds. *La Religion*. Paris: Editions du Seuil, 1996.

Dooley, Mark, and Liam Kavanagh. *The Philosophy of Derrida*. Montreal: McGill–Queen's University Press, 2007.

Drabinski, John E. *Sensibility and Singularity: The Problem of Phenomenology in Levinas*. Albany: State University of New York Press, 2001.

Dreher, Jochen. "The Symbol and the Theory of the Life-World: 'The Transcendence of the Life-World and Their Overcoming by Signs and Symbols.'" *Human Studies* 26 (2003): 141–63.

Drummond, John J. *Husserlian Intentionality and Non-Foundational Realism: Noema and Object*. Dordrecht: Kluwer Academic, 1990.

———. "The 'Spiritual' World: The Personal, the Social and the Communal." In *Issues in Husserl's* Ideas II, ed. Thomas Nenon and Lester Embree. Dordrecht: Kluwer Academic, 1996.237–54.

———. "Time History and Tradition." In *The Many Faces of Time*. Vol. 41 of *Contributions to Phenomenology*, ed. John Barnett Brough and Lester Embree. Dordrecht: Kluwer Academic, 2000.127–47.

Dudiak, Jeffrey. *The Intrigue of Ethics: A Reading of the Idea of Discourse in the Thought of Emmanuel Levinas*. New York: Fordham University Press, 2001.

Dummett, Michael. "A Defense of McTaggart's Proof of the Unreality of Time."*Philosophical Review* 69:4 (Oct. 1960). 497–504.

Eaglestone, Robert. "Postmodernism and Ethics against the Metaphysics of Comprehension." In *The Cambridge Companion to Postmodernism*, ed.Stephen Connor. Cambridge: Cambridge University Press, 2004. 182–95.

Eliade, Mircea. *The Sacred and the Profane: The Nature of Religion.* Trans. Willard R. Task. London: Harcourt Brace Jovanovich, 1959.

Fink, Eugen, and Edmund Husserl. *Sixth Cartesian Meditation: The Idea of a Transcendental Theory of Method.* Trans. Ronald Bruzina. Bloomington: Indiana University Press, 1995.

Gibbs, Robert. *Correlations in Rosenzweig and Levinas.* Princeton: Princeton University Press, 1992.

Gyllenhammer, Paul R. "The Passivity of Optimalizing Practices: A Development of Husserl's Transcendental Aesthetics." *Journal of the Southwestern Philosophical Society* 19.1 (2003): 97–105.

Hart, Kevin. "Without." In *Cross and Khora: Deconstruction and Christianity in the Work of John D. Caputo,* ed. Neal DeRoo and Marko Zlomislič. Eugene, Ore.: Pickwick, 2010. 80–108.

Heidegger, Martin. *Being and Time.* Trans. Joan Stambaugh. Albany: State University of New York Press, 1996.

———. *Pathmarks.* Ed. William McNeil. Cambridge: Cambridge University Press, 1998.

———. "Phenomenology and Theology." Trans. James G. Hart, John Maraldo, and William McNeil. In *Pathmarks,* ed. William McNeil. Cambridge: Cambridge University Press, 1998. 39–62. Originally published in *The Piety of Thinking: Essays by Martin Heidegger,* trans. and ed. James G. Hart and John Maraldo. Bloomington: Indiana University Press, 1976.

———. *The Piety of Thinking: Essays by Martin Heidegger.* Trans. and ed. James G. Hart and John Maraldo. Bloomington: Indiana University Press, 1976.

———. *Sein und Zeit.* Tübingen: Max Niemeyer, 1993.

Henry, Michel. "The Critique of the Subject." Trans. Peter T. Connor. In *Who Comes after the Subject?,* ed. Eduardo Cadava, Peter Connor, and Jean-Luc Nancy. New York: Routledge, 1991. 157–66.

Hobson, Marianne. *Jacques Derrida: Opening Lines.* London: Routledge, 1998.

Hodge, Joanna. *Derrida on Time.* London: Routledge, 2007.

———. "Excesses of Subtlety: The Current Reception of Edmund Husserl." *Journal of the British Society for Phenomenology* 35.2 (2004): 208–13.

Husserl, Edmund. "The Origin of Geometry." Trans. David Carr. In *Edmund Husserl's* Origin of Geometry: *An Introduction,* by Jacques Derrida. Trans. John P. Leavey. Lincoln: University of Nebraska Press, 1989. 157–80. Originally published in *The Crisis of the European Sciences and Transcendental Phenomenology.* Evanston: Northwestern University Press, 1970.

———. *Philosophie der Arithmetik: Psychologische und logische Untersuchungen.* Vol. 1. Halle-Saale: C.E.M. Pfeffer, 1891.

———. "Philosophy as a Rigorous Science." In *Phenomenology and the Crisis of Philosophy.* Trans. Quentin Lauer. New York: Harper Torchbooks, 1965. 71–147.

James, William. *The Principles of Psychology*. Vol. 1. Cambridge, Mass.: Harvard University Press, 1981.

Janicaud, Dominique."The Theological Turn of French Phenomenology." Trans. Bernard G. Prusak. In *Phenomenology and the "Theological Turn": The French Debate*, by Dominique Janicaud et al. New York: Fordham University Press, 2000. 16–103.

Janicaud, Dominique, et al. *Phenomenology and the "Theological Turn": The French Debate*. New York: Fordham University Press, 2000.

Johnson, Galen, ed. *The Merleau-Ponty Aesthetics Reader: Philosophy and Painting*. Evanston, Ill.: Northwestern University Press, 1993.

Kant, Immanuel. *Religion within the Limits of Reason Alone*. Trans. Theodore M. Greene and Hoyt H. Hudson. New York: HarperOne, 1960.

Kaufmann, Fritz. "On Imagination." *Philosophy and Phenomenological Research* 7 (1947): 369–75.

Kearney, Richard. *Anatheism: Returning to God after God*. New York: Cambridge University Press, 2010.

———. "Epiphanies of the Everyday: Toward a Micro-eschatology." In *After God: Richard Kearney and the Religious Turn in Continental Philosophy*, ed. John Panteleimon Manoussakis. New York: Fordham University Press, 2006. 3–20.

———. *The God Who May Be: A Hermeneutics of Religion*. Bloomington: University of Indiana Press, 2001.

———. "The Kingdom: Possible and Impossible." In *Cross and Khora: Deconstruction and Christianity in the Work of John D. Caputo*, ed. Neal DeRoo and Marko Zlomislič. Eugene, Ore.: Pickwick, 2010. 118–39.

———. *On Stories*. London: Routledge, 2002.

———. *Poetics of Imagining: Modern to Postmodern*. New York: Fordham University Press, 1988.

———. *Strangers, Gods and Monsters*. London: Routledge, 2003.

Kierkegaard, Søren. *Philosophical Fragments and Johannes Climacus*. Trans. Howard V. Hong and Edna H. Hong. Princeton: Princeton University Press, 1985.

Kircher, Tilo, and Anthony S. David, eds. *The Self in Neuroscience and Psychiatry*. Cambridge: Cambridge University Press, 2003.

Kortooms, Toine. *Phenomenology of Time: Edmund Husserl's Analysis of Time-Consciousness*. Dordrecht: Kluwer Academic, 2002.

Kuspit, Donald. "Fiction and Phenomenology."*Philosophy and Phenomenological Research* 29.1 (1968): 16–33.

Landgrebe, Ludwig. *The Phenomenology of Edmund Husserl: Six Essays*. Ed. Donn Welton. Ithaca: Cornell University Press, 1981.

Large, William. "On the Meaning of the Word Other in Levinas." *Journal of the British Society for Phenomenology* 27.1 (1996): 36–52.

Lawlor, Leonard. *Derrida and Husserl: The Basic Problem of Phenomenology*. Bloomington: Indiana University Press, 2002.

―――. "Temporality and Spatiality: A Note to a Footnote in Derrida's *Writing and Difference.*" *Research in Phenomenology* Volume 12(1982): 149–65.

―――. *This Is Not Sufficient: An Essay on Animality and Human Nature in Derrida.* New York: Columbia University Press, 2007.

Levinas, Emmanuel. *Basic Philosophical Writings.* Ed. Adriaan T. Peperzak, Simon Critchley, and Robert Bernasconi. Bloomington: Indiana University Press, 1996.

―――. *Collected Philosophical Papers.* Ed. and trans. Alphonso Lingis. The Hague: Martinus Nijhoff, 1987.

―――. "Dialogue on Thinking the Other." In *Entre Nous: On Thinking-of-the-Other.* Trans. Michael B. Smith and Barbara Harshav. New York: Columbia University Press, 1998. 201–6.

―――. *Difficult Freedom: Essays on Judaism.* Trans. Seán Hand. Baltimore: Johns Hopkins University Press, 1990, 1997.

―――. *Entre Nous: Thinking-of-the-Other.* Trans. Michael B. Smith and Barbara Harshaw. New York: Columbia University Press, 1998.

―――. "Entretien." In *Répondre d'autrui: Emmanuel Levinas.* Ed. Jean-Christophe Aeschlimann. Boudry-Neuchâtel: Editions de la Baconniere, 1989. 9–16.

―――. "Is Ontology Fundamental?" In *Entre Nous: On Thinking-of-the-Other.* Trans. Michael B. Smith and Barbara Harshaw. New York: Columbia University Press, 1998. 1–11.

―――."Language and Proximity."In *Collected Philosophical Papers.* Ed.and trans. Alphonso Lingis. The Hague: Martinus Nijhoff, 1987. 109–26.

―――."Lévy-Bruhl and Contemporary Philosophy." In *Entre Nous: Thinking of the Other.* Trans. Michael B. Smith and Barbara Harshav. New York: Columbia University Press, 1998. 39–51.

―――. "The Name of a Dog, or Natural Rights." In *Difficult Freedom: Essays on Judaism.* Trans. Seán Hand. Baltimore: Johns Hopkins University Press, 1997. 151–53.

―――. *Of God Who Comes to Mind.* Trans. Bettina Bergo. Stanford: Stanford University Press, 1998.

―――. "The Paradox of Morality: An Interview with Emmanuel Levinas." In *The Provocation of Levinas: Rethinking the Other,* ed. Robert Bernasconi and David Wood. New York: Routledge, 1988. 168–80.

―――. "Philosophy, Justice, and Love." In *Entre Nous: On Thinking-of-the-Other.* Trans. Michael B. Smith and Barbara Harshav. New York: Columbia University Press, 1998. 103–22.

―――. "Preface to the German Edition of *Totality and Infinity.*" In *Entre Nous: Thinking-of-the-Other.* Trans. Michael B. Smith and Barbara Harshav. New York: Columbia University Press, 1998. 197–200.

Llewelyn, John. "Am I Obsessed by Bobby? (Humanism of the Other Animal)." In *Re-Reading Levinas,* ed. Robert Bernasconi and Simon Critchley. Bloomington: Indiana University Press, 1991. 234–45.

———. *The Middle Voice of Ecological Conscience: A Chiasmatic Reading of Responsibility in the Neighbourhood of Levinas, Heidegger and Others*. New York: Palgrave MacMillan, 1991.

Luft, Sebastian, and Pol Vandevelde, eds. *Epistemology, Archaeology, Ethics: Current Investigations of Husserl's Corpus*. London, Continuum, 2010.

Manning, Robert. *Interpreting Otherwise than Heidegger*. Pittsburgh: Duquesne University Press, 1993.

Manoussakis, John Panteleimon, ed. *After God: Richard Kearney and the Religious Turn in Continental Philosophy*. New York: Fordham University Press, 2006.

———. *God after Metaphysics: A Theological Aesthetic*. Bloomington: Indiana University Press, 2007.

———. "Toward a Fourth Reduction?" In *After God: Richard Kearney and the Religious Turn in Continental Philosophy*, ed. John Panteleimon Manoussakis. New York: Fordham University Press, 2006. 21–33.

Marion, Jean-Luc. *Being Given: Toward a Phenomenology of Givenness*. Trans. Jeffrey L. Kosky. Stanford: Stanford University Press, 2002.

———. *God without Being: Hors-Texte*. Trans. Thomas A. Carlson. Chicago: University of Chicago Press, 1995.

———. *The Idol and Distance: Five Studies*. Trans. Thomas A. Carlson. New York: Fordham University Press, 2001.

———. *In Excess: Studies in Saturated Phenomena*. Trans. Robyn Horner and Vincent Berrand. New York: Fordham University Press, 2002.

———. *Reduction and Givenness: Investigations of Husserl, Heidegger, and Phenomenology*. Trans. Thomas A. Carlson. Evanston, Ill.: Northwestern University Press, 1998.

———. "The Saturated Phenomena." Trans. Thomas A. Carlson. In *Phenomenology and the "Theological Turn": The French Debate*, by Dominique Janicaud et al. New York: Fordham University Press, 2000. 176–216.

Marrati, Paola. *Genesis and Trace: Derrida Reading Husserl and Heidegger*. Stanford: Stanford University Press, 2005.

McInerney, Peter K. "About the Future: What Phenomenology Can Reveal." In *The Many Faces of Time*. Vol. 41 of *Contributions to Phenomenology*, ed. John Barnett Brough and Lester Embree. Dordrecht: Kluwer Academic, 2000. 113–26.

McTaggart, J.M.E. *The Nature of Existence*. Cambridge: Cambridge University Press, 1927.

———. "The Unreality of Time." *Mind* 17 (1908). 457–74.

Meinong, Alexius. "On Objects of Higher Order and Their Relationship to Internal Perception." In *Alexius Meinong: On Objects of Higher Order and Husserl's Phenomenology*, ed. M.-L. Schubert Kalsi. The Hague: Martinus Nijhoff, 1978. 137–208.

Mensch, James R. *Husserl's Account of Our Consciousness of Time*. Milwaukee, Wisc.: Marquette University Press, 2010.

————. "Husserl's Concept of the Future." *Husserl Studies* 16 (1999): 41–64.

————. "Instincts."Unpublished manuscript. 2008.

Merleau-Ponty, Maurice. "Indirect Language and the Voices of Silence." In *Signs*. Trans. Richard C. McCleary. Evanston, Ill.: Northwestern University Press, 1964. 39–83.

————. *Phenomenology of Perception*. Trans. Colin Smith. 1962; London: Routledge, 2002.

————. *Signs*. Trans. Richard C. McCleary. Evanston, Ill.: Northwestern University Press, 1964.

Milbank, John. *Theology and Social Theory: Beyond Secular Reason*. Oxford: Blackwell, 1990.

Mirvish, Adrian. "The Presuppositions of Husserl's Presuppositionless Philosophy." *Journal of the British Society for Phenomenology* 26.2 (1995): 147–70.

Mohanty, Jitendra Nath. *The Concept of Intentionality*. St. Louis, Mo.: Warren H. Green, 1972.

————. *Edmund Husserl's Theory of Meaning*. The Hague: Martinus Nijhoff, 1964.

Moltmann, Jürgen. *The Coming of God: Christian Eschatology*. Trans. Margaret Kohl. Minneapolis: Fortress, 1996.

————. *Theology of Hope*. Trans. James W. Leitch. Minneapolis: Fortress, 1993.

Mouffe, Chantal, ed. *Deconstruction and Pragmatism*. New York: Routledge, 1996.

————. *The Democratic Paradox*. London: Verso, 2000.

Naas, Michael. *Taking on the Tradition: Jacques Derrida and the Legacies of Deconstruction*. Stanford: Stanford University Press, 2003.

Nenon, Thomas, and Lester Embree, eds. Issues *in Husserl's* Ideas II. Dordrecht: Kluwer Academic, 1996.

Olthuis, James H., ed. *Religion with/out Religion: The Prayers and Tears of John D. Caputo*. New York: Fordham University Press, 2002.

Peperzak, Adriaan. *Beyond: The Philosophy of Emmanuel Levinas*. Evanston, Ill.: Northwestern University Press, 1997.

————. *To the Other: An Introduction to the Philosophy of Emmanuel Levinas*. West Lafayette, Ind.: Purdue University Press, 1994.

Plantinga, Alvin. *Warrant and Proper Function*. Oxford: Oxford University Press, 1993.

Plato. *Complete Works*. Ed. John M. Cooper. Indianapolis: Hackett, 1997.

————. *Parmenides*. Trans. Mary Louise Gill and Paul Ryan. In *Complete Works*, ed. John M. Cooper. Indianapolis: Hackett, 1997. 359–97.

————. *Timaeus*. Trans. Donald J. Zeyl. In *Complete Works*, ed. John M. Cooper. Indianapolis: Hackett, 1997. 1224–91.

Quine, W.V.O. *Word and Object*. Cambridge, Mass.: MIT Press, 1960.

Rand, Richard, ed. *Futures: Of Jacques Derrida*. Stanford: Stanford University Press, 2001.

Rapaport, Herman. *Heidegger and Derrida: Reflections on Time and Language*. Lincoln: University of Nebraska Press, 1989.

Richardson, William J. *Heidegger: Through Phenomenology to Thought*. New York: Fordham University Press, 1993.

Ricoeur, Paul. *History and Truth*. Evanston, Ill.: Northwestern University Press, 1965.

———. *Husserl: An Analysis of His Phenomenology*. Trans. Edward G. Ballard and Lester E. Embree. Evanston, Ill.: Northwestern University Press, 2007.

———. *Oneself as Another*. Trans. Kathleen Blamey. Chicago: University of Chicago Press, 1992.

Rodemeyer, Lanei. "Developments in the Theory of Time-Consciousness: An Analysis of Protention." In *The New Husserl: A Critical Reader*, ed. Donn Welton. Bloomington: Indiana University Press, 2003. 125–54.

Rolland, J. *Emmanuel Levinas: Les Cahiers de La nuit surveillée*, no. 3. Lagrasse, France: Verdier, 1984.

Romano, Claude. "Awaiting." Trans. Ryan Coyne. In *Phenomenology and Eschatology: Not Yet in the Now*, ed. Neal DeRoo and John Panteleimon Manoussakis. Aldershot, England: Ashgate, 2009. 35–52.

Rorty, Richard. "From Ironist Theory to Private Allusions: Derrida." In *Contingency, Irony, Solidarity*. Cambridge: Cambridge University Press, 1989. 122–37.

———. *Philosophy and the Mirror of Nature*. Princeton: Princeton University Press, 1979.

Ryan, William F. "Passive and Active Elements in Husserl's Notion of Intentionality." *Modern Schoolman* 55 (1977): 37–55.

Sallis, John. *Chorology: On Beginning in Plato's Timaeus*. Bloomington: Indiana University Press, 1999.

———. ed. *Deconstruction and Philosophy: The Texts of Jacques Derrida*. Chicago: University of Chicago Press, 1987.

Santilli, Paul Chester. "The Notion of Style in Merleau-Ponty." PhD dissertation, Boston College, 1976.

Saraiva, Maria Manuela. *L'Imagination selon Husserl*. The Hague: Martinus Nijhoff, 1970.

Sartre, J.-P. *Being and Nothingness: A Phenomenological Essay on Ontology*. Trans. Hazel E. Barnes. New York: Washington Square Press, 1992.

———. *L'Être et le néant: Essai d'ontologie phénoménologique*. Paris: Gallimard, 1943.

———. *Imagination: A Psychological Critique*. Trans. F. Williams. Ann Arbor: University of Michigan Press, 1962.

Scheler, Max. *Gesammelte Werke II. Der Formalismus in der Ethik und die Materiale Werkethick: Neuer Versuch der Grundlegung eines ethischen Personalismus*. Ed. Maria Scheler. Bern: Franke, 1954.

Schubert Kalsi, Marie-Louise. *Alexius Meinong: On Objects of Higher Order and Husserl's Phenomenology*. The Hague: Martinus Nijhoff, 1978.

Simmons, J. Aaron. *God and the Other: Ethics and Politics after the Theological Turn*. Bloomington: Indiana University Press, 2010.

Singer, Linda. "Merleau-Ponty on the Concept of Style." In *The Merleau-Ponty Aesthetics Reader: Philosophy and Painting*, ed. Galen Johnson. Evanston, Ill.: Northwestern University Press, 1993. 233–44.

Smith, James K.A. "Determined Hope: A Phenomenology of Christian Expectation." In *The Future of Hope: Christian Tradition amid Modernity and Postmodernity*, ed. Miroslav Volf and William Katerberg. Grand Rapids, Mich.:Eerdmans, 2004. 200–227.

———. *The Fall of Interpretation: Philosophical Foundations for a Creational Hermeneutic*. Downer's Grove, Ill.: InterVarsity, 1999.

———. *Jacques Derrida: Live Theory*. New York: Continuum, 2005.

———. "The Logic of Incarnation: Toward a Catholic Postmodernism." In *The Logic of Incarnation: A Critique of Postmodern Religion*, ed. Neal DeRoo and Brian Lightbody. Eugene, Ore.: Pickwick, 2008. 3–37.

———. "Re-Kanting Postmodernism? Derrida's Religion within the Limits of Reason Alone." *Faith and Philosophy* 17.4 (2000): 558–71.

Sokolowski, Robert. *The Formation of Husserl's Concept of Constitution*. The Hague: Martinus Nijhoff, 1964.

———."Immanent Constitution in Husserl's Lectures on Time." *Philosophy and Phenomenological Research* 24.4 (1964): 530–51.

———. *Introduction to Phenomenology*. Cambridge: Cambridge University Press, 2000.

Spiegelberg, Herbert. *The Phenomenological Movement: A Historical Introduction*. 2 vols. The Hague: Martinus Nijhoff, 1965.

Steinbock, Anthony J. *Home and Beyond: Generative Phenomenology after Husserl*. Evanston, Ill.: Northwestern University Press, 1995.

Stern, L.W. "Psychische Präsenzzeit." *Zeitschrift für Psychologie und Physiologie der Sinnesorgane* 13 (1897): 325–49.

Strasser, Stephan. "Antiphénoménologie et phénoménologie dans la philosophie d'Emmanuel Levinas."*Revue Philosophique de Louvain* 75 (Feb. 1977): 101–25.

Taylor, Mark C., ed. *Deconstruction in Context: Literature and Philosophy*. Chicago: University of Chicago Press, 1986.

Tito, Johanna M. "In Praise of Presence: Rethinking Presence with Derrida and Husserl." *Philosophy Today*, 45:2 Summer 2001, 154–67.

Tymieniecka, A.-T., ed. *Analecta Husserliana*. Vol. 34. Boston: Kluwer Academic, 1991.

Volf, Miroslav, and William Katerberg, eds. *The Future of Hope: Christian Tradition amid Modernity and Postmodernity*. Grand Rapids, Mich.: Eerdmans, 2004. 200–227.

Ward, Graham. "Questioning God." In *Questioning God*, ed. John D. Caputo, Michael Scanlon, and Mark Dooley. Bloomington: Indiana University Press, 2001. 274–90.

Welton, Donn, ed. *The New Husserl: A Critical Reader*. Bloomington: Indiana University Press, 2003.

Westphal, Jonathan, and Carl Levenson, eds. *Time*. Indianapolis: Hackett, 1993.

Westphal, Merold. "The Welcome Wound: Emerging from the il y a Otherwise." *Continental Philosophy Review* 40 (2007): 211–30.

Wittgenstein, Ludwig. "St. Augustine's Puzzle about Time." In *The Blue Book*. Oxford: Blackwell, 1958.

Wood, David. *The Deconstruction of Time*. Atlantic Highlands, N.J.: Humanities Press International, 1989.

Wood, David, and Robert Bernasconi, eds. *Derrida and Différance*. Evanston, Ill.: Northwestern University Press, 1988.

Wyschogrod, Edith. *Emmanuel Levinas: The Problem of Ethical Metaphysics*. New York: Fordham University Press, 2000.

Zahavi, Dan, ed. *Exploring the Self: Philosophical and Psychopathological Perspectives on Self-Experience*. Amsterdam: John Benjamins, 2000.

———. "Husserl's Intersubjective Transformation of Transcendental Philosophy." *Journal of the British Society of Phenomenology* 27.3 (1996): 228–45.

———. *Husserl's Phenomenology*. Stanford: Stanford University Press, 2003.

———. "Phenomenology of Self." In *The Self in Neuroscience and Psychiatry*, ed. Tilo Kircher and Anthony S. David. Cambridge: Cambridge University Press, 2003. 56–75.

———. "Self and Consciousness." In *Exploring the Self: Philosophical and Psychopathological Perspectives on Self-Experience*, ed. Dan Zahavi. Amsterdam: John Benjamins, 2000. 55–74.

———. *Self-Awareness and Alterity: A Phenomenological Investigation*. Evanston, Ill.: Northwestern University Press, 1999.

———. ed. *Self-Awareness, Temporality and Alterity: Central Topics in Phenomenology*. Dordrecht: Kluwer Academic, 1998.

———. "Time and Consciousness in the Bernau Manuscripts." *Husserl Studies* 20 (2004): 99–118.

Index

futurity: as absolute surprise, 73–74, 78, 84–91, 99; awaiting and, 83–90, 132, 135; being-for-beyond-my-death (*see* being-for-beyond-my-death); centrality to phenomenological method, 50, 69–70, 92, 95, 100–101, 133–35; diachrony and, 82–85 (*see also* futurity, prehistory and); elements of 131–32 (*see also* anticipation; expectation; protention); eschatological, 47, 121–26, 130, 133 (*see also* eschatology; Levinas, Emmanuel, eschatology and); futuration of the future and, 83, 94; as imperative, 83; intentionality and, 14, 22–24, 45, 75, 133–38; as interruptive, 84, 130, 133; past as "absolute future," 118–22; prehistory and, 69, 77–82; promise and, 51–52, 92–95, 99, 114, 127–28; as relation to the Other, 73–75

Gefühl, 32
Gegenstandlichkeit, 33–35
genesis: in Husserl, 28, 39–40, 99–105
genetic phenomenology, 28–36, 101
givenness, 47–52, 67, 134, 141; self-givenness, 101, 141–44, 149–52, 189n45

Hamlet, 118–19, 127, 133, 184–85n8
hauntology, 118–19, 126
Heidegger, Martin, 3–4, 58–59, 72, 85, 173n6, 185n16, 186n8, 188n23
Henry, Michel, 7, 176n7, 180n35, 186n8, 190nn51, 56
history, 28, 74, 80–82, 142–51, 165n14; transcendental, 149
hope, 42–49, 121–22, 125, 167n2, 168nn4, 7
Horizons: in constitution, 19, 36, 51, 63, 80, 84, 108, 142–43; eschatological, 132; of expectation, 37–38, 46–47, 51, 58, 103, 148; infinity and, 107–8; lost, 60, 63–64; messianisms and, 122–23; responsibility for, 147–48; retentional, 19, 46, 58, 89; of sensation, 64–66; transcendent, 62–65

hospitality, 121–22
hostage, 78–84, 91, 152
Husserl, Edmund: *Analyses Concerning Active and Passive Synthesis*, 22–26, 29–39, 43, 163nn33, 38, 167n27; *Bernau Manuscripts on Time Consciousness*, 6, 19–22, 161nn20–21, 162n29; content/apprehension schema, 16, 23, 28, 52, 162n22; *Crisis of the European Sciences*, 144–47, 152, 158n22, 167n27, 187n17, 190n51; empirical type and, 32–35; *Experience and Judgment*, 30, 33, 165nn7, 9; feeling and, 32; *Formal and Transcendental Logic*, 33, 50, 148, 186n8; historical influences of (*see* Kant, Immanuel; Meinong, Alexius; Stern, L.W.); *Ideas I*, 6, 60, 101, 140–41, 146, 148, 159n7, 166n21, 178n6; *Ideas II*, 63, 171n17, 187n17; impression and, 15, 62–65; infinite regress problems in, 16, 20–22; narrowness of consciousness in, 48–53; *On the Phenomenology of the Consciousness of Internal Time*, 5, 15–20, 24, 26, 28–31, 59, 63, 87, 101, 158n2, 159nn4, 6, 8, 161n18, 162nn24, 27, 32; symphony example in, 17–18, 26, 163n33; tendency and, 30, 32, 37

Ideality, 110, 117, 121, 124, 130, 147, 181n4
il y a, 71–73, 77–79, 89–91, 171n15, 173n6, 176n8
impression, 15, 19–20, 62–65, 88; sensation and, 15
induction, 37
inference, 46–51, 126, 147, 183n32
infinite, 21–22, 66–68, 70, 76–77, 104–9, 117, 144–47, 162n27, 169n16, 175n29, 179n14, 188n26, 191n58. *See also* Husserl, Edmund, infinite regress problems in
infinity, 22, 68, 76, 108, 117–18, 146, 175n1, 189n45, 190n51
instincts, 33, 161n20, 166n19, 176n6

intentionality: double, 16–18, 24–27, 63, 101, 143; as futural, 75, 133–35, 146; horizontal and transverse, 16, 63, 89, 101–2, 143; importance to phenomenology, 59–62, 95, 101–8; nonobjectifying, 143; nontheoretical, 60–62, 78; as openness, 20–23, 40, 62, 108–9, 137–39, 146–47; passive, 30, 90, 104, 147; promise and, 92–95, 137–38; protention as necessary for, 22–24, 26; as relationship between constituting and constituted, 101–2, 107–8, 137; as traditionality, 147; transcendental, 104, 133–34

interest [*Interesse*], 34

interiority, 66–67

internal time-consciousness, 5, 13–16, 24–31, 39, 59, 88, 100–104, 145, 159n5, 161–62n21, 164n2. *See also* impression, sensation and; protention; retention

intuition: clarifying and confirming modes of, 6, 23–26, 38–44, 52, 89–94, 143–44; domain of, 21–22, 39–40; fulfilling mode of (*see* intuition, clarifying and confirming modes of); historical, 142; nonintuitive differentiation, 21–22, 39–40, 145–46; zero of, 21

ipseity, 66–67, 88, 91–94, 113, 137, 175n25, 176n3

Jemeinigkeit, 3, 172n32

judgment, 33–35

justice, 119–25, 130, 191n61

Kant, Immanuel, 39–40, 102, 124–25, 184nn26–27, 188n27; idea in the Kantian sense, 108–9, 145–46, 149, 189n45; neo-Kantianism, 52, 102, 133, 177n20

Kearney, Richard, 160n12

Lacoste, Jean-Yves, 2, 47–52, 156n8, 173n7

Levinas, Emmanuel: caress, 74–75; the concrete and, 61, 76, 83, 108, 145; critiques of phenomenology, 57–59

(*see also* Levinas, Emmanuel, differences from Heidegger); Desire, 75, 85, 89–94, 175n30; "Diachrony and Representation," 80–87, 94; differences from Heidegger, 57–59, 62–64, 71–73, 79, 84–85, 173n6, 174n20; elemental and, 75–77; eschatology and, 2–3, 7, 69, 79, 182n16; *Existents and Existence*, 77–78, 173n2; expiation, 81–82; face to face encounter, 65–67, 73–78, 149, 172n29, 174n19, 185n18; *God, Death and Time*, 69–70, 82–84, 91, 175n28; hostage, 78–84, 91; hypostasis, 71–73, 77–79, 89; *il y a*, 71–73, 77–79, 89–91 (see also *il y a*); influence on Derrida, 105–7; as influenced by Husserl, 59–68, 88–92; "Intentionality and Sensation," 61, 64; ipseity and, 66–67, 88, 91–94, 113, 137, 175n25, 176n3; nourishment and, 71–72, 75–76; obsession, 78–80; *Otherwise than Being*, 58–59, 67, 70, 80–82, 87, 137, 172n32, 174n23, 175n25, 185n15; as phenomenologist (*see* Phenomenology, in Levinas); "The Ruin of Representation," 59, 64–67, 102, 107; separation and, 66–67, 76–78, 91, 106–8; *Time and the Other*, 70–83, 89, 168n4, 174n18; *Totality and Infinity*, 65, 69–70, 75–81, 170n8, 174nn17–19, 175n29, 177n15 "The Trace of the Other," 75–79, 83, 89, 123, 174n23

life: cognitive/mental, 25, 61, 64; egological, 106, 108; empirical/human, 72, 127, 151–52; ultratranscendental concept of, 113, 117, 134, 151–52, 180n35

lifeworld, 145–51, 185n18; as root of scientific objectivity, 146–47

Marion, Jean-Luc, 2, 157n14, 168n3, 172n33, 180n25, 187n16, 190n51

materiality, 71–72, 75–78, 145

meaning, as distinct from sense, 33–34, 171n14

Meinong, Alexius, 14, 24, 159n11

Merleau-Ponty, Maurice, 2, 176nn2, 10
messianic, 118–23; as holding together
Husserlian constitution and
Levinasian surprise, 9, 110, 115,
118–20, 123–26; messianicity as
distinct from messianisms, 120–23
Moltmann, Jürgen, 168n7

neo-Kantianism, 52, 102, 133, 177n20
norms, 147–50, 190n53
nourishment, 71–72, 75–76

objectivity, 34
omnitemporality, 117, 144
optimalization, 91, 138, 146, 186n19
other in me, 9, 91–92, 126–27, 152–53,
177n15, 180n27

Passive synthesis, 29–36, 62; elements of,
25, 30; relation to active synthesis, 29,
31–36; relation to internal time-
constitution, 24–27, 31, 144–45
passivity: in each level of constituting
consciousness, 8, 57; more passive
than any passivity, 57, 65, 83, 87;
radicality of, 80; relation with activity,
9, 63, 131; subject as, 62–65, 79–81
perception, 14–18, 23–26, 30–39, 43, 60,
141–44, 166n20, 169n14
phenomenology: "crisis" in, 104; in
Derrida, 100–110, 123–26; dialectic/
tension at the heart of, 103–10, 116,
123; eidetic, 101–4, 112, 165n10; as
ethical, 52–53, 73, 118, 135–38
(see also ethical relation; ethics,
as first philosophy; ethics, as
nonepistemological focus of
phenomenology); genetic, 28–36,
101; intersubjectivity and, 103,
120–23, 131, 134–35; in Levinas,
57–68, 77, 89–92; lost/forgotten
horizons of, 60–64, 76; method of,
1–5, 95, 134–35, 140–43, 149–53;
presuppositions of, 107–10, 112, 142;
"principle of principles," 60–61, 101,
140–43, 151; as promissory discipline,
52, 135, 140, 148–53; reduction and
(see reduction); scope of, 9, 149–53;

"theological turn" and, 2, 118, 156n8,
190n52 (see also relevant figures listed by
name); transcendental, 13, 25, 28,
40–41, 63–64, 102–13, 133–35; and
undecidability, 143–44
Phenomenology and Eschatology, 184n7.
See also Lacoste, Jean-Yves
Plantinga, Alvin, 184n33, 184n5 (chap. 9)
plurality, 72, 78
politics, 5, 10, 119, 152–53, 183n31
pre-experience, 47–51, 88–90, 109,
138–39
pre-givenness, 47–51, 63, 109
presence, 49–51, 79–80, 109–31, 139–40
primal impression. See impression
promise, 9, 51–52; centrality to
phenomenological method, 51–52,
92–95, 114, 132–33; as double
affirmation (yes, yes), 127; elements of,
51–52, 93–95, 130–31; futurity and,
94–95, 99, 114, 132–33; as guiding
social institutions, 151–52; justice and,
125; promissory discipline, 9, 135,
140–53; self as, 94, 132–33; as
transcendental, 126
protention: distinctions from retention,
14, 17–24; emptiness of, 23–27, 36,
43; "striving" character of, 14, 22–24,
35–36, 43, 89

reduction, 102–3, 122, 134, 144
Reiz, 30
repetition, 48, 119, 133
reproductive association, 30, 36
responsibility, 67, 71, 79–88, 90–94, 119,
126–27, 137, 146–48, 185n15
retention, 14–24; as a modifying act, 16
revenant, 118, 181n13, 184n37
Rorty, Richard, 152

Sartre, Jean-Paul, 2, 160n12, 187n16
sedimentation, 142–44, 186n8, 187n13
selbstgegebenheit [self-givenness], 101, 144
sense, 61, 102–5, 116, 143–44, 147,
166n21; as distinct from meaning,
33–34, 171n14; reactivation of,
142–44, 151
sensibility, 62–65, 76–78

separation, 66–67, 76–78, 91, 106–8

Sinnbildung [making-sense], 143–44

Sinngebung [sense-bestowal], 61–67, 78–79, 89–90, 92–94, 171nn14–15, 173n1

Smith, James K.A., 182n22

Stern, L.W., 14, 158n1

subject: as constituted, 8, 52–53, 64, 80, 87; constituted/constituting, 52–53, 61, 88–92, 101–5, 137; as constituting, 8, 39–40, 52–53; as created/creature, 81, 94; as futural, 85; historicity of, 30; openness of, 20–23, 40, 57, 59, 64, 71–72, 87, 92–95, 126–28, 138–39; as promise, 94, 127–28, 132–33; solitude of, 70–78, 91; temporal, 24–26, 36, 58; transcendence of, 95

supplement, original, 111, 116–19, 142

synopsia, 91, 175n28, 176n12

teleology, 104, 119–20, 128, 132–33, 182n16

tendency, 30, 32, 33

Tendenz, 30

testimony, 148, 177n15, 183n31

to-come, 78, 83, 93–94, 115, 120, 191n58

trace, 94; as constitutive of subjectivity, 77–82, 116; as nonintentional, 80; of the Other, 69, 77–82

tradition, 10, 112, 142–53, 186n7, 188nn28, 31, 189nn43, 45, 190n51

transcendental origin of the world, 105–7, 112, 133–35

transcendental unity of apperception, 83

trustworthiness, 51–52, 126, 131–32, 147, 183n32, 191n58

unity: in difference (see *différance*); in multiplicity, 30

vorgegeben [pregiven], 63

Wood, David, 152, 157n16, 158n19

World: as "concrete," 61; as constitutive of the subject, 80, 89, 104–5, 134; as correlate of absolute consciousness, 37; environing, 33; as foreign to the subject, 62–64; passive constitution of, 9, 33–37; phenomenological definition of, 33, 36–37; subject's openness onto, 40, 62, 71–72, 89, 95, 131–32; transcendental constitution of, 106, 133–35

Zahavi, Daniel, 158n2, 164n40, 164n4 (chap. 2), 165n16, 189n47

zero point of the world, 106, 117

Perspectives in Continental Philosophy
John D. Caputo, series editor

Jean-Luc Marion, *The Idol and Distance: Five Studies.* Translated with an introduction by Thomas A. Carlson.

Jeffrey Dudiak, *The Intrigue of Ethics: A Reading of the Idea of Discourse in the Thought of Emmanuel Levinas.*

Robyn Horner, *Rethinking God as Gift: Marion, Derrida, and the Limits of Phenomenology.*

Mark Dooley, *The Politics of Exodus: Søren Kierkegaard's Ethics of Responsibility.*

Merold Westphal, *Overcoming Onto-Theology: Toward a Postmodern Christian Faith.*

Edith Wyschogrod, Jean-Joseph Goux, and Eric Boynton, eds., *The Enigma of Gift and Sacrifice.*

Stanislas Breton, *The Word and the Cross.* Translated with an introduction by Jacquelyn Porter.

Jean-Luc Marion, *Prolegomena to Charity.* Translated by Stephen E. Lewis.

Peter H. Spader, *Scheler's Ethical Personalism: Its Logic, Development, and Promise.*

Jean-Louis Chrétien, *The Unforgettable and the Unhoped For.* Translated by Jeffrey Bloechl.

Don Cupitt, *Is Nothing Sacred? The Non-Realist Philosophy of Religion: Selected Essays.*

Jean-Luc Marion, *In Excess: Studies of Saturated Phenomena.* Translated by Robyn Horner and Vincent Berraud.

Phillip Goodchild, *Rethinking Philosophy of Religion: Approaches from Continental Philosophy.*

William J. Richardson, S.J., *Heidegger: Through Phenomenology to Thought.*

Jeffrey Andrew Barash, *Martin Heidegger and the Problem of Historical Meaning.*

Jean-Louis Chrétien, *Hand to Hand: Listening to the Work of Art.* Translated by Stephen E. Lewis.

Jean-Louis Chrétien, *The Call and the Response.* Translated with an introduction by Anne Davenport.

D. C. Schindler, *Han Urs von Balthasar and the Dramatic Structure of Truth: A Philosophical Investigation.*

Julian Wolfreys, ed., *Thinking Difference: Critics in Conversation.*

Allen Scult, *Being Jewish/Reading Heidegger: An Ontological Encounter.*

Richard Kearney, *Debates in Continental Philosophy: Conversations with Contemporary Thinkers.*

Jennifer Anna Gosetti-Ferencei, *Heidegger, Hölderlin, and the Subject of Poetic Language: Towards a New Poetics of Dasein.*

Jolita Pons, *Stealing a Gift: Kierkegaard's Pseudonyms and the Bible.*

Jean-Yves Lacoste, *Experience and the Absolute: Disputed Questions on the Humanity of Man.* Translated by Mark Raftery-Skehan.

Charles P. Bigger, *Between Chora and the Good: Metaphor's Metaphysical Neighborhood.*

Dominique Janicaud, *Phenomenology "Wide Open": After the French Debate.* Translated by Charles N. Cabral.

Ian Leask and Eoin Cassidy, eds., *Givenness and God: Questions of Jean-Luc Marion.*

Jacques Derrida, *Sovereignties in Question: The Poetics of Paul Celan.* Edited by Thomas Dutoit and Outi Pasanen.

William Desmond, *Is There a Sabbath for Thought? Between Religion and Philosophy.*

Bruce Ellis Benson and Norman Wirzba, eds., *The Phenomenology of Prayer.*

S. Clark Buckner and Matthew Statler, eds., *Styles of Piety: Practicing Philosophy after the Death of God.*

Kevin Hart and Barbara Wall, eds., *The Experience of God: A Postmodern Response.*

John Panteleimon Manoussakis, *After God: Richard Kearney and the Religious Turn in Continental Philosophy.*

John Martis, *Philippe Lacoue-Labarthe: Representation and the Loss of the Subject.*

Jean-Luc Nancy, *The Ground of the Image.*

Edith Wyschogrod, *Crossover Queries: Dwelling with Negatives, Embodying Philosophy's Others.*

Gerald Bruns, *On the Anarchy of Poetry and Philosophy: A Guide for the Unruly.*

Brian Treanor, *Aspects of Alterity: Levinas, Marcel, and the Contemporary Debate.*

Simon Morgan Wortham, *Counter-Institutions: Jacques Derrida and the Question of the University.*

Leonard Lawlor, *The Implications of Immanence: Toward a New Concept of Life.*

Clayton Crockett, *Interstices of the Sublime: Theology and Psychoanalytic Theory.*

Bettina Bergo, Joseph Cohen, and Raphael Zagury-Orly, eds., *Judeities: Questions for Jacques Derrida.* Translated by Bettina Bergo and Michael B. Smith.

Jean-Luc Marion, *On the Ego and on God: Further Cartesian Questions.* Translated by Christina M. Gschwandtner.

Jean-Luc Nancy, *Philosophical Chronicles.* Translated by Franson Manjali.

Jean-Luc Nancy, *Dis-Enclosure: The Deconstruction of Christianity.* Translated by Bettina Bergo, Gabriel Malenfant, and Michael B. Smith.

Andrea Hurst, *Derrida Vis-à-vis Lacan: Interweaving Deconstruction and Psychoanalysis.*

Jean-Luc Nancy, *Noli me tangere: On the Raising of the Body.* Translated by Sarah Clift, Pascale-Anne Brault, and Michael Naas.

Jacques Derrida, *The Animal That Therefore I Am.* Edited by Marie-Louise Mallet, translated by David Wills.

Jean-Luc Marion, *The Visible and the Revealed.* Translated by Christina M. Gschwandtner and others.

Michel Henry, *Material Phenomenology.* Translated by Scott Davidson.

Jean-Luc Nancy, *Corpus*. Translated by Richard A. Rand.

Joshua Kates, *Fielding Derrida*.

Michael Naas, *Derrida From Now On*.

Shannon Sullivan and Dennis J. Schmidt, eds., *Difficulties of Ethical Life*.

Catherine Malabou, *What Should We Do with Our Brain?* Translated by Sebastian Rand, Introduction by Marc Jeannerod.

Claude Romano, *Event and World*. Translated by Shane Mackinlay.

Vanessa Lemm, *Nietzsche's Animal Philosophy: Culture, Politics, and the Animality of the Human Being*.

B. Keith Putt, ed., *Gazing Through a Prism Darkly: Reflections on Merold Westphal's Hermeneutical Epistemology*.

Eric Boynton and Martin Kavka, eds., *Saintly Influence: Edith Wyschogrod and the Possibilities of Philosophy of Religion*.

Shane Mackinlay, *Interpreting Excess: Jean-Luc Marion, Saturated Phenomena, and Hermeneutics*.

Kevin Hart and Michael A. Signer, eds., *The Exorbitant: Emmanuel Levinas Between Jews and Christians*.

Bruce Ellis Benson and Norman Wirzba, eds., *Words of Life: New Theological Turns in French Phenomenology*.

William Robert, *Trials: Of Antigone and Jesus*.

Brian Treanor and Henry Isaac Venema, eds., *A Passion for the Possible: Thinking with Paul Ricoeur*.

Kas Saghafi, *Apparitions—Of Derrida's Other*.

Nick Mansfield, *The God Who Deconstructs Himself: Sovereignty and Subjectivity Between Freud, Bataille, and Derrida*.

Don Ihde, *Heidegger's Technologies: Postphenomenological Perspectives*.

Françoise Dastur, *Questioning Phenomenology*. Translated by Robert Vallier.

Suzi Adams, *Castoriadis's Ontology: Being and Creation*.

Richard Kearney and Kascha Semonovitch, eds., *Phenomenologies of the Stranger: Between Hostility and Hospitality*.

Michael Naas, *Miracle and Machine: Jacques Derrida and the Two Sources of Religion, Science, and the Media*.

Alena Alexandrova, Ignaas Devisch, Laurens ten Kate, and Aukje van Rooden, *Re-treating Religion: Deconstructing Christianity with Jean-Luc Nancy*. Preamble by Jean-Luc Nancy.

Emmanuel Falque, *The Metamorphosis of Finitude: An Essay on Birth and Resurrection*. Translated by George Hughes.

Scott M. Campbell, *The Early Heidegger's Philosophy of Life: Facticity, Being, and Language*.

Françoise Dastur, *How Are We to Confront Death? An Introduction to Philosophy*. Translated by Robert Vallier. Foreword by David Farrell Krell.

Christina M. Gschwandtner, *Postmodern Apologetics? Arguments for God in Contemporary Philosophy*.

Ben Morgan, *On Becoming God: Late Medieval Mysticism and the Modern Western Self.*

Neal DeRoo, *Futurity in Phenomenology: Promise and Method in Husserl, Levinas, and Derrida.*

Sarah LaChance Adams and Caroline R. Lundquist, eds., *Coming to Life: Philosophies of Pregnancy, Childbirth and Mothering.*